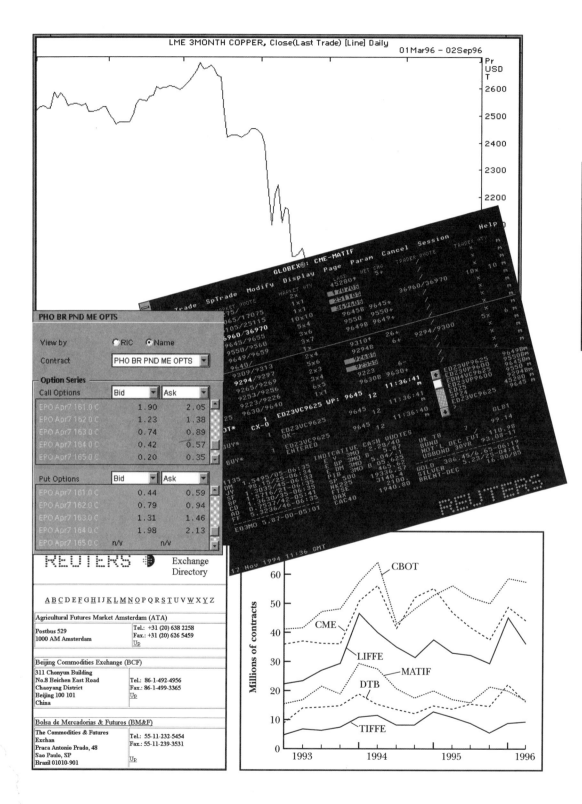

An Introduction to

Derivatives

John Wiley & Sons (Asia) Pte Ltd
Singapore   New York   Chichester
Brisbane   Toronto   Weinheim

Other titles in the series

You can get more information about the other titles in the series from the Reuters Financial Training series companion web site at *http://www.wiley-rft.reuters.com.*

Acknowledgments

The publishers and Reuters Limited would like to thank the following people for their invaluable assistance in this book:

Chong Siew Hoon of CSH Consultancy Services for her review of the book and constructive feedback.

Keith Rogers who wrote and produced the original version of the book.

Charles Kaplan, President of Equity Analytics Ltd. for use of his Glossary of Options And Futures Related Terms at the back of this book.

Numa Financial Systems Ltd for use of their Directory of Futures & Options Exchanges at the back of this book.

The logos on page 16 are registered trademarks. No trademark or logo may be reproduced or copied without the exchange's permission.

Published in 1999 by John Wiley & Sons (Asia) Pte Ltd
2 Clementi Loop, #02-01, Singapore 129809, Singapore.

Other Wiley Editorial Offices
John Wiley & Sons, Inc., 605 Third Avenue, New York,
NY 10158-0012, USA
John Wiley & Sons Ltd, Baffins Lane, Chichester, West Sussex PO19
1UD, England
John Wiley & Sons (Canada) Ltd, 22 Worcester Road, Rexdale,
Ontario M9W 1L1, Canada
Jacaranda Wiley Ltd, 33 Park Road (PO Box 1226), Milton,
Queensland 4064, Australia
Wiley-VCH, Pappelallee 3, 69469 Weinheim, Germany

Library of Congress Cataloging-in-Publication Data

An introduction to derivatives.
        p. cm. – (The Reuters financial training series)
    Includes bibliographical references.
    ISBN 0-471-83176-X (cloth)
    1. Derivative securities. 2. Options (Finance) 3. Futures.
I. Reuters ltd. II. Series.
HG6024.A3I59 1998
332.64'5 – dc21   98-55177
                                                      CIP

ISBN 0-471-83176-X

Typeset in 10/12 point New Baskerville
Printed in Singapore by Craft Print Pte Ltd
10 9 8 7 6 5 4 3 2 1

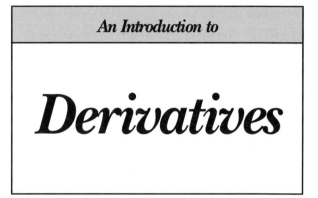

An Introduction to

Derivatives

Contents

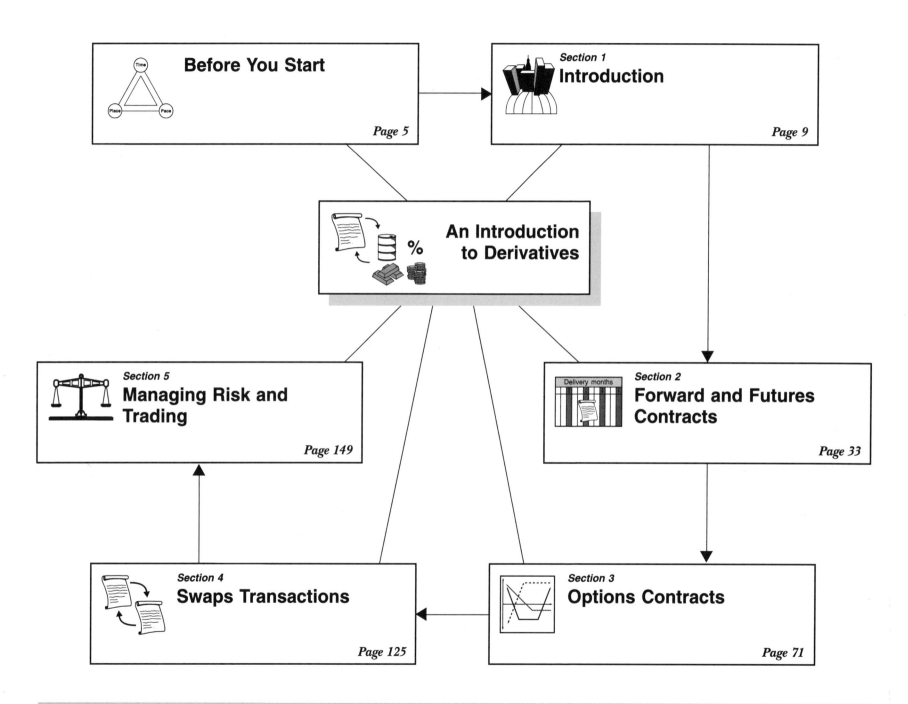

Contents

Contents

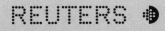

Who Should Use This Book?

This book is designed to provide an overview of the derivatives markets for a variety of readers: salespeople, support and operations staff, trainers, managers or the average investor who wants to learn how to use derivatives in his own trading strategy. Also, anyone about to begin an in-depth study of derivatives would find this book to be a useful primer. Derivatives are a very complicated subject and the reader will be able to find volumes of information on the subject with which to continue studying.

Derivatives are a fundamental tool in many trading strategies and while derivatives have long been in existence, their uses continue to expand as the financial markets evolve. While some types of derivatives are very basic, others are quite complicated and anyone who uses derivatives needs to understand their potential risks and rewards to use them effectively.

This book covers the use of derivatives in four market areas:
- Money markets and foreign exchange
- Debt
- Equities
- Commodities, energy and shipping

What Will You Find in This Book?

This book provides a new approach to gaining some basic familiarity with the essential concepts of derivatives. The book is written in a very accessible style with jargon kept to a minimum.

Most importantly, the book includes a range of materials to help you reinforce what you are learning. Each section offers a solid explanation of basic concepts, followed by actual examples for the reader to work through. Additional exercises and quick quizzes enable the reader to further enhance learning. Finally, each chapter includes a graphic overview — a visual outline — of what has been covered for quick yet thorough review and ends with a listing of additional reference materials.

In addition, the **RFT Web Site** has been created as this series of books' companion web site where additional quiz questions, updated screens and other information may be found. You can find this web site at **http://www.wiley-rft.reuters.com**.

How is This Book Organised?

This book has five sections:

Overview
This section introduces you to the basic concepts and principles of derivatives and a brief history of their development.

Forward and Futures Contracts
This section addresses the concept of trading forward, that is, buying or selling an asset at a specified future date, either Over-The-Counter (OTC) or on an exchange.

Options Contracts
This section deals with the basic terminology used in buying and selling options, options pricing, option sensitivities or greeks, and some of the more important trading strategies. Options can be traded either Over-The-Counter (OTC) or on exchanges.

Swaps Transactions
This section describes swaps involving interest rates, currencies, commodities and equities. Swaps transactions are not new but they are becoming increasingly more important as OTC derivatives.

Risk Management and Trading
This section deals with the various types of risk and how they affect trading and traders in general. In addition, exchange trading and how clearing houses function are explained in more detail.

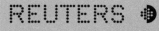

Throughout the book you will find that important terms or concepts are shown in bold, for example, **underlying**. You will also find that activities included to enhance your learning are indicated by the following icons:

This indicates the definition of a term that you must know and understand to master the material.

This means stop and think about the point being made. You may want to jot a few words in the box provided.

This indicates an activity for you to do. It is usually something written – for example, a calculation.

This indicates the main points of the section.

This indicates questions for you to answer to help you to review the material. The answers are also provided.

This indicates the one-page summary that provides a quick overview of the entire section. This page serves as an excellent study tool.

How to Use This Book

Before you start using this book, decide what you want from the material. If you are using this book as part of your work, discuss with your manager how he/she will help by giving time for study and giving you feedback and support. Although your learning style is unique to you, you will find that your learning is much more effective if you allocate reasonable sized periods of time for study. The most effective learning period is about 30 minutes – so use this as a basis. If you try to fit your learning into odd moments in a busy schedule you will not get the best from the materials or yourself. You might like to schedule learning periods into your day just as you would business meetings.

Remember that the most effective learning is an interactive process and requires more than just reading the text. The exercises in this book make you think through the material you have just read and then apply your understanding through basic activities. Take time to do the exercises. This old Chinese saying sums up this concept:

> **I hear and I forget**
> **I see and I remember**
> **I do and I understand**

The various types of activities and their icons have already been mentioned – even thinking is an activity.

Try to make sure your study is uninterrupted. This probably means that your workplace is not a good environment! You will need to find both the time and place where you can study – you may have access to a quiet room at work, you may have a room at home, you may need to use a library.

It's important to remember that learning is not a race – everyone learns at their own rate. Some people find things easy, some not quite so easy. So don't rush your learning – make sure you get the most from the book. You should now have enough information to plan the use of your book and the Web materials – remember it's your learning.

This section of the book should take about one hour of study time. You may not take as long as this or you may take a little longer – remember your learning is individual to you.

'Derivatives are like NFL quarterbacks. They get too much of the
credit and too much of the blame'

Gerald Corrigan, former President, Federal Reserve Bank of New York

What Are Derivatives?

Derivatives and derivatives trading have made the international and financial headlines recently because they have involved spectacular losses or institutional collapses. But market players have traded derivatives successfully for centuries and the daily international turnover in derivatives trading runs into billions of US dollars. Are derivatives instruments that can only be traded by experienced, specialist traders? Are derivatives to be avoided and left to the 'rocket scientists?'

Although it is true that complicated mathematical models are used for pricing some derivatives, the basic concepts and principles underpinning derivatives and their trading are quite easy to grasp and understand. Indeed, derivatives are used increasingly by various market players including governments, corporate treasurers, dealers and brokers and individual investors.

The purpose of this book is to introduce the basic concepts and principles of derivatives and their trading by considering:

- What are derivatives?

- Why have derivatives at all?

- Who uses derivatives?

- How are derivatives traded and used?

Before moving on to look at the questions above, how much do you know already about derivatives? Write down any answers you have to the questions opposite – no answers are given because the text that follows covers everything.

 Use the space here to write down any thoughts you may have concerning the following questions.

What are derivatives?

Why do derivatives exist?

How are derivatives traded?

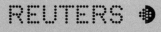

The following examples may help you understand some of the derivatives that are the subject of this book.

Example 1

It is early September and you decide you want to buy a new car. You select the type of car you want and go to your local dealer. At the dealer's showroom you decide on the exact specification of your car – colour, engine size, wheel trim etc – and more importantly the price is set. The dealer tells you that if you place the order today and place a deposit, then you can take delivery of the car in 3 months time. If in 3 months time the dealer is offering a 10% discount on all new cars, or the price of the model has increased, it does not matter. The price you pay for the car on delivery has been agreed and fixed between you and the dealer. You have entered into a **forward** contract – you have the **right** and **obligation** to buy the car in 3 months.

Example 2

Suppose now you had gone to the showrooms and seen the car you wanted was on offer at £20,000, but you must buy the car today. You don't have that amount of cash available and it will take you a week to organise a loan. You could offer the dealer a deposit and enter into a one week forward contract. But, there is something else you could offer.

This time you offer the dealer £100 if he will just keep the car for a week and hold the price. At the end of the week the £100 is his whether or not you buy the car. This is a tempting offer and the dealer accepts your offer. You have entered into an **option** contract – in this case it is termed a **call** option. This means you have the **right** to buy the car in a week but **not the obligation**.

If during the week you discover a second dealer offering an identical model for £19,500 then you don't take up your option with the first dealer. The total cost of buying the car is now £19,500 + £100 = £19,600 – cheaper than the first price you were offered.

If you cannot find the car at a cheaper price and buy the car from the first dealer, then the car will cost a total of £20,100. If you decide not to buy at all you will lose your £100 to the car dealer.

In both Examples 1 and 2 you are **hedging** against a price rise in the car. There are risks and rewards involved for you that are outlined in the tables below:

Forward Contract	
Risks	**Rewards**
The dealer will not deliver your car on time or go out of business before the delivery date	The price of the car may increase in the future
The price of the car may be cheaper in the future	

Option Contract	
Risks	**Rewards**
The dealer will not hold the car	You find a car at a cheaper price
You may not find the car at a cheaper price	

Example 3

The car you have bought a call option for is very much in demand and there is a sudden price rise to £22,000. A friend of yours also wants the same car and hears that you have an option to buy the car for £20,000 in a week's time. After visiting the bank you decide that you cannot really afford to buy the car so you sell the option to buy to your friend for £200. This means that the car dealer still gets his sale, your friend gets the car he wants and you make £100 on selling your option. In this case you have **speculated** on your contract and made a 100% profit.

For both the forwards and option contracts described, delivery of the car was for a **future** date and the prices of the deposit and option were based on the **underlying asset** – the car.

What then is a derivative? Within the financial markets a derivative may be defined as follows:

> A **derivative** is a financial contract, between two or more parties, which is **derived** from the future value of an underlying asset.

The original trading of derivatives involved a commodity such as rice, tulip bulbs or wheat as the underlying asset. Today, some underlying assets are still commodities but in addition almost any other **financial measure** or **financial instrument** can be used. For example there are derivatives based on debt instruments, interest rates, stock indices, money market instruments, currencies and even other derivative contracts!

There are four main types of derivatives traded today which are covered in the following sections of this book:

- Forward contracts

- Futures contracts

- Option contracts

- Swap transactions

Some Derivative Definitions

At this stage, in order for you to understand the following *Overview* materials, you need to know the basic definitions of the four types of derivatives (the full explanation of their pricing, use, trading strategies, etc is in later sections).

> A **forward contract** is a transaction in which the buyer and the seller agree upon the delivery of a specified quality and quantity of asset (usually a commodity) at a specified future date. A price may be agreed on in advance or at the time of delivery.

> Do you understand the definition? Write down any concerns you may have here.

In *Example 1* you entered into a forward contract. The terms of the deal were privately negotiated with the dealer and you paid a deposit as a form of collateral that you would honour the contract.

But what would have happened if the car you ordered did not arrive on time or it was not quite the specification you ordered? You would have to resolve the problem with the dealer.

For the more general case of commodities such as food, metals, oil etc contracts with standard conditions for amount, quality, delivery date etc were introduced in market places known as **exchanges**. The contracts traded were known as **futures contracts**.

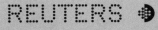

Introduction

The price of a futures contract is agreed on an exchange floor in a process whereby buyers and sellers shout their orders and quotes publicly. In today's markets, it is also common for contract details to be determined electronically through an automated trading system. This means that once a contract is agreed upon everyone on the floor knows the price paid. This transparency in futures contracts prices is one of the main differences from forward contracts where prices are privately negotiated.

 An **option contract** confers the **right**, but not the obligation, to **buy (Call)** or **sell (Put)** a specific underlying instrument or asset at a specific price – the **strike** or **exercise price** – up until or on a specific future date – the **expiry date**. The price to have this right is paid by the buyer of the option contract to the seller as a **premium**.

 A **futures contract** is a firm contractual agreement between a buyer and seller for a specified asset on a fixed date in the future. The contract price will vary according to the market place but it is fixed when the trade is made. The contract also has a standard specification so both parties know exactly what is being traded.

 Do you understand the definition? Write down any concerns you may have here.

 Do you understand the definition? Write down any concerns you may have here.

 A **swap transaction** is the simultaneous buying and selling of a similar underlying asset or obligation of equivalent capital amount where the exchange of financial arrangements provides both parties to the transaction with more favourable conditions than they would otherwise expect.

 Do you understand the definition? Write down any concerns you may have here.

REUTERS

A Brief History of Derivatives

The following brief history may help your understanding of the development and use of derivatives over the centuries – as you will see, fortunes have been won and lost in the markets for hundreds of years!

1630s	Tulips

In the late 1630s Tulipomania – Dutch Tulip bulb mania – was sweeping through Holland and England. In Holland options on Tulip bulbs had been written in Amsterdam in the early 1600s and in England forward contracts were being written at the Royal Exchange by the 1630s. The spectacular trading and gains made in trading Tulip bulbs was followed by an equally spectacular market crash and lost fortunes in 1636-37.

The Royal Exchange, established in 1571 to promote international trade

One of the most precious bulbs was that of the *Semper Augustus* tulip. In 1636 there were only two bulbs of this species in the whole of Holland. A speculator offered 12 acres of building ground for a single bulb. Another story involving a *Semper Augustus* bulb concerns a sailor who brought news to a rich merchant who had a bulb proudly displayed on his shop counter. As a reward for bringing the news the merchant gave the sailor a herring for his breakfast. The sailor was partial to onions and seeing the 'onion' on the counter slipped it into his pocket. On discovering his loss the merchant rushed into the street and found the sailor finishing his breakfast of herring and 'onion'. The sailor's breakfast could have paid the whole crew of his ship for a year! The unfortunate sailor spent a few months in prison for stealing the bulb.

1630s	Rice

One of the first examples of futures trading was in the Yodoya Rice Market in Osaka, Japan. Landlords, who had collected a share of the rice harvest as rent, found weather and other conditions too unpredictable. So the landlords, who needed cash, shipped the rice for storage in city warehouses. They then sold warehouse receipts – **rice tickets** – which gave the holder the right to receive a certain amount of rice, of a certain quality, at a future date at an agreed price. The landlords received a steady income and merchants had a steady supply of rice plus an opportunity to profit by selling the tickets.

In an effort to predict future prices, a successful merchant and money lender from the **Honma** family named **Munehisha** is popularly recorded as having invented the Candlestick method of plotting price movement – the birth of Charting or Technical Analysis.

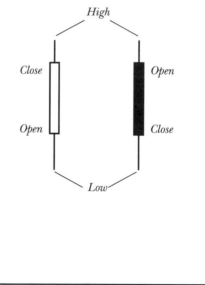

If the Close price is lower than the Open price, then the colour of the candle is red or black. If the Close is higher than the Open, then the candle is hollow or white.

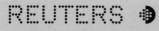

Early 1800s	Puts and Calls

The trading of Puts and Calls on shares was already established on the London Stock Exchange but not without its problems! In 1821 feelings were running high concerning the question of option dealings – also known as Puts and Calls. The exchange committee received the following request from a number of its members:

'The outright abolition of puts and calls which are now so frequent as to constitute the greater part of the business done in the House and which operate materially against the interests of those who do not comply with this practice.'

There were members who took a more positive attitude towards options trading and the situation was resolved.

New Stock Exchange from Ackermann's 'Microcosm of London' by T. Rowlandson (1756-1827) & Pugin, A.C. (1762-1832) Guildhall Library, Corporation of London/Bridgeman Art Library, London

Early 1800s	Puts and Calls

The history of modern futures trading can be traced to the middle of the nineteenth century and the development of the grain trade in Chicago. In 1848 the **Chicago Board of Trade (CBOT)** was formed to provide a place where buyers and sellers could exchange commodities. Originally trading was spot and then **'to arrive'** – these were contracts where the delivery of a commodity was specified at a predetermined rate and future date. The earliest recorded CBOT forward contract was made on 13th March 1851 for 3000 bushels of corn to be delivered in June. The problems with these early cash forward contracts were that they had no standard conditions nor were the contracts always fulfilled. In 1865 CBOT formalised grain trading by introducing agreements called **futures** contracts which standardised:

- The quality of grain
- The quantity of grain
- The time and location for grain delivery

The price of the futures contract was open to negotiation on the exchange floor. It is these early grain futures contracts which have formed the basis of the financial and commodities futures used today.

 The American Civil War provided an opportunity for the 'rocket scientists' of the day to create a derivative to meet the needs of the day. The Confederate States of America issued a dual currency optionable bond which allowed the Southern States to borrow money in sterling with an option to pay back the loan in French francs. But, the holder of the bond had the option to convert the repayment into cotton!

Options were traded on commodities and shares on US exchanges by the 1860s and the Put and Call Brokers and Dealers Association was established in the early 1900s.

The 1970s	Financial Futures

After a long period during which futures and options trading was variously regulated and banned by different governments worldwide, the **International Monetary Market (IMM)**, a division of the **Chicago Mercantile Exchange (CME)**, was established in 1972. This was the first exchange to trade **financial futures** contracts – currency futures. Up until this time futures contracts had just been traded on commodities.

During the same year CBOT was refused permission to start trading futures on shares and in response created the **Chicago Board Options Exchange (CBOE)** for options trading in 1973. This was also the year that Fischer Black and Myron Scholes published their option pricing formula.

$$\text{Call price} = SN(d_1) - Ke^{-rT}N(d_2)$$

$$d_1 = \frac{\ln(S/K) + (r + \sigma^2/2)T}{\sigma\sqrt{T}}$$

$$d_2 = d_1 - \sigma\sqrt{T}$$

By the late 1970s exchange traded financial futures were well established and traded on exchanges worldwide.

1980s on	Swaps and OTC Derivatives

Exchange trading involves **open outcry** where the traders shout their orders to each other on an exchange floor. In contrast privately negotiated derivatives contracts can be conducted face-to-face or using the phone, telex etc. These contracts are known as **Over-The-Counter (OTC)**.

Although privately negotiated OTC forwards and options contracts had been in existence for a long time, the 1980s was the period when OTC derivatives trading expanded considerably. It was also the period when swaps first became important.

Some of the first swaps involved swapping interest rate repayments on loans in which one party exchanged its fixed rate of interest with another party having variable interest rate payments.

In this brief history a number of exchanges have been mentioned. To complete this section see the timeline which illustrates many of the worldwide exchanges now trading derivatives and the dates when they were established.

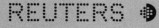

Timeline

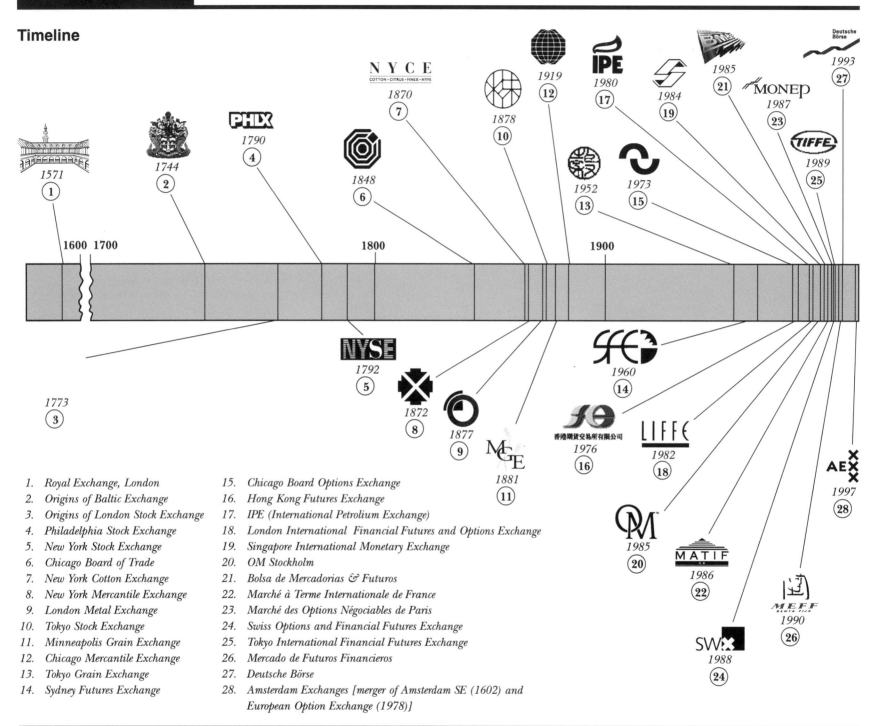

1. Royal Exchange, London
2. Origins of Baltic Exchange
3. Origins of London Stock Exchange
4. Philadelphia Stock Exchange
5. New York Stock Exchange
6. Chicago Board of Trade
7. New York Cotton Exchange
8. New York Mercantile Exchange
9. London Metal Exchange
10. Tokyo Stock Exchange
11. Minneapolis Grain Exchange
12. Chicago Mercantile Exchange
13. Tokyo Grain Exchange
14. Sydney Futures Exchange
15. Chicago Board Options Exchange
16. Hong Kong Futures Exchange
17. IPE (International Petrolium Exchange)
18. London International Financial Futures and Options Exchange
19. Singapore International Monetary Exchange
20. OM Stockholm
21. Bolsa de Mercadorias & Futuros
22. Marché à Terme Internationale de France
23. Marché des Options Négociables de Paris
24. Swiss Options and Financial Futures Exchange
25. Tokyo International Financial Futures Exchange
26. Mercado de Futuros Financieros
27. Deutsche Börse
28. Amsterdam Exchanges [merger of Amsterdam SE (1602) and European Option Exchange (1978)]

Why Have Derivatives?

The earlier examples of forward and option contracts discussed some of the risks and rewards involved when buying the car. There are obviously similar risks for the dealer – will the buyer be able to pay for the car etc?

Derivatives are very important financial instruments for risk management as they allow risks to be separated and more precisely controlled. Derivatives are used to shift elements of risk and therefore can act as a form of insurance.

This shift of risk means that each party involved in the contract should be able to identify all the risks involved **before** the contract is agreed.

It is also important to remember that derivatives are derived from an underlying asset, so that the risks in trading derivatives may **change** depending upon what happens to the underlying asset. For example, if the settlement price of a derivative is based on the commodity's cash price, which changes on a daily basis, then the derivative's risks are also changing on a daily basis. This means that derivative risks and positions must be monitored constantly as the amounts to be gained or lost can be sizable.

Before moving on, who do you think uses derivatives? Write down any answers you have as to who might use forwards, futures, options and swaps – no answers are given because the text that follows covers everything.

 Who do you think uses derivative instruments? Write down any ideas you may have here.

Forwards/futures?

Options?

Swaps?

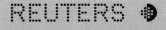

Who Uses Derivatives?

Derivatives can be used by a party who is exposed to an unwanted risk to pass this risk on to another party willing to accept it. Originally producers of commodities used forward and futures contracts to **hedge** prices and therefore reduce their risk.

Suppose you are a farmer growing rice or corn and you want to protect the future value of your harvest against price fluctuations. You can do this by hedging your position. In other words you sell your crop today for a price which is for a guaranteed amount for delivery of the crop and payment in the future. If the cash price of your crop at delivery is more than your guaranteed amount you cannot gain. You have an obligation to fulfil the contract and a right to receive the agreed delivery price. Any loss or gain in the cash market is offset by a gain or loss for the futures contract.

However if you had used an option contract you could have bought a contract where you had the right but not obligation to sell your crop in the future. If the future cash prices were better than the option price, then you could take advantage of them. Also, using an option limits any losses you may incur. Manufacturers using commodities also use derivatives to hedge their positions in order to predict and stabilise their production costs.

If commodity producers want to hedge their positions, then who takes on the other side of the contract? In many cases it could be other hedgers, for example, manufacturers, or it could be **speculators**. A speculator takes an opposite position to a hedger and exposes him/herself in the hope of profiting from price changes to his or her advantage.

There are also **arbitrageurs** who trade derivatives with a view to exploit any price differences within different derivatives markets or between the derivative instruments and cash or physical prices in the underlying assets.

The recent growth in swaps and OTC options instruments has been attributed to their increasing use by governments, international corporations and major institutional and financial investors. These various groups use derivatives to help achieve the following objectives:

- Lower international funding costs

- Provide better rates of exchange in international markets

- Hedge price risks

- Diversify funding and risk management

The number of different derivative instruments and volume of derivatives contracts traded are both increasing dramatically every year. The following chart lists the top ten international exchanges volumes of futures and options traded for 1995.

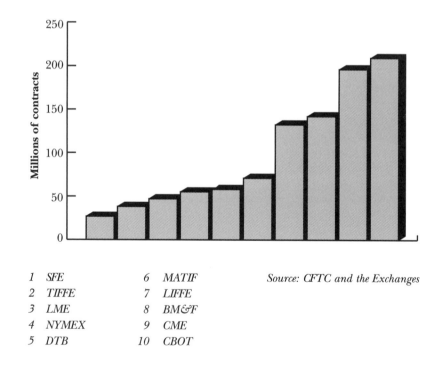

1	SFE	6	MATIF
2	TIFFE	7	LIFFE
3	LME	8	BM&F
4	NYMEX	9	CME
5	DTB	10	CBOT

Source: CFTC and the Exchanges

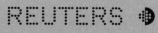

However, associated with this growth have been a few notable bank collapses and corporate losses involving billions of US dollars. In some cases the losses were incurred very rapidly, as in the case of the Barings Bank collapse, while other losses appear to have resulted from years of trading irregularities, as in the case of the Sumitomo Corporation.

Look at the following summary of derivatives before judging derivatives and how they are used:

- Derivatives do carry a risk – that's why they were devised. The risks associated with derivatives must be identified and managed.

- Many corporations and organisations use derivatives very successfully and benefit from their use.

- Unfortunately there is still a lack of understanding of derivatives within the markets and by the very nature of speculation, losses can be huge. When institutional collapses and losses occur, the organizations should carefully examine their risk management procedures, including the role that derivatives play.

Some people may suggest that derivatives trading is just another form of gambling and serves no useful purpose. Perhaps the following quote may help to clarify the usefulness of derivatives.

Betting on a horse, that's gambling; betting you can make three spades, that's entertainment; betting that cotton will go up three points, that's business. See the difference?

In an article by Robert Pardo, Technical Analysis of Stocks and Commodities Vol 3:5 (177 - 183), 1985

The huge losses referred to previously have both been attributed to 'rogue' or 'maverick' traders. Look at the events surrounding the Sumitomo Corporation case as shown in the chart below.

The chart contains daily closing Copper prices on the LME between March and September 1996. From mid-May to the end of June there was a dramatic fall in prices.

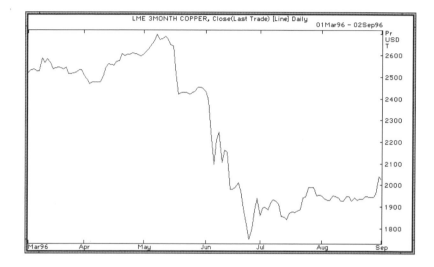

The chart shows there was a clear down trend with a near perfect classical chart wave pattern. What caused such a dramatic plunge in prices?

You only had to look at the financial and international headlines during that period to see that another 'rogue' trader had been discovered to be trading irregularly, inflicting huge losses on his organisation. The Japanese giant Sumitomo Corporation had lost a staggering $2.6 billion in trading copper on the LME and in trading OTC forward and futures contracts.

In the recent past there have been other organisations who have suffered losses due to poor financial controls and trading practices.

Look at the following table of financial disasters attributed to trading derivatives improperly.

1993	Metallgesellschaft AG loses 1.8 billion deutsche marks from oil futures trading.
1994	Chile Copper Corporation (CODELCO) loses some $200 million from irregular futures trading in copper and precious metals.
1995	Barings Bank collapses owing more than $1 billion on financial derivative contracts made by a single trader based in the bank's Singapore branch.

You should now have some understanding of who uses derivatives but how exactly are they traded?

Floor traders on LIFFE

Sydney Futures Exchange floor

Electronic trading at OM Stockholm

How are Derivatives Traded?

Traders are the market players who buy and sell derivatives contracts on behalf of their clients or on their own account in the financial and commodity markets. There are three basic ways in which trading can take place:

- Over-The-Counter (OTC)

- On an exchange floor using open outcry

- Using an electronic, automated matching system such as GLOBEX

Derivatives traders can operate across all the markets buying and selling futures, options, swaps contracts etc.

In some markets **brokers** act as intermediaries between traders and clients. Brokers do not usually trade on their own account but earn commissions on the deals that they arrange.

Traders and brokers both need up-to-date financial data, such as Reuters and other services provide, including:

- Information on the underlying instruments

- Technical analysis

- Prices from exchanges and contributors

- News

Open Outcry

The primary role of an exchange is to provide a safe environment for trading. Exchanges have approved members and rules governing matters such as trading behaviour and the settlement of disputes. Open outcry involves traders or brokers operating on an exchange floor where they communicate their deals by shouting at each other and using hand signals. On exchanges such as LIFFE, CME and SIMEX the floor is a very colourful, noisy place where at times the exchange activities seem to be in chaos! The floors of some of the smaller exchanges are not quite so colourful or noisy but an open outcry is still used.

The SIMEX trading floor

OTC

This method originates from the days when instruments were literally bought over the counter of a bank, for example. The present day meaning describes markets which have no specific locations, have fewer rules governing trading and which may be more international in character. Trading takes place directly between dealers and principals via a telephone and computer network rather than via a highly regulated exchange floor.

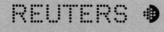

Automated Matching Systems

Many exchanges use an automated matching system to extend their trading hours. The systems are either provided as a joint venture such as GLOBEX, a Reuters/MATIF/SIMEX venture, or specific to an exchange such as Automated Pit Trading (APT) on LIFFE.

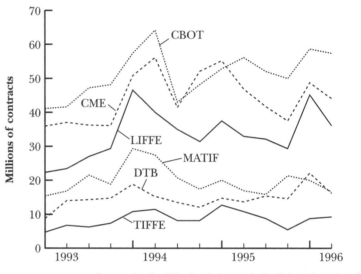

The automated matching systems operate using the same trading rules used for floor trading. They also offer the advantage of anonymity in trading and so are sometimes known as **electronic brokers**. There are three characteristics of an automated matching system:

- Users send their bids and offers to a central matching system

- The bids and offers are distributed to all other market participants

- The system identifies possible trades based on price, size, credit and any other rules relevant to the market

Exchange Based v OTC Trading

Although exchange based trading involves millions of contracts monthly involving the equivalent of billions of US dollars, the importance of the OTC markets is increasing as derivatives are better understood by the markets and the financial needs of market players change. The chart below shows the total quarterly turnover by millions of contracts for six of the major international exchanges.

Source: Bank of England Quarterly Bulletin, November 1996

Within the OTC markets **plain vanilla** instruments for forwards, swaps and options are traded most frequently. Plain vanilla instruments have no special features and are traded to more or less standardised contract specifications and market conventions. Instruments with more specialised features are known as **exotics**.

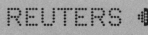

The following tables show that currently, interest rate instruments dominate the worldwide OTC and exchange traded derivatives. The values given as outstandings are the notional or face value of OTC contracts not yet settled or completed.

Although interest rate derivatives are very important worldwide as exchange based derivatives, the table below of the top ten individual contracts for April 1996 shows that bond and stock index derivatives are also important. It is also important to remember that different exchanges tend to specialise in different derivatives and are constantly introducing new products and deleting products which are not supported by the markets.

Derivatives Traded	Outstandings USD Billions	Turnover USD Billions
OTC	**38,304**	**193**
Currency swaps	8,741	4
Currency options	1,968	40
FRAs	4,588	65
Interest Rate Swaps	18,265	63
Interest Rate Options	3,548	21
Equity derivatives	805	–
Commodity derivatives	389	–
Exchange based	**16,581**	**1136**

Contract	Exchange	Average Daily Turnover USD Billions
3-Month Eurodollar	CME	33,151,598
Average Interest Rate Option	BBF	29,567,630
US T-Bonds	CBOT	29,519,887
S&P 100 Index Option	CBOE	21,419,286
Interest Rate	BM&F	18,537,128
US Dollar	BM&F	16,489,524
German Government Bond	LIFFE	14,969,359
Notional Bond	MATIF	13,042,395
3-Month Euromark	LIFFE	12,930,772
IBEX 35	MEFF	10,683,428

Futures Industry Magazine June/July 1996 Vol 6, Number 6, Page 7. The magazine is produced by the Futures Industry Association (FIA).

Contract	Exchange	Average Daily Turnover USD Billions
3 Month Interest Rate		
Eurodollar	CME	337.2
Sterling	LIFFE	39.2
Euromark	LIFFE	65.1
PIBOR	MATIF	52.2
Euroyen	TIFFE	231.3
Government Bond futures		
US T-Bond	CBOT	32.4
Bund	DTB	7.5
Bund	LIFFE	19.2
Notionnel	MATIF	11.9

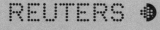

The main differences mentioned so far between exchange traded and OTC derivatives are summarised in the following table.

Exchange traded	OTC

• Derivatives available:
  • Futures
  • Options
	• Derivatives available:
	  • Forwards
	  • Options
	  • Swaps

• Derivatives traded on a competitive floor, open outcry and electronically	• Derivatives traded on a private basis and individually negotiated
• Standardised and published contract specifications	• No standard specifications although plain vanilla instruments are common
• Prices are transparent and easily available	• Prices are less transparent
• Market players not known to each other	• Market players must be known to each other
• Trading hours are published and exchange rules must be kept	• Commoditised vanilla contracts trade 24 hours a day while less liquid and customised one-time deals trade during local times.
• Positions can easily be traded out	• Positions are not easily closed or transferred
• Few contracts result in expiry or physical delivery	• Majority of contracts result in expiry or physical delivery

OTC trading by its very nature is private and contract details are not usually openly discussed. Exchange trading on the other hand is usually a very noisy, colourful, apparently chaotic affair. Traders shout at each other in open outcry and use hand signals to indicate their intentions.

In an amusing article written by Joseph Wilson entitled 'Into the Pit' he describes his first day as a member of the International Options Market (IOM), Chicago Mercantile Exchange. This short extract may give you some indication of the excitement of pit trading.

'My palms are sweating. My heart begins to race. The pit starts to rock back and forth as bids and offers are shouted. People are pushing and shoving each other to get good positioning. I am somewhere between total excitement and sheer panic.'

Part of the CME trading floor

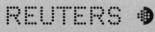

In another article 'She flashes signals from the pit at CBOT', Marie Pawlyk, a T-Bond pit trader explains the importance of hand signals in trading.

'Hand signals are vital. They are the fastest way to place an order in the shortest time in a constantly changing market where every second can be expensive.'

Hand signals being used to relay information on the CBOT trading floor

Summary

You have now finished the first section of the book and you should have an understanding of the following:

- What are derivatives?

- Why have derivatives at all?

- Who uses derivatives?

- How are derivatives traded?

The question remaining is how are derivatives used? The remaining sections of the book deal with derivatives and trading techniques in more detail. The following sections are concerned with:

- Forward and futures contracts

- Options contracts

- Swaps transactions

- Managing risk and trading

As a check on your understanding of this section, you should try the Quick Quiz Questions. You may also find the Overview Section to be a useful learning tool.

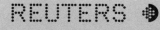

Quick Quiz Questions

1. Which of the following is **not** set by an exchange for trading derivatives?

    ❑ a) Contract amount
    ❑ b) Contract expiry date
    ❑ c) Contract delivery conditions
    ❑ d) Contract price

2. You have bought a LIFFE contract which gives you the right to buy 10,000 long-term gilts priced at 96 in the next 3 months. However you do not have to buy the gilts if you do not wish to. What kind of contract have you bought?

    ❑ a) An options contract
    ❑ b) A futures contract

3. Which of the following exchanges was the first to trade financial futures contracts in 1972?

    ❑ a) LIFFE
    ❑ b) IMM
    ❑ c) CBOT
    ❑ d) CBOE

4. Which of the following exchanges was the first to trade 'modern' standardised futures contracts in 1865?

    ❑ a) CBOE
    ❑ b) CME
    ❑ c) CBOT
    ❑ d) LME

5. What was the original use of forward and futures contracts in the commodities markets?

6. What are the main differences between trading derivatives open outcry and OTC?

You can check your answers on page 28.

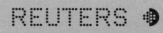

Overview

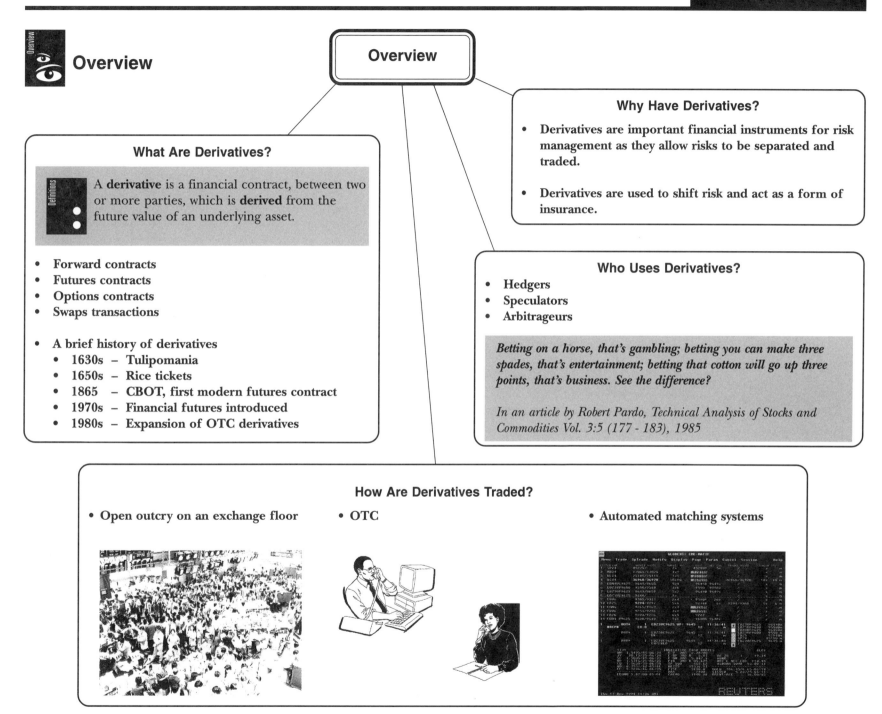

Overview

What Are Derivatives?

> A **derivative** is a financial contract, between two or more parties, which is **derived** from the future value of an underlying asset.

- Forward contracts
- Futures contracts
- Options contracts
- Swaps transactions

- A brief history of derivatives
  - 1630s – Tulipomania
  - 1650s – Rice tickets
  - 1865 – CBOT, first modern futures contract
  - 1970s – Financial futures introduced
  - 1980s – Expansion of OTC derivatives

Why Have Derivatives?

- Derivatives are important financial instruments for risk management as they allow risks to be separated and traded.

- Derivatives are used to shift risk and act as a form of insurance.

Who Uses Derivatives?

- Hedgers
- Speculators
- Arbitrageurs

> *Betting on a horse, that's gambling; betting you can make three spades, that's entertainment; betting that cotton will go up three points, that's business. See the difference?*
>
> *In an article by Robert Pardo, Technical Analysis of Stocks and Commodities Vol. 3:5 (177 - 183), 1985*

How Are Derivatives Traded?

- Open outcry on an exchange floor
- OTC
- Automated matching systems

Quick Quiz Answers

✓ or ✗

1. d   ❏

2. a   ❏

3. b   ❏

4. c   ❏

5. Your answer should have included something similar to the following:

    • To hedge prices and therefore the risk of holding the commodity

    • The producer can sell today for a guaranteed price in the future

    ❏
    ❏

6. Your answer should have included something similar to the following:

    • OTC are privately negotiated contracts between two parties who know each other: open outcry takes place publicly on an exchange floor between any approved traders
    • OTC contract details are not reported or published: open outcry trades are reported by the exchange and the results are transparent

    ❏
    ❏

How well did you score? You should have scored at least 6. If you didn't, you should study the material again.

Further Resources

Books

Derivatives Handbook: Risk Management and Control
Robert J. Schwartz and Clifford W. Smith (ed.), John Wiley & Sons,
Inc., 1997
ISBN 0 471 15765 1

Derivatives: The Theory and Practice of Financial Engineering
Paul Wilmott, John Wiley & Sons, Inc., 1998
ISBN 0 471 98389 6

Derivatives Demystified: Using Structured Financial Products
John C. Braddock, John Wiley & Sons, Inc., 1997
ISBN 0 471 14633 1

Merton Miller on Derivatives
Merton H. Miller, John Wiley & Sons, Inc., 1997
ISBN 0 471 18340 7

The Theory of Futures Trading
Asia Publishing House, 1965

Understanding Derivatives
Bob Reynolds, FT/Pitman Publishing, 1995
ISBN   0 273 61378 2

A Short History of Financial Euphoria
John K. Galbraith, Whittle Books/Penguin Books, 1994
ISBN   0 14 023856 5

Extraordinary Popular Delusions and the Madness of Crowds
Charles Mackay, Wordsworth Editions Ltd, 1995 – originally
published in 1841
ISBN   0 85326 349 4

Publications

Chicago Mercantile Exchange
- A World Marketplace

Chicago Board of Trade
- Action in the Marketplace
- The Commodity Trading Manual Chicago Board of Trade, 1989

Options Clearing Corporation
- Characteristics and Risks of Standardised Options

London International Financial Futures and Options Exchange
- LIFFE: An Introduction

Credit Suisse
- A Guide to foreign exchange and the money markets
  Credit Suisse Special Publications, Vol. 80, 1992

Swiss Bank Corporation
- Financial Futures and Options

Internet

RFT Web Site
- **http://www.wiley-rft.reuters.com**
This is the series' companion web site where additional quiz
questions, updated screens and other information may be found.

Derivatives Research Unincorporated
- http://fbox.vt.edu:10021/business/finance/dmc/DRU/contents.html
A good collection of well explained articles.

AIB: Derivatives in Plain English
- http://cgi-bin.iol.ie/aib/derivs-pe/

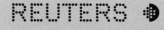

Your notes

 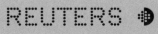

This section of the book should take between two and a half and three hours of study time. You may not take as long as this or you may take a little longer – remember your learning is individual to you.

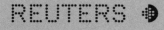

'*It's tough to make predictions, especially about the future*'

Lawrence P. 'Yogi' Berra, American baseball player and philosopher

 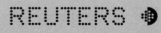

Introduction

The concept of trading forward, that is, buying and selling an asset for delivery at a **future date**, originated in the early commodity markets.

In principle there are two basic markets in which trading assets and financial instruments can take place. These are the:

- Spot, cash or physical markets

- Forward or futures markets

Spot, Cash or Physical Markets

In these markets, traders buy and sell the actual – **physical** – commodity and typically settle the transaction two business days later for **cash**. This is why the markets are also known as the cash markets. You are probably familiar with the **spot** FX markets where currencies are the commodities being bought and sold.

Typically cash or spot trading is OTC but occasionally some commodities such as tea, pepper and spices are still traded in salesrooms or at auction. Trades are non-standardised and each deal is individually negotiated specifying a particular delivery date, location, quality and quantity of commodity.

The parties to the trade must be very clear on the contract terms as there is a degree of risk involved in all OTC transactions which has to be assessed by both sides. Will the seller deliver and will the buyer pay on delivery?

As the contracts are private, the specific terms are not reported or made transparent by the counterparties. However, some exchanges, market-makers and official organisations quote spot prices for physical delivery **two business days** from the quote date – similar to the conditions used in the FX markets.

For energy products spot deliveries vary from 2 to 15 days – market places differ so you will have to be careful when using the term spot or cash.

You can find cash or spot prices for a range of commodities in the financial press such as the *Financial Times* or *The Wall Street Journal,* or by using an electronic data service, such as Reuters.

The screen displayed shows the **Latest Spot** prices of all the major currencies against the USD.

```
FX=                   Latest Spots
RIC              Bid/Ask   Contributor   Loc Srce Deal   Time  High      Low
GBP=      ↓   1.6908/18    DRESDNER       FFT DRE1 DRFF   06:49 1.6915    1.6875
GHC=      ↑   2110/2140    MERCHANT BNK   ACC NSAY        16:37
GIP=      ↑   1.6861/      RRU            LON EXOF        13:27
GMD=      ↓   9.8700/00    CEDEF          LON CEDD CEDX   08:49
GNF=      ↑   1090.5/01.5  W.A.D.S        CKY 1ZAF        18:35
GRD=      ↑   274.78/4.88  BARCLAYS       ATH BBXG BBIG   06:49 276.69    274.69
GTQ=      ↓   5.9012/      RRU            LON EXOG        13:36
GWP=      ↑ 35000.13/      RRU            LON EXOG        13:36
GYD=      ↑   142.30/      RRU            LON EXOG        15:21
HKD=      ↑   7.7410/20    FST CHICAGO    LON CHIC FNCD   06:41 7.7425    7.7413
HNL=      ↓   13/          RRU            LON EXOG        13:36
HRK=      ↓   6.2042/09    SOC GENERALE   ZAG SGHR SGZH   06:46 6.2362    6.2309
HTG=      ↑   16.6834/     RRU            LON EXOG        13:36
HUF=      ↓   187.98/8.03  MKB RT.        BUD MKBQ HFTB   06:49 188.70    187.94
IDR=      ↓   2430.40/0.90 DBS            SIN DBSS DBSS   06:47 2430.50   2429.29
IEP=      ↑   1.5231/51    ULSTER BANK    DUB UBFY UIBI   06:49 1.5231    1.5205
ILS=      ↑   3.5518/61    MARITIME BK    TLV MARB MARI   06:49 3.5741    3.5435
INR=      ↓   35.780/790   ANZ            BOM GBBY GBBY   06:46 35.787    35.580
IQD=      ↓   1200.0/      RRU            LON EXOG        16:15
IRR=      ↓   3000.00/     BNP            NYC      BNPY   20:37
ISK=      ↓   70.22/0.60   SEDLABANKI     RVK ICEX        11:00
ITL=      ↑   1703.00/4.50 BARCLAYS       LON BAXX BBIL   06:49 1708.00   1702.10
```

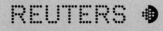

Look at the base and precious metal spot prices shown below.

```
0850 METALS OVERVIEW CASH QUOTES IN USD
XAU      339.10/339.50 GOLD PER TROY OZ
XAG        4.64/4.66   SILVER PER TROY OZ
XPT      373.00/374.00 PLATINIUM PER TROY OZ
XPD      157.75/158.75 PALLADIUM PER TROY OZ
CU       2520.0/25.0   LME COPPER OFFICIAL PER TONNE
AL       1606.0/06.5   LME ALUMINIUM OFFICIAL PER TONNE
ZN       1247.0/48.0   LME ZINC OFFICIAL PER TONNE
NI       7320/7330     LME NICKEL OFFICIAL PER TONNE
PB       626.00/6.50   LME LEAD OFFICIAL PER TONNE
SN       5685/5686     LME TIN OFFICIAL PER TONNE
AA       1475.0/77.0   LME ALUMINIUM ALLOY OFFICIAL PER TONNE


 FOR INFO SEE <S99B>
```

Depending on the market place you are considering you may have to be careful about the term **spot**. For some futures contracts the term spot is used to denote the **first contract month** – so be careful!

```
    ENERGY OVERVIEW          GMT
 BRENT DTD   17.94/98   28APR97 14:55
 IPE BRENT     18.24    28APR97 19:09
 IPE GASOIL   165.50    29APR97 08:36
 WTI CUSHG   19.80/90   28APR97 14:09
 NYMEX WTI     19.87    29APR97 06:50
 NYMEX No2     56.60    28APR97 21:48
 NYMEX ULD     62.25    29APR97 05:12
 NYMEX PRO               28APR97 18:40
 NYMEX NGS      2.082   28APR97 22:59
 CASH DUBAI  17.05/09   28APR97 14:55
                        28APR97 10:53


 FOR INFO SEE <S999>
```

It is important to remember that these cash or spot prices provide a **guide** only – they are not necessarily the prices used for a transaction.

For some commodities and energy products the majority of trading takes place using derivatives contracts – only about 10% of trading is for spot transactions. So why are spot prices important?

As you have seen already producers and users of commodities, such as rice, corn and crude oil, are always seeking ways to lock in future income or costs so that they can plan their businesses better. Commodity prices are unpredictable and volatile. The prices are dependent on factors such as weather conditions, crop disasters, political events, worker strikes etc. Buyers and sellers of commodities constantly seek to protect themselves against these risks of price volatility. If an oil producer can establish a price for crude oil today for future delivery, then this helps the producer predict cash flows and manage future financial commitments. Similarly, if a refinery can fix the price of future crude oil deliveries, then the prices of energy products can be established in advance.

The first solution to the producers and users dilemma was relatively simple. A **forward** contract was established between seller and buyer for the delivery of the commodity at a pre-determined rate and at a future date. One of the first modern **'to arrive'** contracts – as forward contracts were known – was agreed at the Chicago Board of Trade in March 1851 for corn (maize) to be delivered in June of that year. As with any OTC transaction these early forward contracts were not without risk – the quality of the commodity delivered was not always as agreed, deliveries were often late and in some cases contracts were never fulfilled.

The rest of this section is concerned with the derivative instruments used for transactions involving delivery of an asset or financial instrument at a future date. These are:

- Forward contracts

- Futures contracts

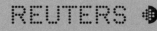

Forward Contracts

Forward contracts exist for a variety of commodities and underlying assets including:

- Metals

- Energy products

- Interest rates – Forward Rate Agreements (FRAs)

- Currency exchange rates – Forward FX transactions

In general, a forward contract is defined as follows:

> A **forward contract** is a transaction in which the buyer and the seller agree upon the delivery of a specified quality and quantity of asset at a specified future date. A price may be agreed on in advance or at the time of delivery.

It is important to remember that forward contracts are OTC transactions.

> Can you remember the differences between OTC and exchange traded contracts?

Forward contracts are not traded on an exchange and do not have standardised, transparent conditions. A forward contract involves a credit risk to both counterparties as in the spot market. In such circumstances the counterparties may require some kind of collateral that the other party will honour the contract.

Forward contracts are not normally negotiable and when the contract is made it has **no value**. No payment is involved as the contract is simply an agreement to buy or sell at a future date. Therefore the contract is neither an asset nor a liability.

A forward contract can be summarised as follows:

Contract agreed today...	...for future date
Terms and conditions agreed: • Price • Quantity and quality • Settlement date • Location for delivery • Any other conditions	On settlement: • Delivery at agreed date, location, terms and conditions • Payment on delivery

But how are forward prices determined? In principle, the forward price for a contract is determined by taking the spot or cash price at the time of the transaction and adding to it a **'cost of carry'**.

Depending on the asset or commodity, the cost of carry takes into account payments and receipts for matters such as storage, insurance, transport costs, interest payments, dividend receipts etc.

> **Forward price = Spot or cash price + cost of carry**

Forward and Futures Contracts

Interesting examples of forward contracts are the benchmark contracts for base metals on the **London Metal Exchange (LME)**. Although these are contracts traded on an exchange with some degree of transparency, the contracts are for 3 months where market players can take positions for any business day out to 3 months forward. This is a similar situation to that found in the OTC Forward FX markets.

Why are the contracts 3 months forward? Three months historically was the time it took for shipments of metals from South America to reach London. The LME is ultimately a physical market whereby all contracts involve the actual delivery or receipt of ingots of metal on the delivery date.

The 3 month LME contracts are rolling contracts which means that the contract expires exactly three months **forward** from the transaction date. For example, a 3 month Copper contract bought on 12th June 1997 expires on 12th September 1997.

Look at the prices of base metal 3 month forward contracts shown on the sample screen to the right before moving on. Pay attention to the two areas marked ∂ and Σ.

These are the IDs of the market-makers

```
LME          LONDON METAL EXCHANGE OVERVIEW        25-APR-1997        GMT: 14:44
TIME--METAL-MMID---3n Bid/Ask MM----LME FLOOR----TIME -METAL-MMID-- Cash to 3s-
14:38  CU  =REFO  ×2366.0/2369.0 | 2368.0/2369.0  14:35  CU  =BILL  b180.0/190.0b
13:58  SN  =AMTL    5715/5735    |       /        11:41  SN   RING       /46   c
14:25  PB  =WOLF  × 629.0/629.5  |  629.0/629.5   13:07  PB  =WOLF  c 11.0/10.5 c
14:30  ZN  =REFO  ×1270.0/1271.0 | 1270.0/1272.0  14:26  ZN   RING  c 21.5/21.0 c
14:40  AL  =WOLF  ×1596.0/1597.0 | 1596.0/1597.0  13:29  AL  =DSML  c 29.0/28.0 c
13:50  NI  BACH   × 7430/7450    |  7420/7440     13:29  NI  =DSML  c 115/112   c
12:34  AA  =WOLF  ×1475.0/1480.0 | 1475.0/1480.0  12:09  AA   RING  c 27.0/
14:37  CS  =WOLF  ×1459.0/1461.0 |
14:37  PS  =WOLF  × 387.5/389.0  (a)                CURRENT SESSION: SN 1st PM
                                                   '=' denotes RING Dealing Member
---GBP--- ---DEM--- ---JPY--- ---CHF--- --FTSE-- --DJI-- --SILVER-- ----GOLD----
1.6240/50 1.7179/86 125.73/78 1.4640/45  4366.8  6730.04   4.74/76   342.30/2.80

LME  (b)--Officials 25-APR-1997----- Stocks --  FOR MORE INFO DOUBLE CLICK ON:
           Cash      3 Months      25-APR-1997
CU     2568.0/2569.0  2368.0/2369.0    145200       QUICK SUMMARY:      <METAL/SUM>
SN     5690/5695      5715/5720         10735       MAIN INDEX:         <METAL1>
PB     624.0/625.0    633.0/634.0      114475       FORWARDS: <O#MCU:><O#MSN:>
ZN    1249.5/1250.0  1272.0/1273.0     434900                 <O#MPB:><O#MZN:>
AL    1568.0/1568.5  1596.0/1597.0     807225                 <O#MAL:><O#MNI:>
NI     7320/7325      7430/7440         50484                 <O#MAA:>
AA    1450.0/1455.0  1479.0/1480.0      68100       NEWS: [MTL] [C]
                                                    WORLD INDICES:     <O#.INDEX>
```

Stock levels for the metals

(a) The best forward 3 month Bid/Ask prices from the different market-makers are displayed here. These prices are used for OTC inter-office trading by members of the LME.

(b) These are the official LME prices used to settle contracts agreed on the exchange floor. You will probably notice that the official prices differ from those quoted by the market-makers.

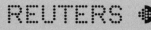

If you look closely at the official prices quoted for base metals on the LME you may notice that for some metals the cash price is higher than the 3 month price whereas for other metals the opposite situation occurs – the 3 month prices are lower than the cash prices.

```
┌─────────────────────────────────────────────────────────────────────┐
│ 0000 LME DAILY OFFICIAL PRICES (+REF PRICES)                    MTLE  │
│             CASH        3 MTHS      15 MTHS    27 MTHS    SETT         │
│ COPPER    2568.0/69.0 2368.0/69.0 2095.0/05.0 2035.0/45.0 2569.0      │
│ (STG EQ)    1582.38      1461.27                                      │
│ TIN        5690/5695    5715/5720   5780/5790              5695       │
│ LEAD      624.00/5.00  633.00/4.00 662.00/7.00            625.00      │
│ (STG EQ)    384.97       391.07                                       │
│ ZINC      1249.5/50.0 1272.0/73.0 1235.0/40.0 1190.0/95.0 1250.0      │
│ ALUMINUM  1568.0/68.5 1596.0/97.0 1620.0/25.0 1605.0/10.0 1568.5      │
│ NICKEL     7320/7325    7430/7440   7685/7705  7865/7885  7325        │
│ AL.ALLOY  1450.0/55.0 1479.0/80.0 1560.0/80.0             1455.0      │
│ SETTLEMENT RATES - GBP  1.6235   DEM  1.7161   JPY  125.63            │
│                                                                       │
│                    25 APR 1997                                        │
└─────────────────────────────────────────────────────────────────────┘
```

Why are some prices lower in 3 months than the present cash prices? Forward prices are derived from the underlying cash prices as has been explained. If a surplus of a commodity is expected in the future then forward prices will fall as the expected spot price will decline. On the other hand if the commodity is predicted to be in short supply in the future the forward price will increase.

Keeping a note of stock availability will help predict forward price rises or falls. Warehouse stock levels for LME metals are indicated next to the official prices on the screen on the previous page.

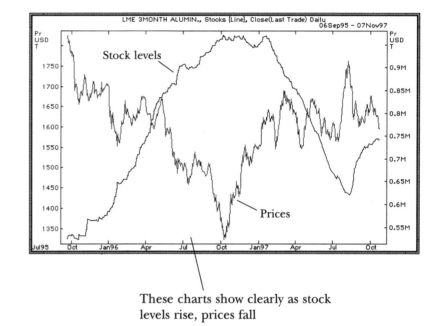

These charts show clearly as stock levels rise, prices fall

Forward and Futures Contracts

In the energy markets there are informal forward markets in crude oils and oil products. Forward markets have developed around **marker** or **benchmark** crude oils such as North Sea Brent Blend (15-day Brent) and West Texas Intermediate (WTI). In many of these forward contracts the parties agree to a cash settlement rather than take physical delivery.

The Brent 15-day market is the largest and most important crude oil forward market in the world. The Brent forward contract gives 15 days notice to the buyer to take delivery of a cargo at Sullom Voe during a notional 3-day loading period. The terms are either accepted or passed to another buyer who can repeat the process forming a 'chain'. This whole process is known as a **book-out**.

The majority of trades use a book-out process which means that the contracts are cleared by the buyers and sellers in a series of trades to cancel mutual contracts by cash settlement.

Before moving on, look at the crude oil forward prices to the right. In this screen, BRENT for JUL/AUG was selected.

```
CRDWLD              World Crudes                    14:53
IPE/   Last  Net  Bid   Ask   Spread  NYM/    Last      High  Low
JUN7  ↑1836  -5   1836  1837  +1.61   JUN7  ↑19.97 -0.06 20.11 19.86
JUL7  ↑1845  -2   1844  1847  +1.51   JUL7  ↑19.96 -0.03 20.05 19.88
AUG7  ↓1851  -4   1850  1856  +1.41   AUG7  ↑19.92 -0.04 19.95 19.88
GBP  1.6241/ 48   JPY  125.77/.82   CHF  1.4650/ 55   DEM  1.7196/ 99
Having trouble finding market report codes? See <NEWSXREF21> to <NEWSXREF
Crude   Deliv            Time  Diff    Deliv              Time
BRENT   DATED  17.98/18.02 14:50 Brent   DTD/JUN  -0.40/-0.30 16:52
BRENT   MAY/JUN 18.18/18.22 14:50 Brent   MAY/JUN  -0.18/-0.12 11:43
BRENT   JUN/JUL 18.33/18.37 14:50 Brent   JUN/JUL  -0.09/-0.06 11:44
BRENT   JUL/AUG 18.41/18.45 14:50 Brent   JUL/AUG  -0.09/-0.06 11:44
BONNY LT        18.38/18.42 14:50 BONNY LT         +0.35/+0.45 11:29
FLOTTA L        16.86/16.90 14:50 FLOTTA           -1.15/-1.10 16:54
FORTIES         18.11/18.15 14:50 Forties          +0.10/+0.15 16:54
EKOFISK         18.16/18.20 14:50 Ekofisk          +0.15/+0.20 16:54
STATFJOR        18.12/18.16 14:50 STATFJOR         +0.13/+0.15 16:18
ES SIDER        17.58/17.62 14:50 ES SIDER         -0.45/-0.35 15:53
DUBAI   JUN  16.83/16.87 14:50 Dubai   JUN/JUL  -0.20/-0.16 08:18
DUBAI   JUL  17.01/17.05 14:50 Dubai   JUL/AUG  -0.09/-0.07 08:18
DUBAI   AUG  17.09/17.13 14:50 Dubai   AUG/SEP  -0.10/-0.08 08:18
OMAN    JUN  17.75/17.85 10:10 OMAN/MPM JUN     -0.25/-0.15 10:10
OMAN    JUL  17.75/17.85 10:10 OMAN/MPM JUL     -0.25/-0.15 10:10
MURBAN  JUN  18.90/19.00 10:10 MURBAN  JUN      -0.05/+0.05 10:10
MINAS   MAY  17.90/18.10 10:28 MINAS Di MAY     +0.10/      10:28
TAPIS   MAY  18.90/19.10 10:28 TAPIS Di MAY     +0.30/      10:28
WTI     MAY  19.75/19.85 14:27                        /        :
```

```
BRT-3M           BRENT         25APR97 14:55

Loc     Delivery      Buy        Sell       C

EUR     JUL/AUG       18.45      18.49

Terms                 Size       Units

FOB SVOE              500KB      D/B

API/Spec  Spec Grav   Benchmark  Date

38.3      0.833       18.47      25APR97
```

The examples used so far have illustrated particular aspects of base metal and energy product forward contracts. However, forward contracts for many other commodities such as wheat, corn, soybeans etc will be similar in principle although the details may differ.

Have a look at the following screen showing spot and forward prices for Pepper. Under the Terms column you will see **CIF** and **FOB**. These terms indicate the types of delivery for different pepper contracts.

CIF and FOB

```
O#PEPPER                  PEPPER PHYSICALS                                          
Commodity        Del.Date      Last          Srce   Terms     Loc  Ccy Units Date
PEP SARAWAK FAQ  SPOT       ↑5350.00   0      RTRS   CIF R/H    MY  USD TONNE 02MAY97
PEP SARAWAK W SP MAY/JUN    ↑5250.00   0      RTRS   CIF R/H    MY  USD TONNE 02MAY97
PEP MUNTOK FAQ   SPOT       ↑5350.00   0      RTRS   CIF R/H    ID  USD TONNE 02MAY97
PEP MUNTOK W SH  MAY/JUN    ↑5250.00   0      RTRS   CIF R/H    ID  USD TONNE 02MAY97
PEP SARAWAK SPEC SPOT       ↑3650.00   0      RTRS   CIF R/H    MY  USD TONNE 02MAY97
PEP SARAWAK B SH MAY/JUN    ↑3525.00   0      RTRS   CIF R/H    MY  USD TONNE 02MAY97
PEP BRAZIL GRD 1 SPOT       ↑3800.00   0      RTRS   CIF R/H    BRA USD TONNE 02MAY97
PEP BRAZIL SHIP  MAY/JUN    ↑3700.00   0      RTRS   CIF R/H    BRA USD TONNE 02MAY97
PEP INDIA SHIP   MAY/JUN    ↓3600.00  -100.00 RTRS   CIF R/H    IND USD TONNE 02MAY97
PEP MUNTOK       SPOT       ↓ 717.50   0      RTRS   FOB SIN    ID  SGD KG100 06MAY97
PEP SARAWAK      SPOT       ↓ 695.00   0      RTRS   FOB SIN    MY  SGD KG100 06MAY97
PEP SARAWAK SPEC SPOT       ↓ 432.00   0      RTRS   FOB SIN    MY  SGD KG100 06MAY97
PEP SARAWAK ASTA SPOT       ↓ 467.00   0      RTRS   FOB SIN    MY  SGD KG100 06MAY97
```

The term **CIF** means **Cost-Insurance-Freight** – in other words the total cost of the contract including delivery is known. In this case the pepper will be delivered to Rotterdam Harbour – R/H.

FOB means **Free-On-Board** – in this case the buyer has to arrange and pay for transportation costs which must therefore be added to the quote price. In this case the pepper will be delivered to Singapore – SIN.

In general, a forward contract can be summarised as follows. Forward contracts are:

- Binding and non-negotiable

- Customised to customer requirements and are not reported

- Negotiable in terms of –

  - contract size

  - delivery grade of asset

  - delivery location

  - delivery date

The major advantage of a forward contract is that it fixes prices for a future date.

The major disadvantage of a forward contract is that if spot prices move one way or the other at the settlement date, then there is no way out of the agreement for the counterparties. Both sides are subject to the potential of gains or losses which are binding.

Is it possible for market players to both fix the forward price of an asset and combine it with the opportunity to take advantage of any future price volatility? The answer as you might expect is yes.

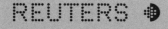

Futures Contracts – Overview

Why Have Futures Contracts?
The disadvantages and the problems posed for the early forward contracts traded to arrive were resolved in the mid-1860s by the introduction of **futures** contracts. In 1865 CBOT laid the foundation to all modern futures contracts by introducing grain agreements which standardised the following:

- The quality of the grain

- The quantity of grain for the contract

- The date and the location for the delivery of the grain

In effect the only condition left for the contract was the price. This was open to negotiation by both sides but was carried out on the floor of the exchange using open outcry. This meant that the prices agreed were available to all traders on the floor – the prices were transparent.

Over the next century or so more and more exchanges were trading futures contracts on a wide variety of commodities. By the early 1970s the world commodity and financial markets had been subjected to dramatic political, economic and regulatory changes leading to the introduction of floating exchange rates and vastly improved communications systems and computers. All these factors combined to produce volatile markets in which producers/users of commodities and issuers/buyers of financial instruments increasingly needed to protect their assets from the risk of price fluctuations.

The need to hedge against risk and the opportunities to speculate have both increased and helped establish the markets in derivative contracts such as futures. What is a futures contract? You have seen the following definition already in Section 1.

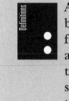
A **futures contract** is a firm contractual agreement between a buyer and seller for a specified asset on a fixed date in the future. The contract price will vary according to the market place but it is fixed when the trade is made. The contract also has a standard specification so both parties know exactly what is being traded.

The definition refers to a 'specified asset', but what exactly is this?

As you are probably aware by now there are two basic types of assets for which futures contracts exist. These are:

- Commodity futures contracts

- Financial futures contracts

Although both contracts are similar in principle, the methods of quoting prices, delivery and settlement terms vary according to the contract being traded.

Do you know any examples of financial futures contracts and the exchanges they are traded on?

 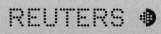

For simplicity the types of contracts available for commodities are summarised in the illustration below.

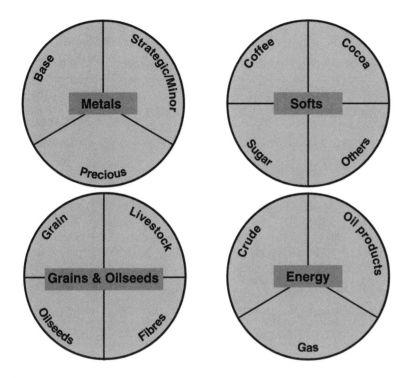

Financial futures comprise the following contracts based on:

- **Interest rates** — eg, short selling

- **Bond prices** — eg, long gilt futures

- **Currency exchange rates**

- **Equity stock indices**

Futures Contracts and Exchanges

Both commodity and financial futures contracts are traded on exchanges worldwide. Futures contracts share the following common features. They are:

- Standardised

- Traded on an exchange

- Open and their prices are published

- Organised by a **clearing house**

The involvement of a clearing house, which differs from exchange to exchange, means that the contract is not directly between the buyer and the seller but between each of them and the clearing house. The clearing house acts as a counterparty to both sides which provides protection to both sides and allows trading to take place more freely.

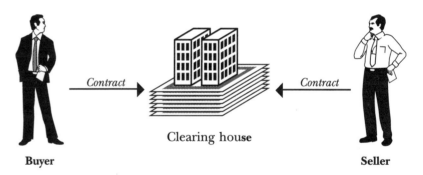

Clearing house

Buyer   **Seller**

It is important to remember that a futures contract does **not** predict what prices will be in the future. It is also important to remember that if a contract is allowed to **expire** this means that delivery must take place under the terms of the contract.

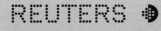

Forward and Futures Contracts

Before moving on, look at the following map of the locations of some of the world's exchanges where futures contracts are traded. Although trading during exchange hours is open outcry and takes place in pits or rings, trading takes place effectively 24 hours per day when combined with automated after-hours trading systems. Many exchanges now have their own systems where previously GLOBEX, a joint Reuters/CME development, was used.

Increasingly exchanges are entering into global partnerships with other exchanges or have Mutual Offset Systems. These systems allow futures contracts to be opened on one exchange, for example, SIMEX, and closed on another, for example, CME.

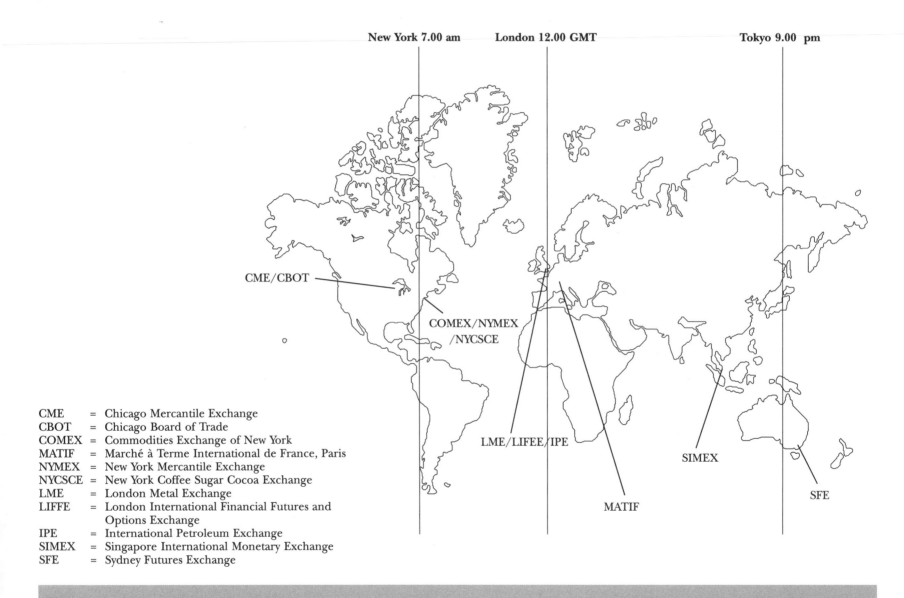

CME	=	Chicago Mercantile Exchange
CBOT	=	Chicago Board of Trade
COMEX	=	Commodities Exchange of New York
MATIF	=	Marché à Terme International de France, Paris
NYMEX	=	New York Mercantile Exchange
NYCSCE	=	New York Coffee Sugar Cocoa Exchange
LME	=	London Metal Exchange
LIFFE	=	London International Financial Futures and Options Exchange
IPE	=	International Petroleum Exchange
SIMEX	=	Singapore International Monetary Exchange
SFE	=	Sydney Futures Exchange

Trading on Margin

When a futures contract is agreed, the full contract price is not paid at that time. Instead, **both** counterparties make an initial 'good faith' or **margin** payment to the clearing house. This **initial margin** or deposit is usually only 5-10% of the total contract value – different exchanges and contracts require different initial margins. The fact that both counterparties deposit initial margin assures the integrity of the contract.

Once a contract has been purchased, it can be sold and closed at any time prior to the settlement date. With this in mind a futures contract is **marked-to-market** on a daily basis. This means the contract value is calculated at the close of exchange trading every day it is open.

All profits and losses are credited to or debited from the counterparties' clearing house accounts daily. Any profits can be withdrawn. If a loss occurs, then extra margin called variation margin is paid to cover this loss. Payment of a variation margin ensures that the initial margin remains at a constant level. These payments are usually required in the same currency as that of the contract.

Only clearing members of the exchange maintain accounts directly with the clearing house. All other market participants will deal through their brokers/clearing members.

This system of maintaining margin ensures the loser can bear any losses and that winners are credited with their gains.

A futures margin payment is in effect a performance pledge that each of the counterparties' obligations will be met.

Minimum initial margins are set by the exchange. Brokers are free to add a mark-up to the minimum prescribed on their clients. Initial margins are subject to change, depending on market volatility and risk perception. Also, in some cases, near month contracts may carry higher margins.

The system is illustrated in the following example for a futures contract for Gold.

On the contract date

1. The Seller sells the Buyer a Gold contract

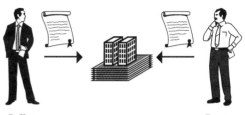

Seller   Buyer

2. Both Buyer and Seller deposit margin with the clearing house

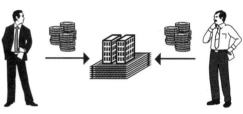

Seller   Buyer

During the contract

Both the Buyer and the Seller have their accounts adjusted daily for profit or loss

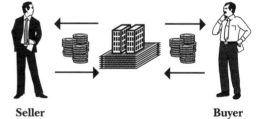

Seller   Buyer

If the contract expires

The Seller delivers a warrant for the Gold to the Buyer. The Buyer pays the Seller the futures contract amount

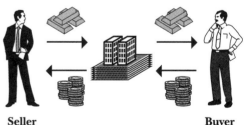

Seller   Buyer

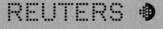

Forward and Futures Contracts

Legend:

Contract

Clearing house

Money
(profit/loss or
contract amount)

Gold warrant

Trading on margin is an example of **gearing** or **leverage**. Gearing allows market players to make larger trades than they could otherwise afford. Small margins can generate large profits but equally large losses can also be had! Problems in the financial and commodity markets may occur because sellers of futures have a limited amount of an asset to protect whereas buyers may purchase a number of contracts on margin for short-term trading. For example, for a buyer required to pay a $1000 margin on a futures contract, this is equivalent to buying $10-20,000 of commodity or financial asset if the contract expires.

You now have considered some of the basic differences between forward and futures contracts. Before moving on try the activity opposite.

Use the space here to write down any thoughts you may have concerning the following question.

What are the differences between forward and futures contracts and the way they are used?

No specific answer is given as it is covered in the following text.

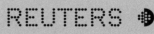

The distinctions between forward and futures contracts are summarised in the table below. However, the main difference is that a **forward contract** is a **one-off OTC** agreement between a buyer and a seller, whereas a **futures contract** is a **repeat offer traded on an exchange**.

Futures contracts...	Forwards contracts...
• Are traded on an exchange	• Are **not** traded on an exchange – OTC
• Use a clearing house which provides protection for both parties	• Are private and are negotiated between the parties with no exchange guarantees
• Require a margin to be paid	• Involve no margin payments
• Are used for hedging and speculating	• Are used for hedging and physical delivery
• Are standardised and published	• Are dependent on the negotiated contract conditions
• Are transparent – futures contracts are reported by the exchange	• Are not transparent as there is no reporting requirement – they are private deals

Who Uses Futures Contracts?

In the table opposite, the terms hedging and speculating appear, with which you may not be familiar. These terms describe two of the three most important market players who are described as:

- Hedgers

- Speculators

- Arbitrageurs

Hedgers

These are market players who wish to protect an existing asset position from future adverse price movements. For example, both producers and consumers of commodities will hedge their positions in the cash or physical markets using futures contracts.

In order to hedge a position, a market player needs to take an equal and opposite position in the futures market to the one held in the cash market. There are two types of hedges, short and long. In a short hedge, you take a short futures position to offset an existing long position in the cash market. For example, a fund manager with a portfolio of stocks could hedge against a decline in stock prices by selling stock index futures contracts. In a long hedge, you take a long futures position to offset an existing short position in the cash market. A crude oil refiner could lock in the buying price by buying crude oil futures contracts today. Whether you are hedging an anticipated cash transaction or a current market position, the purpose of hedging is the same - any loss you make in one market is offset by a profit made in the other market. The hedging positions are summarised in the tables opposite.

Forward and Futures Contracts

Short Hedge

Short Hedge		
in the cash market...	**so in the futures market**	**Resulting hedge**
are **long** because they hold the commodity	sellers need to be **short** or **sell** futures contracts, in other words **go short**.	The positions are opposite so it protects the seller's risk against declining prices in the cash market. Any cash price move **down** is offset by futures contract earnings.

If the prices for the asset **fall** in the cash market then at the time the market player decides to sell futures, any loss on the cash market is offset by the profit made by the gains from the futures contract. The diagrams below show how the loss in the cash market is offset by the gains in the futures markets.

Short Hedge – seller of an asset in futures market

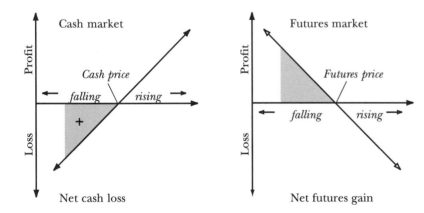

Long Hedge

Long Hedge		
in the cash market...	**so in the futures market**	**Resulting hedge**
are **short** because they need to buy the commodity	buyers need to be **long** or **buy** futures contracts, in other words **go long**.	The positions are opposite so it protects the buyer's risk against rising prices in the cash market. Any cash price move **up** is offset by futures contract earnings.

If prices for the asset **rise** in the cash market, then at the time the market player decides to buy futures, any loss in the cash market is offset by the profit made from the gains from the futures contract. The diagrams below show how the loss in the cash market is offset by the gains in the futures markets.

Long Hedge – buyer of an asset in futures market

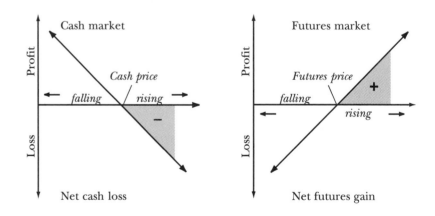

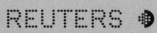

By using futures contracts, hedging removes the opportunity to profit if future cash prices rise but provides the required protection if future cash prices fall. In this respect hedging is in effect an insurance contract which locks in the future price of a commodity or financial asset.

Speculators

Speculators accept the risk that hedgers wish to transfer. Speculators have no position to protect and do not necessarily have the physical resources to make delivery of the underlying asset nor do they necessarily need to take delivery of the underlying asset. They take positions on their **expectations** of future price movements and in order to make a profit. In general they:

- **Buy** futures contracts – go long – when they expect futures prices to **rise**

- **Sell** futures contracts – go short – when they expect futures prices to **fall**

Speculators provide **liquidity** to the markets and without them the price protection – insurance – required by hedgers would be very expensive. There are three types of speculators:

- Scalper
- Day Trader
- Position Trader

Of all speculators, scalpers have the shortest horizon over which they plan to hold a futures position. A scalper goes for minimum price fluctuations on heavy volumes, taking small profits or small losses. They rarely hold positions overnight.

Day traders attempt to profit from the price movements that may take place over the course of one trading day. The day trader closes his or her position before the end of each trading each day so that he or she has no position in the futures market overnight.

A position trader is a speculator who maintains a futures position overnight. On occasion, speculators may hold positions for weeks or even months. There are two types of position traders, those holding an outright position and those holding a spread position. Of the two strategies, the outright position is far riskier.

An outright position trader who is bullish on the US stock market would buy the S&P 500 Stock Index futures contract. If he is right in his market view, the S&P 500 futures price would rise and he can then liquidate his position and reap his profit. However, if his view is wrong, and stock prices decline, the outright position trader may suffer significant losses.

The more risk-averse position traders may prefer to trade spreads. Spreads involve the simultaneous purchase and sale of two or more contract maturities for the same underlying deliverable instrument (known as intra-commodity spreads) or two or more contracts written on different, but related, underlying instruments (also known as inter-commodity spreads). The spread trader's risk is that of the relative price, change of different contract months or different, related instruments of the same maturity.

Arbitrageurs

These are traders and market-makers who deal in buying and selling futures contracts hoping to profit from **price differentials** between markets and/or exchanges.

Relationship between Cash and Futures Prices

For most commodities the futures price is usually **higher** than the current spot price. This is because there are costs associated with storage, freight and insurance etc which have to be covered for the futures delivery. When the futures price is higher than the spot price the situation is known as **contango**.

If a chart is drawn of spot and futures prices then as the futures expiry date is approached the plots converge. This is because the costs diminish over time and become zero at the delivery date. The difference between the futures and spot prices at any time is called the **basis**. A contango chart for a 3 month futures contract might look something like this:

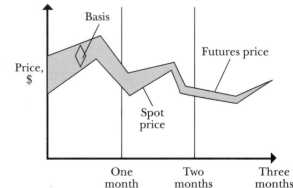

Forward and Futures Contracts

	Cash	3 Months
CU	3083.0/3085.0	2967.0/2968.0
AL	1799.0/1800.0	1820.0/1821.0
AA	1590.0/1600.0	1630.0/1640.0
ZN	1031.0/1032.0	1052.0/1053.0
NI	8630/8635	8730/8740
PB	622.0/622.5	635.0/636.0
SN	6955/6965	6840/6850

If you look at these metal prices you will see that the futures prices for Aluminium (AL), Aluminium Alloy (AA), Zinc (ZN), Nickel (NI) and Lead (PB) are all higher than the spot prices. However, the prices for Copper (CU) and Tin (SN) are lower.

When the futures price is **lower** than the spot price the market is said to be in **backwardation**. Backwardation occurs in times of shortage caused by strikes, undercapacity etc but the futures price stays steady as more supplies are expected in the future.

For metals you can see at a glance whether the market prices are in backwardation (b) or contango (c) – the price differences between the cash and futures prices on the right side of the screen use the letters **b** and **c** for each metal. The difference between the prices is known as the **spread**; b and c are known as the spread symbols.

– Cash to 3s––
b110.0/120.0b
/20.0 c
c 35.0/30.0 c
c 21.0/20.0 c
c 127/124 c
c 13.5/12.5 c
b 120/130 b

Charts of future prices over time are similar to yield curves for money market and debt market financial instruments. **Contango** markets indicate the future prices are at a **premium** to cash markets; **backwardation** markets indicate a **discount** to cash prices.

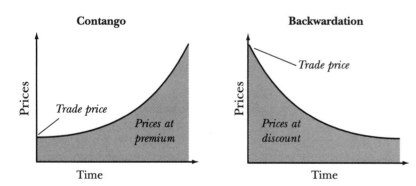

Basis is particularly important when considering commodities such as grain where the futures contract specifies delivery to an exchange such as the Chicago Board of Trade. The following example may help you to understand the importance of basis.

Example

The December futures price for corn is $2.58 per bushel and the cash price in Chicago is $2.38 per bushel. However, in Smallville, USA, the local cash price is only $2.18 – a price which reflects no transport costs, lower storage costs etc. The basis for a Smallville farmer over Chicago futures is therefore 40¢.

If the futures price remains constant but both the Chicago and Smallville cash prices rise by 2¢, then the local basis falls to 38¢. The local basis figures are illustrated in the chart below.

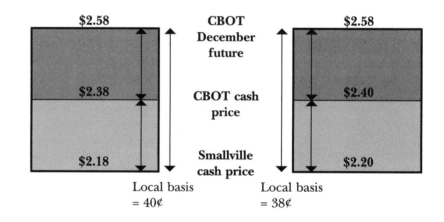

Local basis and basis patterns are very important to producers and are used in decisions such as:

- Accepting/rejecting cash offers for a commodity

- Whether and when to store crops

- When and in what delivery month to hedge

- When to close or lift a hedge

- When to turn an advantageous basis situation into a profit

Hedging Strategies

Hedging
There are three basic types of hedge that market players operate depending on their position. In other words the hedge depends on their decision to buy or sell a futures contract. The hedging strategies are:

- Short or seller's hedge
- Long or buyer's hedge
- Cross hedge

Trading Strategies
Market players employ these hedges to achieve the following trading strategies:

a) Outright trading
b) Spread trading
c) Arbitrage

Outright trading
Outright trading is when a trader assumes a long position (bullish) or a short position (bearish) with the motive of profit maximization.

In October, a trader who is bullish on Eurodollar futures buys ten contracts of the December Eurodollar futures at 95.25. The profit and loss on his trade is given in the following table.

If December Eurodollar futures rose to 95.69	If December Eurodollar futures declined to 95.04

Bought 10 Dec ED 95.25
Sold 10 Dec ED 95.69
Profit = (9569-9525) x
    US$25 x 10 = US$11,000
	Bought 10 Dec ED 95.25
	Sold 10 Dec ED 95.04
	Loss = (9504-9525) x
	    US$25 x 10 = -US$5,250

Spread trading
Spreading is a form of speculative trading that involves the simultaneous purchase and sale of related contracts. The spreader's aim is to profit from a change in the difference (ie spread) between the two futures contracts, not the outright futures prices.

There are two basic types of spread trading in common use:

- Intracommodity spreads
- Intercommodity spreads

An intracommodity spread occurs when the spreader trades the same futures contract but on different delivery months on the same exchange. These are also known as "time spreads" or "calendar spreads."

> eg   BUY MARCH EURODOLLAR
> SELL JUNE EURODOLLAR

An intercommodity spread occurs when the spreader takes a long position in one contract and a short position in a different but economically related contract.

> eg   BUY MARCH EURODOLLAR
> SELL MARCH EUROYEN

Spreading strategies assume that prices of both the long and short contracts are related and will usually move in line with one another. If the trader believes that the current price relationship between the two contracts is out of line, he will buy the relatively underpriced contract and sell the relatively overpriced contract.

If the markets move as expected the dealer profits from the change in the price relationship between the contracts rather than the more volatile movements in absolute price. Spread trading is generally considered to be less risky than taking outright positions, hence it usually incurs lower margins.

Spreads are used for many futures contracts. The following table indicates some of the more common spread trading contracts.

Futures contracts	Typical spreads
Commodities	**Softs** – Cocoa, Coffee, Sugar, Orange juice **Grains** – Soybeans, corn, wheat, oats **Livestock** – Cattle, live hog
Interest rates	T-Bills over Eurodollars (TED) Notes over Bonds (NOB)
Currency	Major currencies – DEM, CHF, GBP, JPY Cross currencies – GBP/DEM, CHF/DEM

Below is a screen for intermonth spreads for the various sugar contracts on different exchanges. The screen also displays spreads for similar contracts over different exchanges – this is discussed later.

```
SUGGLOBE                      WORLD SUGAR SUMMARY                    18:17
LCE5  Last   Net   Bid/Ask    Vol   Sprd  11v5 NY11  Last   Net  High  Low   Sprd
AUG7 ↑310.5 -1.7  310.3 310.5 1711 -10.0  2.81 MAY7 ↓11.15 -0.18 11.45 10.95 -0.18
OCT7 ↓300.5 -4.1  300.3 300.5  770  -1.2  2.82 JUL7 ↓10.92 -0.07 11.09 10.92 -0.14
DEC7 ↓299.3 -2.8  299.0 299.3  134    0   2.85 OCT7 ↓10.77 -0.04 10.88 10.77 -0.06
MAR8 ↑299.3 -2.0  299.0 299.3   50  -0.3       MAR8 ↓10.75 -0.07 10.84 10.75 -0.05
MAY8 ↓299.0 -2.2  298.5 299.5   15              MAY8 ↓10.76 -0.09 10.80 10.76 -0.06
AUG8              298.0 300.5                   JUL8         -0.08               -0.07
Par  Last   Net   Bid/Ask    Vol   Sprd  5vPar NY14  Last   Net  High  Low   Sprd
OCT7 ↑304.5 -0.5  300.5 301.5  110  -7.20 -0.50 JUL7 ↓21.80 +0.04 21.81 21.80  0.11
DEC7 ↑302.0 +0.3  298.0 301.0    1  -2.50 -1.10 SEP7  21.90       21.90 21.90  0.22
MAR8 ↓301.0 -0.5  298.5 301.0   44  -1.00       NOV7         -0.02              -0.05
MAY8              298.5 301.5             0.50  JAN8         +0.01               0.02
AUG8              300.0 301.5                   MAR8         +0.01               0.24
OCT8              294.0 297.0                   MAY8         +0.03               0.08
          Key Foreign Exchange Rates            NYWS  Last   Net  High  Low   Sprd
                                                JUL7
                                                OCT7
GBP  1.6248  1.6253   DEM  1.7296 1.7306        DEC7
JPY 126.96  127.06    CHF  1.4721 1.4726        MAR8
FRF  5.8304  5.8327   BRL  1.0631 1.0636        MAY8                       = = =
       Global Sugar Physical Prices <OHSUGAR>   Sugar News [SUG]  Softs News [SOF]
            Full Sugar Index <SUGAR1>   New Speed Guide Page <COMMOD>
```

The ways traders use intracommodity spreads depend on whether the market is contango or backwardation and is summarised below.

For a Contango Situation		
Where	**If the market view is that basis will...**	**Then for futures contracts**
Near month price is **less** than far month	**Narrow**	Buy near month Sell far month
	Widen	Sell near month Buy far month

For a Backwardation Situation		
Where	**If the market view is that basis will...**	**Then for futures contracts**
Near month price is **more** than far month	**Narrow**	Sell near month Buy far month
	Widen	Buy near month Sell far month

Arbitrage

There are a two main forms of arbitrage employed.

- Futures – Futures Arbitrage
- Cash – Futures Arbitrage/Cash-and-carry Arbitrage

Futures – Futures arbitrage occurs when dealers attempt to profit from the change in price differentials between two exchanges eg, LIFFE and NYCSCE cocoa or between two products, eg, Arabica and Robusta coffee.

Cash-and-carry arbitrage involves the purchase of a physical commodity against the forward sale of that commodity on the futures market. The display below illustrates examples of exchange spreads for similar products and the intermonth spreads for the same contract on the same exchange.

```
OILOIL                        IPE - NYMEX Futures                        14:50
Brent Last  Net  Bid   Ask   Vol   Sprd WTI/Bt WTI   Last   Net  High  Low   Sprd
JUN7 ↓1835   -6  1833  1837  7121 -0.10  1.61 JUN7 ↑19.96 -0.07 20.11 19.86    0
JUL7 ↑1845   -2  1843  1845  3159 -0.06  1.51 JUL7 ↑19.96 -0.03 20.05 19.88  0.04
AUG7 ↓1851   -4  1850  1854   380        1.41 AUG7 ↓19.92 -0.04 19.95 19.88  0.04
SEP7                   1858              1.35 SEP7 ↓19.88 -0.04 19.88 19.88  0.08
OCT7                                     1.35 OCT7 ↓19.80 -0.10 19.84 19.80 -0.02
NOV7                                     1.38 NOV7 ↓19.82 -0.06 19.88 19.82  0.02
Gasoil Last  Net  Bid   Ask   Vol   Sprd Gsl/HO Heat Last   Net  High  Low   Sprd
MAY7 ↑16600 +125 16600 16625 3917 -0.25 -2.72 MAY7 ↑ 5570  -19  5600  5530  1.65
JUN7 ↑16625 +125 16625 16650 2357 -1.50 -0.99 JUN7 ↑ 5405   -3  5415  5380     0
JUL7 ↑16775 +125 16750 16800  860 -1.75 -0.51 JUL7 ↑ 5405   -8  5410  5385 -0.55
AUG7 ↑16950 +100 16900 16950  819 -1.75 -0.50 AUG7 ↑ 5450  -13  5465  5440 -0.40
SEP7 ↑17125  +75 17075 17150   10 -1.50 -0.34 SEP7 ↓ 5500  -33  5535  5500 -0.80
OCT7 ↓17275  +50 17250 17300   33       -0.66 OCT7 ↓ 5580  -28  5610  5580 -0.65
Unld Swap FOB ARA Bid   Ask                   Unld Last   Net  High  Low   Sprd
MAY          196.00 97.00                     MAY7 ↑ 6265  -19  6315  6230  0.95
JUN          192.50 93.50                     JUN7 ↑ 6170  -15  6215  6150  1.05
GBP  1.6242  1.6247      DEM  1.7190 1.7200    JUL7 ↑ 6065  -12  6110  6050  1.10
JPY  125.73  125.83      CHF  1.4649 1.4654    AUG7 ↑ 5955   -8  5960  5940  1.25
FRF  5.8030  5.8050      NLG  1.9338 1.9348    SEP7 ↓ 5830   -5  5850  5830 = = =
Help:<ENERGY>  Other key pages:<OILAXS><NYMOIL><IPEOIL><OILARB><OILSPD><CRDWLD>
Having trouble finding market report codes? See <NEWSXREF21> to <NEWSXREF26>
```

These figures show the spreads for futures prices between those for IPE Brent crude and the NYMEX contracts for the equivalent crude, WTI

These figures show the intermonth spreads for IPE Brent and Gasoil futures

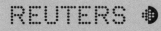

Off-Setting Contracts

As the expiry date of a futures contract approaches, the contract price gradually tends to the current cash price. In other words the basis or spread approaches zero. On expiry the futures contract price **equals** the cash price.

For this reason, unless the buyer or seller wishes to take or make delivery of the underlying asset, the vast majority – over 95% – of futures contracts are **closed out** before the agreed expiry date is reached.

Off-setting or closing out involves taking an **equal and opposite position for exactly the same contract**.

The difference in price from the original contract transaction to that when the contract is off-set represents the gain or loss on the trade. The process for a buy/sell close out is illustrated below – for a sell/buy close out the positions are reversed.

Position	For the **same contract month**	Commodity or asset **delivery**
Initial	**Buy** futures contract	Agree to **take**
To off-set	**Sell** futures contract	Agree to **make**
Result	Positions cancel = **Close out**	Positions cancel = **Close out**

If the original contract price was $100.00 and the position was closed out at $102.00, then a **profit** of $2.00 is made. If the position is closed out at $98.00, then the result is a loss of $2.00.

Your notes

Commodity and Energy Futures Contracts

As you have seen, commodity futures contracts are some of the oldest traded derivatives.

The chart opposite lists some of the commodity and energy futures contracts available on a selection of exchanges.

See if you can find the exchange listing a futures contract for National Catastrophe Insurance.

Chicago Board of Trade	LIFFE
Soybean	No.7 Cocoa
Corn	Robusta coffee
Wheat	No.5 White sugar
Kilo Gold	No.7 Premium sugar
1000 oz Silver	Potato
	Wheat
Chicago Mercantile Exchange	Barley
	BIFFEX
Live cattle	
Live hog	**International Petroleum Exchange**
Frozen pork bellies	
Broiler chickens	Brent crude oil
Random length lumber	Gas oil
	Natural gas
Coffee Sugar & Cocoa Exchange	
	London Metal Exchange
Cocoa	
Coffee C	Aluminium Alloy
Sugar No.11	Aluminium
Sugar No.14	Copper
White sugar	Lead
	Nickel
New York Mercantile Exchange	Tin
	Zinc
Light sweet crude oil	
Heating oil	**SIMEX**
Unleaded gasoline	
Natural gas	Brent crude oil
Liquefied Petroleum Gas	Gold
Electricity	
Platinum	
Palladium	

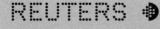

Commodity and energy contracts' details vary from type to type and from exchange to exchange. The following example is taken from the specification for a CME contract and indicates the terms and conditions involved with a typical commodities futures contract.

CME Frozen Pork Bellies Futures	
Trading unit	40,000 lbs USDA inspected pork bellies
Price quote	$ per hundred pounds or cents per pound
Minimum price fluctuation (Tick)	.025 = $10.00/tick 2.5¢/100lbs or .025¢/lb
Daily price limit	2.00 = $800.00 $2.00/100lbs 2.0¢/lb
Contract months	Feb, Mar, May, July, Aug
Trading hours (Chicago time)	9.10am - 1.00pm Last day 9.10am - 12.00pm
Last day of trading	The business day immediately preceding the last 5 business days of the contract month
Delivery days	Any business day of the contract month
Delivery points	Consult CME for list of current warehouses

This is the standard contract size.

The futures price is quoted as either $/100lbs or ¢/lb.

This is smallest amount a contract can change value. Because the contract conditions are standardised the tick value has a specific value.

This is the maximum daily allowable amount a futures price may advance or decline in any one day's trading session.

This is the trading cycle of contract months.

Exchange trading hours – open outcry.

This is the last day and time trading can take place.

This is the day contracts are settled.

The locations specified for physical delivery.

Futures prices are published in the financial press and appear something like the information for CME Pork Bellies futures shown here:

Livestock					
Pork Bellies (CME) 40,000lbs.; cents per lb					
	Open	High	Low	Settle	Change
Feb	43.80	44.35	43.15	43.77	−.35
Mar	43.80	43.77	42.80	43.42	−.50
May	44.15	44.65	43.65	44.30	....
July	44.50	44.75	43.90	44.62	+.07
Aug	41.70	42.00	41.50	41.90	+.22

Using this information, if you wished to purchase a CME Pork Bellies futures contract for August, the implied payment for 40,000lbs of pork bellies is 40,000 x 41.90¢ = $16,760.

 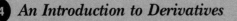
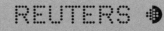

Financial Futures Contracts

The worldwide economic and political upheavals of the early 1970s meant that many large organisations and governments were exposed to rapid changes in interest rates and foreign exchange rates. In order to hedge asset positions and protect against position exposures, exchanges introduced a variety of currency and interest rate futures contracts. These contracts were based on the principles established for commodity futures but were referred to as **financial futures** in order to distinguish them.

Over the next decade a variety of financial futures contracts were introduced – some are now discontinued and no longer traded. The introduction of new contracts on exchanges is a constant process – as worldwide financial conditions change so does the need to hedge and protect assets.

There are three broad types of financial futures as follows:

- **Currency futures**. These were first introduced by the International Monetary Market division of the Chicago Mercantile Exchange in 1972.

- **Interest rate futures**. These were first introduced by the Chicago Board of Trade as futures on Government National Mortgage Association (GNMA) certificates known as **Ginnie Maes** in 1975. These contracts are no longer traded but many exchanges now trade interest rate futures on both short- and long-term assets. Contracts on long-term assets having bonds as the underlying instrument are also known as **bond futures**.

- **Equity index futures**. These were introduced by the International Options Market division of the Chicago Mercantile Exchange as contracts on the Standard & Poor's 500 Index in 1982. In the same year the Kansas Board of trade introduced a contract on the Value Line Index.

The table below lists some of the financial futures contracts available on a selection of exchanges – the list is by no means exhaustive.

Chicago Board of Trade	LIFFE
US Treasury Bond 30-day Fed Funds	*Short term interest rate* Three month Sterling Three month Euromark Three month Eurodollar *Government bonds* Long gilt German Government bond *UK Stock Indices* FT-SE 100
Chicago Mercantile Exchange	
Interest rate (IMM) One month LIBOR 13 week T-Bills *Currencies (IMM)* Deutschemark Yen Swiss franc British pound *Indices (IOM)* S&P 500 Index Nikkei Stock Average FT-SE 100 Share Index	**SIMEX**
	Interest rate Eurodollar Euroyen Euromark Japanese Government bonds *Stock Indices* Nikkei 225 Average Nikkei 300

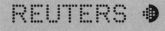

Forward and Futures Contracts

Just as for commodity and energy contracts, details for financial futures vary from type to type and from exchange to exchange. The following example is taken from the specification for a LIFFE contract and indicates the terms and conditions for a short-term interest rate futures contract.

LIFFE 3-month Sterling Interest Rate Future		
Unit of Trading	£500,000	This is the standard contract size.
Delivery Months	Mar, Jun Sept, Dec	This is the trading cycle of contract months.
Delivery Day	First business day after the last trading day	This is the day contracts are settled.
Last Trading Day	11.00 Third Wednesday of delivery month	This is the last day and time on which trading can take place.
Quotation	100 minus rate of interest	The futures price is quoted according to the type of future – short or long-term.
Minimum price movement (Tick size and value)	0.01 (£12.50)	This is the smallest amount a contract can change value and the 'tick' size.
Trading hours	07.15 – 16.02 London time	Exchange trading hours – open outcry.
APT Trading hours	16.27 – 17.57	Computer-based trading system hours.

Futures prices are published in the financial press and appear something like the information for LIFFE 3 month Sterling futures shown here:

LIFFE 3 month Sterling Futures £500,000 points of 100%				
	Open	High	Low	Settle
Mar	93.74	93.76	93.74	93.75
Jun	93.55	93.57	93.55	93.56
Sep	93.35	93.37	93.33	93.35
Dec	93.20	93.21	93.17	93.18

Here is an example of the contract specification for the SIMEX Nikkei 225 Stock Index Futures.

Nikkei 225 Stock Index		
Unit of Trading	¥500	This is the standard contract size.
Delivery Months	Mar, Jun Sept, Dec	This is the trading cycle of contract months.
Trading hours	8.55am – 11.15am 12.15pm – 3.15pm 4.00pm – 8.00pm* (electronic trading hours)	Exchange trading hours – open outcry except where noted.
Minimum price movement (Tick size and value)	0.01 (¥2,500)	This is the smallest amount a contract can change value and the 'tick' size.
Last Trading Day	11.00 The day before the second Friday of the contract month	This is the last day and time on which trading can take place.

 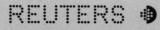

Financial futures are used by market players to protect their assets against adverse price movements. The positions they take depend on market volatility and are summarised in the table below.

Financial futures contract	Sell short to protect against	Buy long to protect against
Interest rate	**Rise** in interest rates	**Fall** in interest rates
Currency	**Fall** in currency	**Rise** In currency value
Equity index	**Fall** in equity index value	**Rise** in equity index value

Your notes

Forward and Futures Contracts

The Importance of Forwards and Futures

In order to assess the importance of exchange traded futures contracts in the commodity and financial markets worldwide it is necessary to compare them with derivatives traded in the OTC markets. However, any comparison is not easy as it is almost impossible to compare like-with-like. For example, futures contracts are not traded OTC.

It is possible to compare the **derivatives** of all types – forwards, futures, options and swaps – traded OTC and on exchanges. But what measures are used to compare statistics? Two commonly used measures are as follows:

- **Notional amounts outstanding**. These are the notional values of trades concluded but not yet settled. The measure provides an indication of market size and an indication of potential transfer to price risk.

- **Turnover**. This provides a measure of market activity and of market liquidity. It is the gross value of trades concluded but not yet settled in terms of the nominal value for forwards, futures and swaps and in terms of notional amounts and premiums paid and received for options.

It is not possible to obtain market data from a single source which covers all aspects of the derivatives markets. The data used for comparisons here has been drawn from the following organisations:

- Bank for International Settlements (BIS)

- Commodities Futures Trading Commission (CFTC)

- The exchanges

OTC v Exchange Traded Derivatives

Although comparisons are difficult the BIS has produced a number of reports from which the following statistics are drawn. The table below summarises some of the data.

Derivatives traded	Outstandings USD billions	Average daily turnover USD billions
OTC	**40,637**	**880**
Currency swaps	1,957	7
Currency options	2,379	41
FRAs	4,597	65
Interest rate swaps	18,283	62
Interest rate options	3,548	21
Equity derivatives	579	–
Commodity derivatives	318	–
Exchange based	**8,186**	**570**

Average daily turnover USD billions	OTC	Exchange traded
Foreign exchange	720	7
Interest rates	160	563
Total	**880**	**570**

BIS: Central Bank Survey of Foreign Exchange and Derivative Market Activity 1995

1. OTC trading dominates the derivative markets in terms of the notional amounts outstanding. However, it must be noted that the foreign exchange data here includes those for forward outright and FX swap transactions. Some of the individual derivative amounts are indicated.

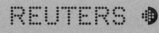

2. Based on average daily turnover amounts, OTC trading accounts for almost two-thirds of worldwide derivatives trading.

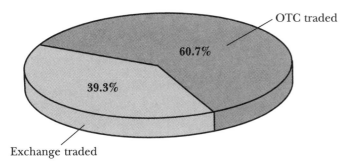

3. The most important OTC and exchange traded derivatives contracts involve foreign exchange and interest rates. In the OTC markets, foreign exchange derivatives trading dominates, accounting for over 60% of the market share. However, for exchange based trading, interest rate derivatives account for almost 99% of the market turnover.

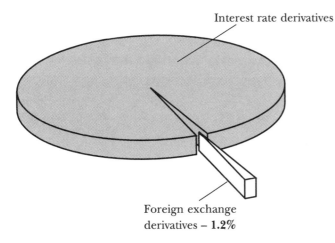

Exchange Traded Futures Contracts

Market statistics on derivatives trading are published by individual exchanges but unfortunately it is not always published in a way which makes for easy comparisons. Information is also available from various news vendors such as Reuters, Telerate, Knight Ridder, and Bloomberg for some exchanges. Exchanges in the US all have to submit statistics to the CFTC – a central government regulatory body. The various exchange statistics are then published annually by the CFTC.

Most exchanges publish their data in terms of the **volume of contracts traded** – usually in millions. This volume represents the total trading activity (total longs OR total shorts) in a specific trading period - day, month, year - for a commodity. Volume data is used for **technical analysis** as it is a measure of the amount of buying and selling taking place in a market.

Volume is used in conjunction with other technical analysis chart patterns and indicators to gauge market signals. The following chart may help with these signals.

Price	Volume	Market
↑	↑	Strong
↑	↓	Warning sign
↓	↑	Weak
↓	↓	Warning sign

The **warning sign** indicates that the trend of the price may change.

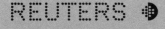

Forward and Futures Contracts

Another useful measure of market activity is **open interest** which is also published by exchanges and used for technical analysis. **Open interest** indicates the liquidity of a market and is the total number of contracts which are still outstanding in a futures market for a specified futures contract. A futures contract is formed when a buyer and a seller take opposite positions in a transaction. This means that the buyer goes long and the seller goes short.

Open interest is calculated by looking at **either** the total number of outstanding long or short positions – not both. Open interest is therefore a measure of contracts that have **not** been matched and closed out. The number of open long contracts must equal exactly the number of open short contracts. It is worth remembering that the reason a player holds an open futures position may be for hedging rather than speculative purposes. The following table summarises how changes in open interest may result.

Action	Resulting Open Interest
New buyer (long) and new seller (short) trade to form a new contract	**Rise**
Existing buyer sells and existing seller buys – the old contract is closed	**Fall**
New buyer buys from existing buyer. The existing buyer closes his position by selling to new buyer	**No change** – there is no increase in long contracts being held
Existing seller buys from new seller. The existing seller closes his position by buying from new seller	**No change** – there is no increase in short contracts being held

Open interest is also used in conjunction with other technical analysis chart patterns and indicators to gauge market signals. The following table may help with these signals.

Price	Open Interest	Market
↑	↑	Strong
↑	↓	Warning sign
↓	↑	Weak
↓	↓	Warning sign

The **warning sign** indicates that the open interest is not supporting the price direction

If you need to know more about technical analysis, refer to *An Introduction to Technical Analysis 0-471-83127-1,* one of the books in this series.

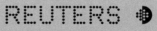

Exchanges vary both in physical floor size and in volumes of contracts traded. It is probably not very surprising to find that the two largest exchanges by floor area – CBOT and CME – have the largest annual futures volume trading figures. Both of these exchanges traded over 150 million contracts in 1995. The following chart shows the volume of contracts traded on 23 exchanges worldwide. The smallest exchange was the Philadelphia Board of Trade with a futures contracts volume of 0.39 million, whereas the largest exchange was CBOT trading 166.52 million futures contracts.

In order to counter the growth and dominance of the OTC derivatives market, exchanges are developing their more traditional role of open outcry pit trading. A recent report by BIS indicated that the best year in terms of turnover for financial futures traded on worldwide exchanges was 1994. The statistics also confirmed the dominance of interest rate futures contracts – almost 95% of the market share in 1995. The following tables have been taken from this report.

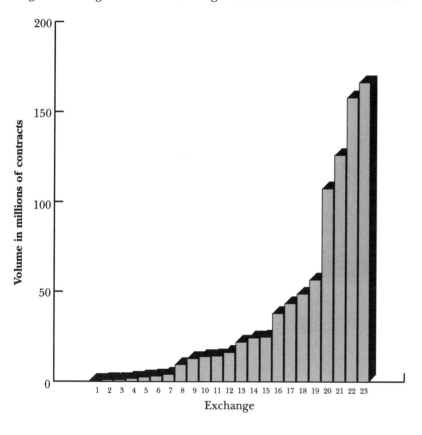

Futures turnover – notional principal USD billions					
Instrument	1991	1992	1993	1994	1995
Interest rate	995.6	1409.7	1750.0	2732.7	2589.1
Currency	26.8	23.2	27.5	32.9	31.9
Equity Index	77.8	59.7	71.7	93.8	114.1
Total	1100.2	1492.6	1849.2	2859.4	2735.1

BIS: International Banking and Financial Markets Developments 1997

Market share of financial futures in 1995

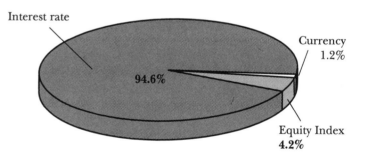

1	PBOT	9	MEFF	17	LME
2	NYFE	10	TGE	18	NYMEX
3	MGE	11	IPE	19	MATIF
4	KBOT	12	COMEX	20	LIFFE
5	SOFFEX	13	SIMEX	21	BM&F
6	MACE	14	SFE	22	CME
7	NYCE	15	DTB	23	CBOT
8	CSCE	16	TIFFE		

Forward and Futures Contracts

The recent BIS report noted the following developments that highlight recent changes in the way derivatives are traded on exchanges.

1. Exchanges such as the CME are working to develop options on a **futures series** of contracts. The result of a bundle of such contracts replicates OTC swaption contracts.

2. Automated trading systems that once supplemented open outcry pit trading out-of-hours are now becoming an integral part of exchange trading. The result of this move is to link exchanges much more with the cash and OTC markets.

   The following charts indicate the volumes of contracts traded open outcry and electronically in 1995 and 1996 for 7 exchanges. On CBOT just over 2% of the total volume of contracts traded – open outcry and electronically – used an electronic system; on MATIF the figure was almost 10% electronically.

3. For a variety of political and economic reasons many exchanges have either entered or are considering strategic alliances/partnerships with other exchanges or brokers. Some exchanges operate Mutual Offset Systems (MOSs) which have already been mentioned. The chart below indicates some of partnerships/MOSs and the contracts involved. The result of these developments has been that global out-of-hours automated systems such as GLOBEX are declining in importance.

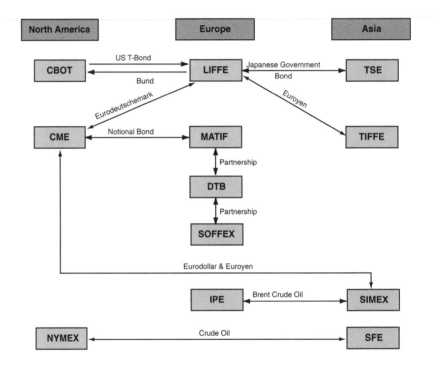

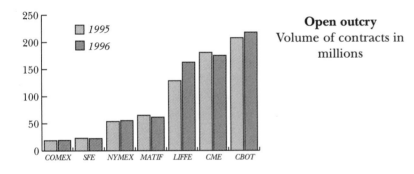

Open outcry
Volume of contracts in millions

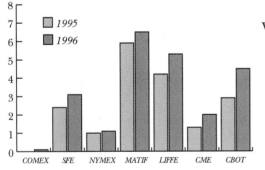

Electronic trading
Volume of contracts in millions

BIS: International Banking and Financial Markets Developments 1997

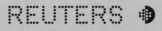

Commodities v Financial Futures Contracts

It is clear from the statistics so far that financial futures trading dominates the market in exchange traded contracts. To emphasise this situation the following table of the top ten individual contracts for year to date, April 1996, traded on worldwide exchanges shows that they were **all** financial derivatives contracts – 8 out of 10 were for financial futures contracts.

Contract	Exchange	Volumes April 1995 – April 1996
3-Month Eurodollar	CME	33,151,598
Average Interest Rate Option	BBF	29,567,630
US T-Bonds	CBOT	29,519,887
S&P 100 Index Option	CBOE	21,419,286
Interest Rate	BM&F	18,537,128
US Dollar	BM&F	16,489,524
German Government Bund	LIFFE	14,969,359
Notional Bond	MATIF	13,042,395
3-Month Euromark	LIFFE	12,930,772
IBEX 35	MEFF	10,683,428

The table below summarises the main differences between financial and commodity futures contracts, which may help in understanding the ways in which the two types of contracts are traded and used.

Financial Futures	Commodities Futures
There are usually a limited range of future dates for delivery based on a 3 month cycle, for example, March, June, September, December.	Many markets have monthly or seasonal delivery dates. Contracts for base metals on the LME use a 3 month forward period and monthly dates thereafter.
Short-term interest rate, currency and equity index futures are cash settled. In 1996 the top short-term interest rate contract was for CME 3 month Eurodollars futures. Of the total 89 million contracts traded only 1% were settled by delivery. Long-term interest rate or bond futures are mostly cash settled but delivery of the underlying government bonds can take place. Most financial futures positions are closed by off-setting.	Commodity and energy contracts specify a delivery location as ultimately the exchanges act as physical markets. Delivery takes place on expiry either directly to the buyer or to a warehouse, silo, storage facility etc. In 1996 the top commodity contract was for CBOT Corn futures. Of the total 20 million contracts traded only 7% were settled by delivery. Commodity futures positions are usually closed by off-setting.
Highly liquid markets for major contracts	
Margin payments mean low credit risks to market players	

Summary

You have now finished the second section of the book and you should have an understanding of the following:

- Forward contracts – what they are and how they are traded

- Futures contracts – both commodity and financial futures, how they are traded and why they are used

- Market players using futures contracts – hedgers, speculators and arbitrageurs

- The importance of futures trading

As a check on your understanding of this section, you should try the Quick Quiz Questions. You may also find the Overview Section to be a useful learning tool.

Your notes

 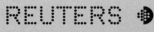

Quick Quiz Questions

1. Which of the following statements concerning commodities and financial **forward** contracts are true?

   ☑ a) They are not traded on an exchange floor
   ☐ b) They involve margin payments
   ☐ c) They have standardised and published contract conditions
   ☑ d) They are privately negotiated deals

2. Which of the following statements concerning commodities and financial **futures** contracts are true?

   ☑ a) They are traded on an exchange floor
   ☐ b) They involve no margin payments
   ☑ c) They are used for speculating and hedging
   ☑ d) They are transparent because the details are reported

3. Which one of the following statements best describes basis?

   ☐ a) The difference between prices for a given delivery month over time
   ☐ b) The difference between cash prices between two exchanges
   ☐ c) The difference between futures prices between two exchanges
   ☑ d) The difference between cash and futures prices

4. What is meant by the term tick when considering a futures contract ?

   ☐ a) It is the price limit of the contract
   ☑ b) It is the smallest amount a contract can change value
   ☐ c) It represents the size of the contract
   ☐ d) It is the current trading month

5. Some LME metal prices have the letters **b** and **c** beside them. What do these letters stand for and can you define the terms?

6. What are the main differences between commodity and financial futures contracts?

You can check your answers on page 67.

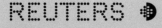

Forward and Futures Contracts

Overview

Forward and Futures Contracts

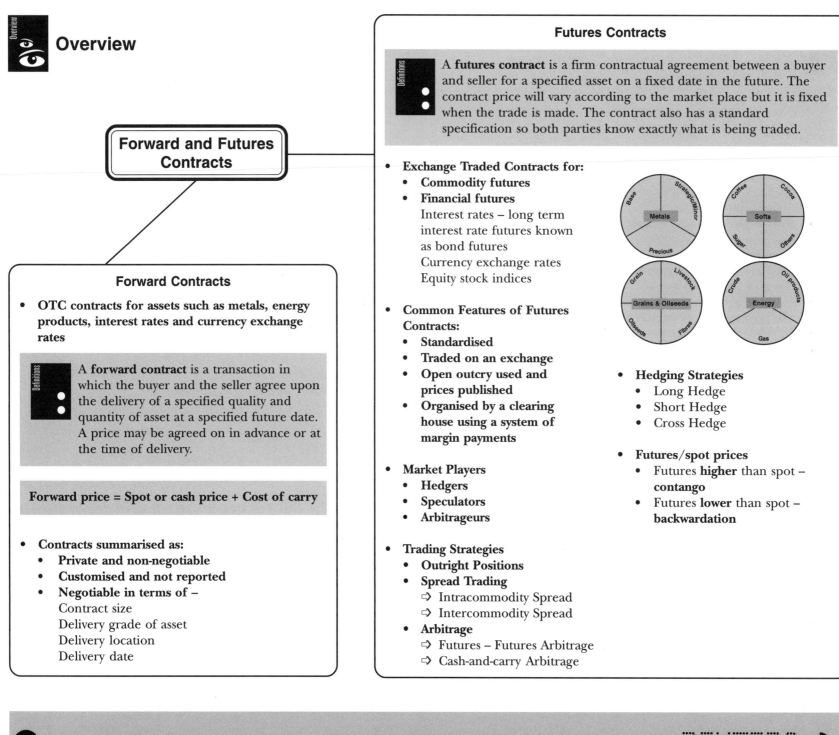

Futures Contracts

A **futures contract** is a firm contractual agreement between a buyer and seller for a specified asset on a fixed date in the future. The contract price will vary according to the market place but it is fixed when the trade is made. The contract also has a standard specification so both parties know exactly what is being traded.

- **Exchange Traded Contracts for:**
  - **Commodity futures**
  - **Financial futures**
    Interest rates – long term interest rate futures known as bond futures
    Currency exchange rates
    Equity stock indices

- **Common Features of Futures Contracts:**
  - **Standardised**
  - **Traded on an exchange**
  - **Open outcry used and prices published**
  - **Organised by a clearing house using a system of margin payments**

- **Market Players**
  - **Hedgers**
  - **Speculators**
  - **Arbitrageurs**

- **Trading Strategies**
  - **Outright Positions**
  - **Spread Trading**
    ⇨ Intracommodity Spread
    ⇨ Intercommodity Spread
  - **Arbitrage**
    ⇨ Futures – Futures Arbitrage
    ⇨ Cash-and-carry Arbitrage

- **Hedging Strategies**
  - Long Hedge
  - Short Hedge
  - Cross Hedge

- **Futures/spot prices**
  - Futures **higher** than spot – **contango**
  - Futures **lower** than spot – **backwardation**

Forward Contracts

- OTC contracts for assets such as metals, energy products, interest rates and currency exchange rates

A **forward contract** is a transaction in which the buyer and the seller agree upon the delivery of a specified quality and quantity of asset at a specified future date. A price may be agreed on in advance or at the time of delivery.

Forward price = Spot or cash price + Cost of carry

- Contracts summarised as:
  - **Private and non-negotiable**
  - **Customised and not reported**
  - **Negotiable in terms of –**
    Contract size
    Delivery grade of asset
    Delivery location
    Delivery date

Quick Quiz Answers

	✓ or ✘
1. a and d	☐
	☐
2. a, c and d	☐
	☐
	☐
3. d	☐
4. b	☐

5. Your answer should have included something similar to the following:

 b = **Backwardation**. This is when the futures price for the commodity is lower than its spot or cash price.

 c = **Contango**. This is when the futures price for the commodity is higher than its spot or cash price.

	☐
	☐

6. Your answer should have included something similar to the following:
 - Financial futures usually have a limited range of delivery dates based on a 3-month cycle: commodity futures often have monthly or seasonal delivery dates
 - Most financial futures are cash settled: commodity futures contracts specify a delivery location

	☐
	☐

How well did you score? You should have scored at least 9. If you didn't you may need to study the materials again.

Further Resources

Books
Getting Started in Futures
Todd Lofton, John Wiley & Sons, Inc., 3rd Edition 1997
ISBN   0 471 17759 8

Analyzing and Forecasting Futures Prices: A Guide for Hedgers, Speculators, and Traders
Anthony F. Herbst, John Wiley & Sons, Inc., 1992
ISBN   0 471 53312 2

Options, Futures and Exotic Derivatives
Eric Briys, John Wiley & Sons, Inc., 1998
ISBN   0 471 96909 5

Reuters Glossary of International Financial and Economic Terms
Ed. Reuters Staff, Longman, 3rd Edition 1994
ISBN   0 582 24871 X

Financial Derivatives: Hedging with Futures, Forwards, Options and Swaps
David Winstone, Chapman & Hall, 1995
ISBN   0 412 62770 1

All About Futures
Thomas McCafferty and Russell Wasendorf, Probus, 1992
ISBN   0 55738 296 4

Guide to Using the Financial Papers
Romesh Vaitiligam, FT/Pitman Publishing, 3rd Edition 1996
ISBN   0 273 62201 3

A – Z of International Finance
Stephen Mahoney, FT/Pitman Publishing, 1997
ISBN   0 273 62552 7

Investments
William F. Sharpe, Gordon J. Alexander, Jeffrey V. Bailey, Prentice Hall International, 5th Edition 1995
ISBN   0 13 183344 8

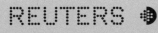

Further Resources (continued)

Options, Futures and Other Derivatives
John C. Hull, Prentice Hall International, 3rd Edition 1997
ISBN   0 13 264367 7

Futures, Options, and Swaps
Robert W. Kolb, Blackwell, 1997
ISBN   1577 180631

Publications

Chicago Mercantile Exchange
- A World Marketplace
- Commodity Futures and Options: Facts and Resources
- Futures and Options Contract Highlights

Swiss Bank Corporation
- Financial Futures and Options

Chicago Board of Trade
- Action in the Marketplace
- Contract Specifications
- Understanding Basis
- Speculating in Futures by Richard L. Sandor

London International Financial Futures and Options Exchange
- Summary of Futures and Options Contracts

Credit Suisse
- A guide to foreign exchange and the money markets
  Credit Suisse Special Publications, Vol.80, 1992

Internet

RFT Web Site
- **http://www.wiley-rft.reuters.com**
This is the series' companion web site where additional quiz questions, updated screens and other information may be found.

Applied Derivatives Trading
- http://www.adtrading.com/
Have a look at the ADT Guide

Derivatives Research Unincorporated
- http://fbox.vt.edu:10021/business/finance/dmc/DRU/contents.html
A good collection of well explained articles

AIB: Derivatives in Plain English
- http://cgi-bin.iol.ie/aib/derivs-pe/

This section of the book should take between three and three and a half hours of study time. You may not take as long as this or you may take a little longer – remember your learning is individual to you.

'Money is better than poverty, if only for financial reasons'

Woody Allen, US film-maker, 'The Early Essays' (1976)

 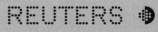

Introduction

Options on commodities and stocks have been used by market players for several centuries. During the Dutch Tulipomania events of the 1630s tulip dealers were granting growers the right to sell their tulip bulb crop to the dealer for a set minimum price. For this privilege the grower paid the dealer a fee. Tulip dealers also paid a fee to growers for the right to buy the bulb crop for an agreed maximum price.

By the early 1820s the London Stock Exchange was trading options on shares and in the 1860s there were OTC options markets on both commodities and stocks in the US. The early exchange traded and OTC options' markets were not without their problems – lack of regulation, contract default etc.

The modern growth of options trading lies in the economic and political events of the 1970s and 1980s with the introduction of foreign exchange and interest rate derivatives in general.

Exchange traded futures contracts on commodities had been established on a number of exchanges in the 1860s but options contracts on commodities were not available until a century or so later. Exchange trading on US stocks started in 1973 when the Chicago Board Options Exchange (CBOE) was established. By 1978 LIFFE was trading options on a small number of UK equities. Trading options on exchanges takes place in much the same way as that for trading futures contracts and uses the same system of contract clearing and delivery.

By the late 1980s and early 1990s the OTC derivatives markets were offering a wide range of options to meet the financial needs of their customers. Since 1991 there has been a dramatic growth in these OTC derivatives markets.

Before moving on try the activity opposite.

What are the main differences between exchange traded and OTC derivatives?

Exchange traded   **OTC**

Compare your answer with the chart on the next page.

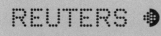

Options Contracts

The main differences mentioned so far between exchange traded and OTC derivatives are summarised in the following table. How well did you do?

Exchange Traded	OTC
Derivatives available: • Futures • Options	Derivatives available: • Forwards • Options • Swaps
Derivatives traded on a competitive floor, open outcry and electronically	Derivatives traded on a private basis and individually negotiated
Standardised and published contract specifications	No standard specifications although plain vanilla instruments are common
Prices are transparent and easily available	Prices are less transparent
Market players not known to each other	Market players must be known to each other
Trading hours are published and exchange rules must be kept	Commoditised vanilla contracts trade 24 hours a day while less liquid and customised one-time deals trade during local times
Positions can easily be traded out	Positions are not easily closed or transferred
Few contracts result in expiry or physical delivery	Majority of contracts result in expiry or physical delivery

As with other derivatives, options are used by market players for:

• Hedging and protecting against adverse price movements in the underlying instrument

• Speculating on increases/decreases in the market price of the underlying instrument

• Arbitrage opportunities between markets and instruments

Exchange traded and OTC options are now available on a wide range of commodity and financial instruments. There are four main types which are broadly classified as follows:

• **Interest rates**
  • Options on interest rate futures
  • Options on FRAs – interest rate guarantees
  • Options on interest rate swaps – swaptions

• **Currency**
  • Options on cash
  • Options on currency futures

• **Equity**
  • Options on individual equities
  • Options on stock index futures

• **Commodities**
  • Options on physicals
  • Options on commodity futures

Although examples of these different types of options are used in the section, you may also find it useful to refer to specific exchange literature where all the option contracts are listed. With the constant need to supply innovative products for the markets some options may seem quite exotic, for example, CBOT's Options on National Catastrophe Insurance futures.

The rest of this section is concerned with the following aspects of options:

- The basic terminology of options

- Why market players buy and sell options

- The basic principles of trading options

- How options are priced

- The risks associated with options and the variables involved – option sensitivities or greeks

- Delta and delta hedging

- Exchange based versus OTC traded options

- Some option trading strategies

- The importance of options in the markets

What Are Options?

So far all of the contracts discussed and mentioned such as spot, forwards and futures commit the counterparties to settle the transaction at agreed contract prices and conditions. The counterparties take on **obligations** when they accept a contract. In other words the counterparties must legally honour and fulfil their part of the contract.

But what if a market player wanted to wait and see if it was advantageous to buy or sell a specific instrument at a future date? In other words the market player would like the **right** but not the obligation to buy or sell if the conditions were advantageous **and** it would be up to the market player whether or not to exercise this right. Contracts granting such rights are the basis of options.

An **option contract** confers the **right**, but not the obligation, to **buy (Call)** or **sell (Put)** a specific underlying instrument at a specific price – the **strike** or **exercise price** – up until or on a specific future date – the **expiry date**.

Calls and puts are the two basic types of options and can themselves both be bought and sold. This means that you can both:

- **Buy** the right to **buy** the underlying instrument – **Buy a call**

- **Sell** the right to **buy** the underlying instrument – **Sell a call**

In a similar way you can **buy a put** or **sell a put.** The buyer of a call or put is referred to as the **holder**, whereas the seller of a call or put is known as the **writer** or **grantor**.

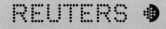

Options Contracts

If the holder decides to buy or sell according to his rights, then he is said to **exercise** the option and the writer has the obligation to deliver – buy or sell according to the contract.

In general, as with forwards and futures contracts, if a market player **buys** a contract he is said to **go long**; if he **sells** they are said to **go short**.

Confused? The following chart is a summary of the rights and obligations of call and put holders and writers, which should help your understanding.

```
                    ┌──────────┐
                    │ Options  │
                    └──────────┘
              ┌───────────┴───────────┐
        ┌──────────┐            ┌──────────┐
        │   Call   │            │   Put    │
        └──────────┘            └──────────┘
```

Buyer/holder Long Call	Seller/writer Short Call	Buyer/holder Long Put	Seller/writer Short Put
Right but not obligation to: • **Buy** underlying instrument • At the **strike price** • If the call is **exercised**	**Obligation** to: • **Sell** underlying instrument • At the **strike price** • If the holder decides to **buy**	**Right** but not obligation to: • **Sell** underlying instrument • At the **strike price** • If the put is **exercised**	**Obligation** to: • **Buy** underlying instrument • At the **strike price** • If the holder decides to **sell**

How does a market player become a holder of an option? How does he or she acquire the rights to buy or sell an underlying instrument at a future date? As you might expect, in order to acquire rights, the buyer of an option has to pay the writer a fee. This fee is called the **premium**.

So by paying a premium to the writer, the holder acquires the rights to exercise the option on or before the expiry date. If the holder exercises an option then the writer has the obligation to fulfil the contract. If the holder does not exercise the option, then he or she just 'walks away' from the contract losing the premium paid.

Exchange Traded Options

Buyers and sellers of exchange traded options can off-set their positions before the expiry date in a similar way to off-setting futures contracts on exchanges. Option writers are usually market-makers hoping to off-set any option risk using their knowledge of the derivatives markets. Option writers face unlimited risks as they have to deliver or take delivery of the underlying instruments no matter what the circumstances!

Option writers who do not own the underlying instruments they are trading are said to issue **naked** or **uncovered** options. Issuing this type of option can lead to very large losses in the event of a market reversal or collapse.

 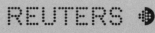

With so many positions that an investor can take, it is important to understand the role of each over time. The following table summarises each position.

Opening purchase	The buyer of an option becomes the **holder**
Opening sale	The seller becomes the **writer** of the option
Closing sale	The holder of an option sells an option identical to that held – this removes the rights of the holder
Closing purchase	The writer buys an option identical to that written – this removes the liabilities of the writer

Options are traded on exchanges using an open outcry system although some worldwide trading also takes place on automated systems after normal trading hours. All deals are registered and settled through a clearing house.

Option writers have to deposit a margin with the clearing house as security that they can meet their obligations. The margin may be in cash or some other financial instrument. If shares are used as the margin the option writer will receive any due dividends etc. Margins are not required for closing sales as the option writer is withdrawing effectively from the market.

In the options markets, buyers **do not** have to deposit a margin – they have to settle their purchase and pay the premium for their contract on most exchanges. However, on LIFFE, options are traded futures style which means that both buyers and sellers pay margin – in this case the buyer does not pay all the premium as a single, up-front payment.

At the expiry date, if the holder of an option wants to exercise the right to buy or sell the financial instrument, then the Clearing house must be instructed accordingly. An **assignment note** is then issued by the clearing house to deliver or receive the financial instrument according to the contract.

The various option positions are summarised in the table below:

Call/Put Buyers	**Call/Put Sellers**
• Pay premium	• Receive premium
• Have the right to buy/sell if they exercise the option	• Have the obligation to sell/buy if required
• Pay no margin on most exchanges	• Pay margin

OTC Traded Options

OTC options are individually negotiated instruments which are not subject to the same contract specifications and margin requirements as exchange traded options.

OTC options have the same definitions for calls/puts, strike price and expiry date as described already. However, OTC option writers **do not** have to pay margin and option buyers, usually, have to pay the premium, in full, at the start of the contract.

In most cases it is not easy to offset a buyer's OTC option position. This is because the offset has to take place with the original seller who may be unwilling to close out a highly customised instrument tailored specifically for the buyer.

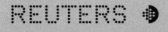

Option Styles

Settlement of options is based on the expiry date. However, there are three basic styles of options you will encounter which affect settlement. The styles have geographical names that have nothing to do with the location where a contract is agreed! The styles are:

- **American**. These options give the holder the right, but not the obligation, to buy or sell the underlying instrument **on or before** the expiry date. This means that the option **can be exercised early**. Settlement is based on a particular strike price at expiration.

- **European**. These options give the holder the right, but not the obligation, to buy or sell the underlying instrument **only** on the expiry date. This means that the option **cannot be exercised early**. Settlement is based on a particular strike price at expiration.

- **Exotic**. These are options with a more complicated structure than a standard call and put, incorporating special elements or restrictions. One type of an exotic option is an Asian option.

It is worth noting the following concerning these different option styles:

- Many exchange traded options are American style, although not all. You will need to check the contract specification to confirm the style being used. This is important as some options on the same underlying instrument are available in American and European styles, for example, PHLX Currency options on cash.

- Most OTC options are European style.

- American style options tend to be more expensive than European style because they offer greater flexibility to the buyer.

- Asian options are becoming more popular in markets where the prices of the underlying instrument can be volatile or susceptible to market manipulation, for example, oil and base metals. Asian option pricing is complex and generally involves using arithmetical averages over the option period involved.

The following table summarises options in terms of buyers/holders and sellers/writers.

	Buyer/holder	Seller/writer
Rights/ obligations	Buyers have rights – no obligations	Sellers have only obligations – no rights
Call	Right to buy/to go long	Obligation to sell/go short on exercise
Put	Right to sell /to go short	Obligation to buy/go long on exercise
Premium	Paid	Received
Exercise	Buyer's decision	Seller cannot influence
Max. loss possible	Cost of premium	Unlimited losses
Max. gain possible	Unlimited profits	Price of premium
Closing position if exchange traded	• Exercise • Offset by selling option in market • Let option expire worthless	• Assignment on option • Offset by buying back option in market • Option expires and keep the full premium

 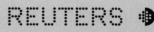

The definition of an option can be summarised as follows:

> An **option** is an agreement by which the buyer of the option pays the seller a **premium** for the **right**, but not the obligation –

To buy/sell	a **call**/**put** option
a specific quantity	contract amount
of a specific instrument	the underlying
on or by a set date	the expiry date depends on the style of the option – **American**/**European**/**Exotic**
at an agreed price	the **strike price**

Finally, it is worth remembering that an option is characterised by:

- The underlying instrument

- A type – call or put

- A style – American/European/Exotic

- A strike price

- An expiry date

Why Do Holders and Writers Use Options?

Hedgers

In the same way that hedgers use futures instruments, so they use options as a risk management tool as a form of insurance to remove or reduce the effects of adverse price movements. The advantages of an option over other derivatives should be clear by now. The holder buys the required protection against risk while retaining the right to benefit from any favourable price movements in the underlying instrument. The advantages of using options for the hedger are obvious, and with the potential for unlimited profits why would anyone want to sell options to hedge?

There are five types of option writers using the markets:

Market-makers

These players manage the risks on their positions by selling and buying options in the markets by quoting two-way prices. They provide liquidity to the markets and profit from small bid/offer price differentials for the option contracts. Because of the risks involved with writing options most market-makers prefer to trade with other market-makers rather than producers, consumers or corporations – in other words if they buy an option will the counterparty be able to fulfil its obligations?

Producers

These are naturally long in the underlying instrument. If they sell a call this means the producer has the obligation to sell the underlying that he holds if the option is exercised. What benefit is this to the producer? If the market price for the underlying remains static or falls, then the holder will not exercise the option at expiry. The producer thus profits from the premium received. However, if prices rise and the option is exercised at expiry, then the producer loses on the option because he has to sell the underlying at a lower price than the current higher price.

Options Contracts

These situations can be illustrated using profit/loss charts which are commonly used when considering options and option trading strategies. These charts are dealt with in more detail later in the section. For now, have a look at the profit/loss chart below for a writer selling a call – a Short Call.

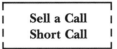

Premium price = maximum profit

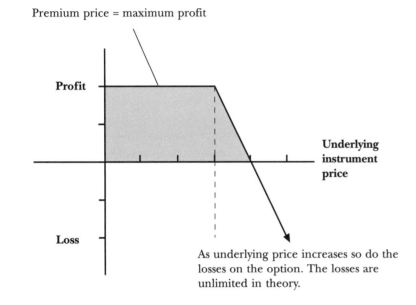

As underlying price increases so do the losses on the option. The losses are unlimited in theory.

Consumers

These are naturally short in the underlying instrument. If they sell a put this means the consumer has the obligation to buy the underlying if the option is exercised. What benefit is this to the consumer? If the market price for the underlying remains static or rises, then the holder will not exercise the option and the consumer profits from the premium received. If the market price falls, then the holder will exercise the option at expiry and the consumer will be obliged to buy the underlying.

This situation can be illustrated using a profit/loss chart in a similar way as before.

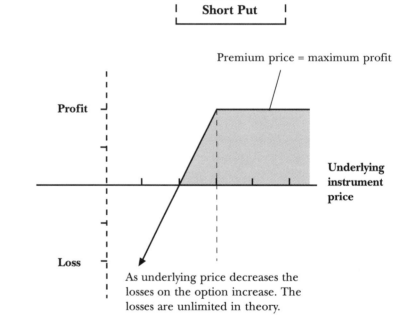

Premium price = maximum profit

As underlying price decreases the losses on the option increase. The losses are unlimited in theory.

Speculators

These market players buy and sell options and take on the risk that hedgers wish to insure against. Speculators use their market knowledge to predict future prices for instruments and set up option trading strategies to profit from their views. These activities are obviously not without risks! Why should a trader use an option rather than a futures contract? The following example illustrates a situation in which an option is more beneficial than a futures contract.

Example

A speculator oil trader is checking news on energy products and sees that oilfield workers in a particular producer country have gone on strike. He suspects that NYMEX Crude oil prices will rise and so buys one lot of the near month futures contract – he buys one lot of 1000 barrels at $19.00 per barrel. The next day his prediction is proven correct and the price of a barrel of NYMEX Crude oil has risen to $22.00. The trader closes out his futures position with a profit of 1000 x $3.00 = $3000.

But supposing the day after buying the futures contract it had been announced that another oil producer was about to increase production figures dramatically with a resulting fall in prices to $16.00 per barrel? In this case the trader would have lost heavily – $3000 – because of the futures contract obligations.

The speculator still has the same objective – to maximise profit and minimise loss, but what can the trader do?

This time the trader uses a call option and buys the right to buy a futures contract at a strike price of $19.00 per barrel and pays a premium of $0.50 per barrel.

If the trader's view is correct and the price rises to $22.00 per barrel, then on exercise of the option, he buys the futures contract at $19.00 and immediately sells it in the markets at $22.00 per barrel. The trader's profit is now the futures profit less the premium paid which is 3000 – 500 = $2500. This is not as much profit as using the futures contract but it still a reasonable amount.

If the prices fall to $16.00 per barrel, then the trader does not exercise the option and walks away from the deal. The trader's loss in this case is a modest $500.

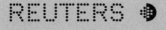

Arbitrageurs

These market players provide liquidity to the options markets by taking advantage of price differences by simultaneously buying/ selling similar options and/or underlying instruments with a view to profit.

Going Short – Going Long

If an option is allowed to expire then it is possible for a market player to end up with a short or long position in two different ways. For example, a market player buys a call option and allows the option to expire. This means that as the holder she now has the right to buy the underlying instrument – **to go long**. Another market player sells a put which the holder exercises. This means that the holder has the right to sell the underlying instrument and that the writer has an obligation to buy the underlying instrument – **to go long**. In both cases the holder of a call and the writer of a put are **long** on exercise and both are hoping for the underlying instrument prices to rise.

Have a look at the following profit/loss charts for a long call and a short put.

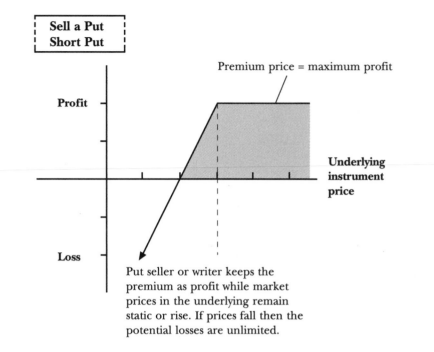

Premium price = maximum profit

Put seller or writer keeps the premium as profit while market prices in the underlying remain static or rise. If prices fall then the potential losses are unlimited.

Conversely, at expiration, the buyer of a put and the seller of a call have the right and obligation respectively to short the underlying instrument.

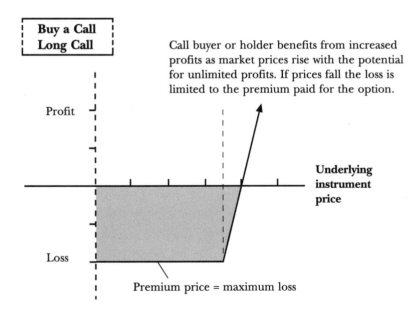

Call buyer or holder benefits from increased profits as market prices rise with the potential for unlimited profits. If prices fall the loss is limited to the premium paid for the option.

Premium price = maximum loss

 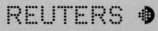

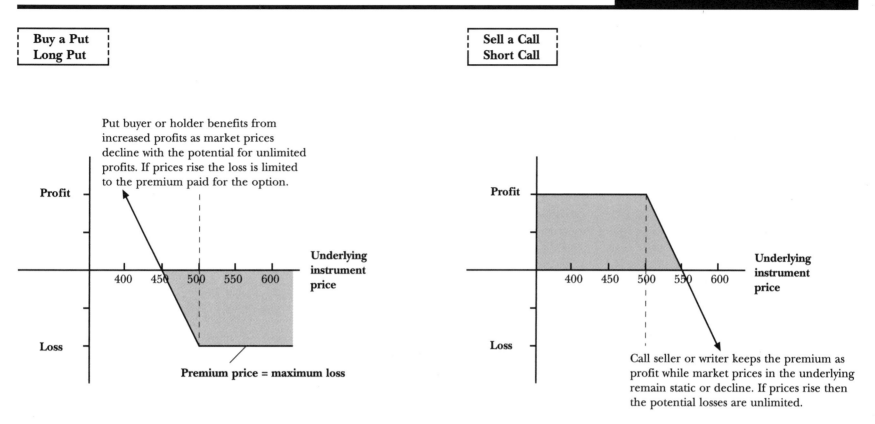

Buy a Put
Long Put

Put buyer or holder benefits from increased profits as market prices decline with the potential for unlimited profits. If prices rise the loss is limited to the premium paid for the option.

Profit

Underlying instrument price

400   450   500   550   600

Loss

Premium price = maximum loss

Sell a Call
Short Call

Profit

Underlying instrument price

400   450   500   550   600

Loss

Call seller or writer keeps the premium as profit while market prices in the underlying remain static or decline. If prices rise then the potential losses are unlimited.

So you can see that the decision on whether a market player wants to go long or short if an option is allowed to expire depends on the rights and obligations the player wishes to assume.

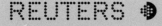

How Options Work

The **fixed** agreed price at which the underlying instrument may be bought (called in) or sold (put out), on exercise of an option, is known as the **strike** or **exercise** price. Typically exchange traded options have exchange determined strike prices above, below and near to the current underlying instrument price.

The **expiry date** is the date and time after which an option may no longer be exercised. Different option contracts have different contract months and depend to a large extent on the underlying instrument. For example, an option on a futures contract will have a **last trading day** dependent on the underlying futures contract's last trading day.

The **premium** is the price paid by the option buyer to the seller for a contract size which is specified as a unit of trading. This unit of trading is again dependent on the underlying instrument. For an option on a futures contract it is usually one futures contract of the underlying; for equities it is typically 100 shares for the American market and 1000 for others. You will need to look at individual contract specifications for specific exchange traded options. All exchanges publish the contract specifications for the options they trade. By their very nature OTC contract conditions are much less transparent and more difficult to find published.

The premium may be considered to be the insurance cost to provide protection against adverse price movements in the underlying instrument.

So far there have been quite a few definitions and terms to understand. Are options so difficult to use in the markets? Interpreting the published information is relatively easy; trading options and determining the strategies to be used are a different matter.

You can see how options are quoted by looking in the financial press such as the *Financial Times* and *The Wall Street Journal*. The following are examples of options for cocoa futures and Deutschemark futures.

Options on cocoa futures

Contract trading unit   Contract price quote

Cocoa (NYCSCE) 10 metric tons; $ per ton

Strike price	Calls - settle			Puts - settle		
	Apr	May	July	Apr	May	July
1350	99	116	150	3	18	33
1400	50	80	123	4	35	56
1450	21	58	97	25	59	80

Expiry months – the actual date is specified by the exchange

Strike prices of futures contracts in $ per ton

How much does it cost to buy a call option for a 10 metric ton cocoa futures contract on or before the July expiry date at a strike price of $1400 per ton?

Using the table, the 1400 July call premium is $123/ton.

Therefore the price of the option for one cocoa futures contract of 10 tons is 10 x 123 = $1230.

Options on Deutschemark futures contracts

Deutschemarks (CME) 125,000 marks; cents per mark

Strike price	Calls Mar	Apr	May	Puts Mar	Apr	May
6700	1.27	1.79	2.03	0.08	0.40	0.65
6750	0.87	1.47	1.72	0.18	0.58	0.83
6800	0.55	1.18	1.42	0.36	0.78	1.03

The strike prices are quoted in American terms as for the futures contract – the USD price of one DEM. For example, $0.6800 per DEM for this strike price.

How much does it cost to sell a put option for a 125,000 DEM futures contract on or before the May expiry date at a strike price of $0.6700? In effect this means that 125,000 DEM will have an effective cost of $83,750 (125,000 x 0.67).

Using the chart the 6700 May Put premium is 0.65¢ per mark.

Therefore the price of the option for one DEM futures contract of 125,000 DEM is 0.0065 x 125,000 = $812.50.

The example here shows a section of the display for Cash GBP options on PHLX.

PHO BR POUND OPTIONS				FOW
View by	○ RIC ● Name		Underlying Instrument	
		RIC	↓ XBP	Name	BRITISH POUND
Contract	PHO BR POUND OPTION ▼	Bid		Ask	
		Last	1.6254	Close	1.6360

Option Series

Call Options	Bid ▼	Ask ▼
XBP Apr7 162.0 C	0.74	0.89
XBP Apr7 163.0 C	0.30	0.45
XBP Apr7 164.0 C	0.12	0.27
XBP Apr7 165.0 C	0.03	0.18
XBP Apr7 166.0 C	n/v	0.14

Put Options	Bid ▼	Ask ▼
XBP Apr7 162.0 C	0.31	0.46
XBP Apr7 163.0 C	0.82	0.97
XBP Apr7 164.0 C	1.59	1.74
XBP Apr7 165.0 C	2.51	2.70
XBP Apr7 166.0 C	3.42	3.67

Single Option Contract

Type	● Calls ○ Puts		
Options	XBP Apr7 164.0 C ▼		
Last Trade		Exchange	PHO
Bid	0.12	Currency	USD
Ask	0.27	Strike	164.00
NetChange		Expiry	12Apr97
PctChange	0	Cnt Size	31250
Open		Volume	0
High		OInt	570
Low		OInt NetChg	40
Close	0.62	Cnt High	2.56

Call and put bid and ask prices for a range of strike prices are shown here

A market-maker will **buy** the option at the **bid price** and **sell** at the **ask price**

Details for a single call or put strike are shown here

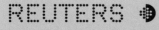

The example here shows options on LIFFE Short Sterling futures.

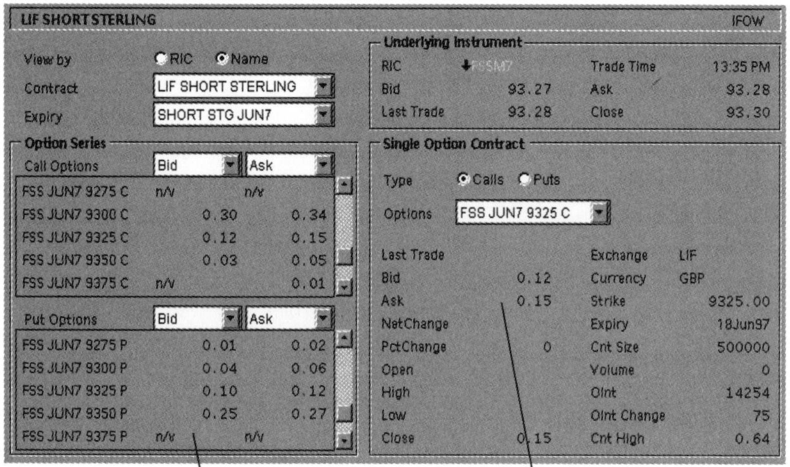

LIF SHORT STERLING				IFOW
View by	○ RIC ● Name	RIC	↓ FSSM7	Trade Time	13:35 PM
Contract	LIF SHORT STERLING	Bid	93.27	Ask	93.28
Expiry	SHORT STG JUN7	Last Trade	93.28	Close	93.30

Option Series

Underlying Instrument

Call Options — Bid / Ask

Call Options	Bid	Ask
FSS JUN7 9275 C	n/v	n/v
FSS JUN7 9300 C	0.30	0.34
FSS JUN7 9325 C	0.12	0.15
FSS JUN7 9350 C	0.03	0.05
FSS JUN7 9375 C	n/v	0.01

Put Options	Bid	Ask
FSS JUN7 9275 P	0.01	0.02
FSS JUN7 9300 P	0.04	0.06
FSS JUN7 9325 P	0.10	0.12
FSS JUN7 9350 P	0.25	0.27
FSS JUN7 9375 P	n/v	n/v

Single Option Contract

Type	● Calls ○ Puts		
Options	FSS JUN7 9325 C		
Last Trade		Exchange	LIF
Bid	0.12	Currency	GBP
Ask	0.15	Strike	9325.00
NetChange		Expiry	18Jun97
PctChange	0	Cnt Size	500000
Open		Volume	0
High		OInt	14254
Low		OInt Change	75
Close	0.15	Cnt High	0.64

Call and put prices for a range of strike prices are shown here

Details for a single call or put strike are shown here

Strike Prices

The most profitable time to exercise an option is taken from the relationship between the strike price and the price of the underlying instrument.

The option which has a strike price at or close to the price of the underlying is known as **At-The-Money, ATM**. For an option which has a strike price such that if the option were exercised immediately a profit would be made, this option is known as **In-The-Money, ITM**. For the situation where no profit would be made immediately, the option is known as **Out-of-The-Money, OTM**.

The further away the strike price is from the ATM position, the deeper ITM or OTM the option is said to be. Have a look at the following chart to see which calls and puts are ITM and OTM depending on their strike price.

Future underlying price at $19		
Call	**Strike**	**Put**
ITM	16 17 18	OTM
ATM	19	ATM
OTM	20 21 22	ITM

Quick Review ?

Satisfy yourself that the strike prices of:
Puts above and calls below the underlying price are ITM.
Puts below and calls above the underlying price are OTM.

It is important to note that the terms ATM, ITM and OTM are considered from the point of view of the **holder** of an option. The following table summarises the strike price and underlying price relationships.

	Call	Put
ITM	Underlying instrument price is **greater** than the strike price	Underlying instrument price is **less** than the strike price
ATM	Underlying instrument price is **equal to** or **near** the strike price	Underlying instrument price is **equal to** or **near** the strike price
OTM	Underlying instrument price is **less** than the strike price	Underlying instrument price is **greater** than the strike price

Premium, Intrinsic Value and Time Value

The premium of an option has two components:

$$\text{Premium} = \text{Intrinsic Value} + \text{Time Value}$$

The **Intrinsic Value, IV**, of an option is the difference between the underlying and the strike prices – the value must always be positive number or zero. The Intrinsic Value is a measure of how much an option is In-The-Money.

$$\text{Intrinsic Value} = \text{Difference between strike and underlying prices}$$

Example
A Euromark June futures price   = 94.96
A Euromark June call option strike price = 94.75
Premium for June call option   = 0.28

Therefore if the buyer of the call were to immediately exercise his or her right to buy the underlying futures contract and sell it immediately in the market the profit is 94.96 – 94.75 = 21 ticks. So for a call option:

$$\text{Intrinsic Value} = \text{Underlying price} - \text{Strike price}$$

The Intrinsic Value of the call option = 0.21

But the premium is quoted at 0.28, so where does the extra amount come from as the premium has additional value over its IV?

This additional component is known as the **Time Value** and is the amount required to compensate for the risk the writer has to take that the option will move ITM before the option expires. For a Call option:

$$\text{Time Value} = \text{Premium} - \text{Intrinsic Value}$$

The Time Value of the call option = 0.07

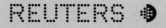

As the time to expiry elapses, so the time value declines until it becomes zero at the expiry date. In other words as the time to expiry reduces there is less and less time for the option to develop IV. The following chart shows the relationship between TV and time to expiry.

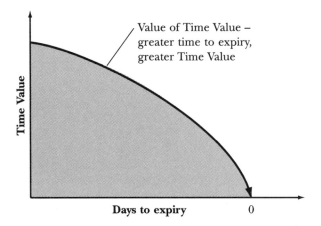

The premium of an ITM option is therefore a combination of intrinsic value and time value.

The premium of an OTM option is therefore entirely a reflection of time value as the intrinsic value is zero.

To understand intrinsic value and time value better, look at the chart opposite.

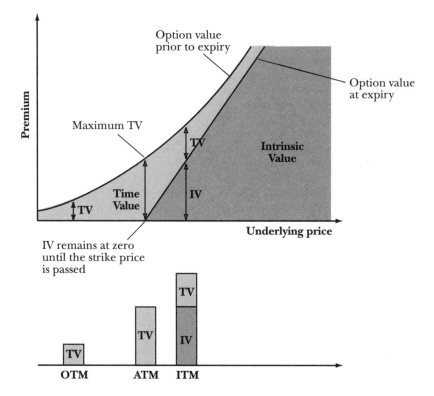

The closer the option strike price is to the underlying market price, the **higher** the time value of the option.

It is worth noting that for put options you will need to reverse some of the definitions and descriptions used so far. For example, for a put option:

Intrinsic Value = Strike price – Underlying price

You should now be clear about the meanings of the terms ATM, ITM, OTM options and about the components of an option's premium – intrinsic value and time value. But how exactly are option premiums calculated?

Pricing an Option

Options are used as risk management tools and the valuation or pricing of the instruments is a careful balance of market factors.

In 1973 Fischer Black and Myron Scholes were the first to provide a reliable mathematical tool by which traders could evaluate option premiums. The key concept of their model was that of a **neutral option hedge**.

Other mathematical models are available today including the following derived from or attributed to:

- Binomial Theory

- Cox Rubenstein

- Garman-Kohlhagen version of Black and Scholes

Traders in different markets may use different models for pricing options and there is no guarantee that two traders will derive the same premium for the same option. However, traders of Currency options almost universally use the Garman-Kohlhagen model.

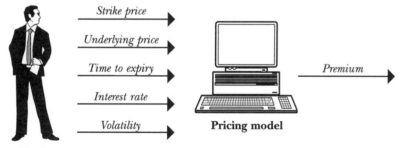

Trader

Strike Price

You have already considered the relationship between strike prices and those of the underlying instrument prices. The differences between these prices determine whether an option is ATM, ITM or OTM and is obviously important in pricing an option. The deeper an option is ITM, the greater its premium will be; conversely, the deeper an option is OTM, the cheaper its premium.

Underlying Price

The premium is affected by the price movements in the underlying instrument.

For call options – the right to buy the underlying at a fixed strike price – as the underlying price rises so does its premium. As the underlying price falls so does the cost of the option premium.

For put options – the right to sell the underlying at a fixed strike price – as the underlying price rises, the premium falls; as the underlying price falls the premium cost rises.

The following chart summarises the above for calls and puts.

Option	Underlying price	Premium cost
Call	↑	↑
	↓	↓
Put	↑	↓
	↓	↑

Options Contracts

Time to Expiry

All other factors being equal the longer an option has to expiry the greater the chance the price of the underlying will move in the holder's favour. This means the **greater** the time to expiry or duration of the option, the **higher** the cost of the option.

The following chart shows the relationship between premium costs and time to expiry.

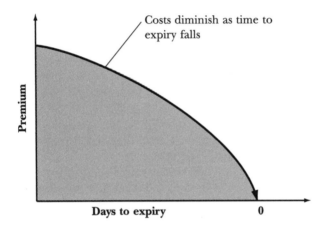

The chart below indicates the effects of time to expiry on the costs of calls and puts.

Option	Time to expiry	Premium cost
Call	↑ ↓	↑ ↓
Put	↑ ↓	↑ ↓

Interest Rates

In general interest rates have the least influence on options and equate approximately to the cost of carry of a futures contract. If the size of the options contract is very large, then this factor may take on some importance.

All other factors being equal as interest rates rise, premium costs fall and vice versa.

The relationship can be thought of as an **opportunity cost**. In order to buy an option, the buyer must either borrow funds or use funds on deposit. Either way the buyer incurs an interest rate cost. If interest rates are rising, then the opportunity cost of buying options increases and to compensate the buyer premium costs fall. Why should the buyer be compensated? Because the option writer receiving the premium can place the funds on deposit and receive more interest than was previously anticipated. The situation is reversed when interest rates fall – premiums rise. This time it is the writer who needs to be compensated.

The following chart indicates the effect of interest rates on the costs of calls and puts.

Option	Interest rates	Premium cost
Call	↑ ↓	↑ ↓
Put	↑ ↓	↓ ↑

Volatility

The volatility factor is a measure of the **rate of fluctuation** of market prices in the underlying instrument. It is the last and most important factor to be calculated in the option model.

Volatility measures **price changes** and does not take into account any price movement **direction**. Have a look at the example below to see what this means.

Example
The chart here shows that the price of the underlying instrument A moves 10 points in 90 days. The price of the underlying instrument B moves 0 points in 90 days.

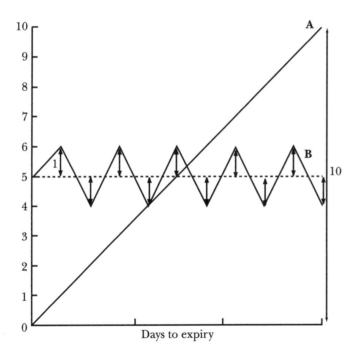

The volatilities of both A and B are similar because on a day-to-day basis B moves up and down at a similar rate to A's gradual rise.

There are two important types of volatility to consider:

- **Historical volatility**

- **Implied volatility**

Historical Volatility
This is the annualised standard deviation of the rate of change of a series of historical prices over a period of time. The historical volatility is used to make an estimate of future volatility.

Implied Volatility
This is the future volatility level that the market believes is a good estimate and is implicit in the option pricing model. The implied volatility is therefore a forecast of the proportional range, up or down, within which the underlying instrument price is expected to finish at expiry. In other words the implied volatility is the collective wisdom of the markets.

The Importance of Implied Volatility
Volatilities are normally expressed as percentages and represent the normal standard deviation or **confidence level** of the underlying.

The confidence level of the volatility forecast being correct for one standard deviation either side of the mean in a statistical normal distribution is 68%. For two standard deviations the confidence level of forecasting the correct volatility range is 95%.

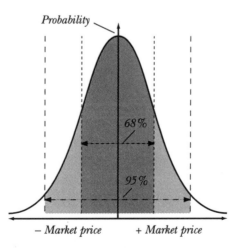

An Introduction to Derivatives 89

Options Contracts

Example

DEM one year interest rates are 4.00% and the one year volatility is forecast at 10%. So the standard deviation is ±0.40 and two standard deviations is ±0.80.

The price ranges for the two confidence levels are shown in the table below:

Confidence level	Interest rate range
68%	3.60 to 4.40 (4.00 ± 0.4)
95%	3.20 to 4.80 (4.00 ± 0.8)

The implied volatility tends to increase slightly for both ITM/OTM strikes the further from the ATM value the strike is. This relationship is often referred to as the **smile curve** because of the obvious analogy!

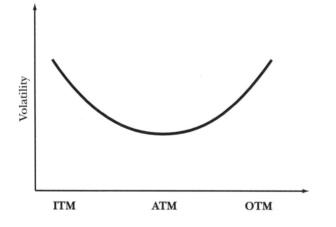

Traders use implied volatilities for an ATM option which trades most actively in conjunction with the smile curve to price an option at a different strike price or different contract month.

OTC option prices are quoted in a different way than that for exchange traded options. OTC market-makers quote in volatility and expect traders to enter these values into their pricing model to calculate the premium. Exchange traded options are quoted as premiums – by knowing the premium it is possible to calculate the implied volatility.

The screens below display the volatility prices as percentages for the major currencies.

```
FXVOL                           FX VOLATILITIES            LINKED DISPLAYS

      DEM      FX OPs        CHF      FX OPs        GBP      FX OPs
1M   9.60     10.00    13:04 10.60   10.90   06:44 9.20     9.60    12:57
2M   9.60     10.00    13:04 10.90   11.20   06:44 9.35     9.75    12:57
3M   9.85     10.10    12:57 11.20   11.50   06:44 9.50     9.90    12:57
6M   9.9      10.2     12:57 11.50   11.80   06:44 9.60    10.00    12:57
9M  10.30     10.60    12:29                     : 9.60     9.90    06:45
1Y   9.95     10.20    12:57 11.70   12.00   06:44 9.70    10.10    12:57
```

```
1257 HSBC MIDLAND            0171-929-2421  NY 212 658-6810   MMDK
TOKYO 010-813-5203-3430                                 SEE MMDA
      GBP/USD   USD/DEM   USD/JPY   DEM/JPY   DEM/ITL  GBP/DEM
1W   8.5/9.5    9.5/10.5  9.0/10.0  9.25/10.2 4.0/5.5  10.0/11.5
1M   9.2/9.6    9.8/10.1  9.55/9.85 9.65/9.95 3.8/4.2  10.0/10.4
2M   9.35/9.75  9.8/10.1  9.7/10.0  9.65/9.95 3.85/4.25 9.8/10.2
3M   9.5/9.9    9.85/10.1 9.8/10.1  9.6/9.9   4.1/4.5   9.7/10.0
6M   9.6/10.0   9.9/10.2  10.4/10.7 9.6/9.9   4.4/4.8   9.5/9.8
1Y   9.7/10.1   9.95/10.2 10.6/10.9 9.5/9.8   4.6/5.0   9.4/9.7
RR   0.1/0.4    0.4/0.7   0.35/0.65 0.3/0.7   0.8/1.3  -0.2/0.2
     GBP PUTS   DEM  PUTS JPY CALLS DEM PUTS DEM CALLS GBP CALLS
SPOT 1.6730     1.7985    115.60    64.50     972.5     3.0080
```

REUTERS

To summarise:

- The higher the volatility of an option, the greater the chance that the underlying price will move through the strike price and therefore become ITM.

Higher volatility = Higher premium

- The lower the volatility of an option, the less the chance there is of the underlying becoming profitable to exercise.

Lower volatility = Lower premium

The table below indicates the effects of volatilities on the costs of calls and puts.

Option	Volatility %	Premium cost
Call	↑ ↓	↑ ↓
Put	↑ ↓	↑ ↓

Option Risks and Sensitivities

Options are used to manage risk in the markets and the importance of the factors used to price options has been discussed. However, it is important to remember that in volatile markets the need to constantly reassess options positions is vital – a large profit can quickly move to a substantial loss. The option risks to holders and writers have already been mentioned but are highlighted here to reinforce their importance.

Holders
The two major benefits of buying options concern:

- Limited price risk

- Leverage

If an option holder does not exercise the option that has been purchased then the loss is limited to the premium paid and is known from the outset of the transaction. Leverage can result in large profits but also has its risks as the following example of a Call option demonstrates.

Example
Investor A invests $10,000 in XYZ Corporation whose shares are currently trading at $100. Investor A buys 100 shares and hopes that the price of shares will rise after 6 months.

Investor B invests $10,000 in buying call options at a strike of $100 with a premium of $10 per share. Investor B buys 10 trading lots of 100 shares per lot – the cost is therefore:

$$10 \times 10 \times 100 = \$10,000$$

Investor B hopes that the price will rise to $120 after 6 months.

Options Contracts

At the end of 6 months the price of XYZ shares has risen to $120. Investor A sells his 100 shares and makes a profit of $2000 – a **20%** return on his investment.

Investor B exercises his option to buy 10 lots of 100 shares per lot at $100 which are then immediately resold in the market for $120 each.

The profit on this transaction is $20,000. If investor B deducts the premium costs from this, then his total profit by using the Call options is $10,000. This represents a **100%** return on his investment and shows how leverage operates – a 100% return compared with a 20% return for the same investment.

However, suppose the price of XYZ shares had only risen to $110 after 6 months. Investor A would still have made a **10%** on his investment on the sale of his shares but on exercise of his options Investor B would have just broken even!

Writers

Writers of covered calls – market players who own the underlying – give up the opportunity to benefit from any increases in the value of the underlying above the option strike price, but continue to bear the risk of price falls in the underlying instrument.

Writers of naked or uncovered calls/puts are in very exposed positions and can incur heavy losses if the value of the underlying instrument is above/below that of the agreed strike price.

Option writers also have risks depending on the style of the option traded. As American options can be exercised any time up to and including the expiry date, these options carry more risk and are therefore more expensive than European style options.

The following are sections of screen dumps showing bid/ask prices for British Pound call and put options on the Philadelphia Stock Exchange. The screens show the difference in prices between American and European style options.

PHO BR PND ME OPTS

View by   RIC   Name
Contract   PHO BR PND ME OPTS

Option Series

Call Options	Bid	Ask
EPO Apr7 161.0 C	1.90	2.05
EPO Apr7 162.0 C	1.23	1.38
EPO Apr7 163.0 C	0.74	0.89
EPO Apr7 164.0 C	0.42	0.57
EPO Apr7 165.0 C	0.20	0.35

Put Options	Bid	Ask
EPO Apr7 161.0 C	0.44	0.59
EPO Apr7 162.0 C	0.79	0.94
EPO Apr7 163.0 C	1.31	1.46
EPO Apr7 164.0 C	1.98	2.13
EPO Apr7 165.0 C	n/v	n/v

PHO BR POUND OPTIONS

View by   RIC   Name
Contract   PHO BR POUND OPTION

Option Series

Call Options	Bid	Ask
CBP Apr7 161.0 C	1.44	1.59
CBP Apr7 162.0 C	0.58	0.73
CBP Apr7 163.0 C	0.15	0.30
CBP Apr7 164.0 C	n/v	0.13
CBP Apr7 165.0 C	n/v	0.14

Put Options	Bid	Ask
CBP Apr7 161.0 C	n/v	0.14
CBP Apr7 162.0 C	0.13	0.28
CBP Apr7 163.0 C	0.74	0.89
CBP Apr7 164.0 C	1.52	1.67
CBP Apr7 165.0 C	n/v	n/v

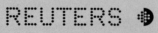

Sensitivities

Do option holders and writers have any other risks to consider? The answer, as you may have predicted, is yes. The following simple model illustrates the general risks associated with derivative instruments. The model shows the level of importance of the risks as concentric circles with the most important at the centre.

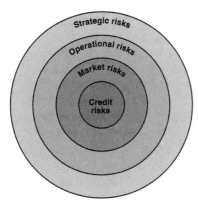

- **Credit risks**
  These are the usual risks associated with counterparty default and which must be assessed as part of any financial transaction. In other words can the counterparty fulfil and honour the trade?

- **Market risks**
  These are associated with all market variables that may affect the value of the contract, for example, a change in the price of the underlying instrument.

- **Operational risks**
  These are the risks associated with the general course of business operations and include legal risks, transmission errors, fraud, theft, etc.

- **Strategic risks**
  Misreading client requirements, entrepreneurial activities, etc, come into this category of risks.

The one area of risk that an institution has **least** control over is that of **market risk**. In other words the value of an option can and will change due to changes in price movements and the other factors described earlier.

The most important risks associated with options arise from the following:

- **Directional risks** resulting from price movements in the underlying

- **Time risks** which arise from the passage of time as the option approaches expiry

- **Volatility risks** which arise from the rate of change of the underlying prices

In the previous section concerning options pricing the affect of these variables was given in simple terms such as 'If the underlying price increases, then the premium increases.' These changes need to be quantified in order to use them in pricing models and to assess the magnitude of their effects.

Each variable or sensitivity associated with options is identified using a Greek or Greek-sounding letter – hence the term **option Greeks**.

The Greeks, associated risks and values are indicated in the table on the next page.

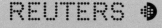

Greek	Risks associated with –	Value equals –
Delta	Change in **price** of underlying instrument	$\dfrac{\text{Change in premium}}{\text{Change in underlying price}}$
Gamma	Change in **delta**	$\dfrac{\text{Change in delta}}{\text{Change in underlying price}}$
Vega	Change in the **volatility** of the underlying instrument price	$\dfrac{\text{Change in premium}}{\text{Change in volatility}}$
Theta	Change in the **time to expiry**	$\dfrac{\text{Change in premium}}{\text{Change in time to expiry}}$
Rho	Change in **interest rate** to fund the underlying instrument	$\dfrac{\text{Change in premium}}{\text{Change in cost of funding}}$

The most important of these variables is delta because it is used to calculate hedging positions. This is important because pricing models such as Black - Scholes are based on a neutral hedge position.

Quick Review

?:?

If you are wondering which of the Greeks is not a Greek letter – it is vega. Vega is sometimes called Epsilon, Kappa, Lambda or Tau which are all Greek letters.

Your notes

Delta and Delta Hedge Ratio

Delta

This is a measure of the sensitivity of the price of an option to a **unit change** in the underlying price.

$$\text{Delta} = \frac{\text{Change in an option premium}}{\text{Change in underlying price}}$$

In other words delta is a measure of the exposure to underlying price movements and is therefore very important. Delta has values of –1 to +1 and the relationship with strike prices is summarised in the chart here.

Option	Delta values		
	OTM	ATM	ITM
Long Call/Short Put	0	+0.50	+1.0
Short Call/Long Put	0	–0.50	–1.0

A delta value of ±0.5 for ATM options also means that there is a 50% chance that the underlying will move up or down from the strike price. To see how delta works have a look at the following example.

Example
A trader is considering buying a call option on a futures contract which has a price of $19.00 per tonne. The premium for the call option with a strike price of $19.00 is $0.80. The delta for this option is +0.5.

This means that if the price of the underlying futures contract rises to $20.00 per tonne – a rise of $1.00 – then the premium will increase by 0.5 x 1.00 = $0.50. The new option premium will be 0.80 + 0.50 = $1.30.

An option which is deep OTM has a low or zero value delta since any change in the underlying has little or no effect on the premium. This means that a market player's exposure or risk to the underlying market is not significant.

An option which is deep ITM has a high value or close to ±1 since any change in the underlying will bring about a more or less point-for-point change in the premium. This results in a market exposure identical to holding an equivalent position in the underlying.

Another way of viewing delta is that it is a measure of the probability that an option will finish ITM.

Options which have a delta close to ±1 will most likely be exercised as they are deep ITM. Options with a delta close to zero will most likely be allowed to expire.

Delta Hedging

The delta value is used in two important ways by market players as a way of calculating a hedging position.

As a practical measure delta is used as a figure that converts an options position into an equivalent futures position. Why would a trader want to do this? Because options market-makers frequently use futures to hedge their options risks.

The equation used to calculate the required futures position is very simple:

Options trading lots x Option delta value = Equivalent futures trading lots at current market price

To see how delta hedging works in practice have a look at the following example.

Example

A trader sells 10 lots of ATM 1900Call options when the underlying futures market price is $19.00. The ATM delta is 0.50. The equivalent futures position is therefore:

$$10 \times 0.50 = 5 \text{ lots of futures}$$

Now suppose the underlying futures price rises to $19.50, the call option still has a strike of $19.00 but the delta value has risen to 0.60.

The equivalent futures position now required by the trader is:

$$10 \times 0.60 = 6 \text{ lots of futures}$$

Neutral Hedging

The neutral options hedge is very important in the risk management of options. It is simply the ratio of options to futures contracts required to establish a **neutral position**. This time delta is viewed as follows:

> **Delta =** **Ratio of the number of underlying instrument contracts that the holder/seller of a call/put option has to sell/buy or own to establish a neutral option hedge**

To see how the neutral hedge works have a look at the following examples.

Example – The perfect hedge

A trader has sold 10 lots of ATM 1900 call options. Each lot has a trading unit of 1000. The option premium is $0.80 and the delta is +0.5.

The trader receives the following premium for selling the options:

$$0.80 \times 10 \times 1000 = \$8,000$$

The trader now needs to hedge his position – but how?

1. He could attempt to buy an opposite position for a similar options contract in the market at a cheaper premium. This is unlikely unless the original sale was overpriced.

2. He could hedge with futures contracts which is the most likely course of events.

The trader has sold call options which means that the holder has the right to buy the underlying if the option is exercised. This means the trader will be short since he has the obligation to sell if the option is exercised.

To delta hedge the trader therefore needs to buy – go long – in futures contracts. But how many contracts are required? As delta is 0.50, 5 lots of futures contracts with a market price of $19.00 are required and bought by the trader. Futures have a delta value of ±1 as they are equivalent to the deepest ITM option possible. The trader's position is now:

Transactions	Price,$	Delta position	
Sell 10 lots Call options	0.80	–10 x 0.5	= –5
Buy 5 lots futures	19.00	+5 x 1.0	= +5
		Net position	= 0

If at expiry the futures price is the same as when purchased and the delta value has not changed, then the buyer would not exercise the options. The trader would close out his futures position by selling in the market at $19.00 and therefore generate $8,000 profit from the premium received for the options.

However this scenario is unlikely!

The only perfect hedge is that found in a Japanese garden.

Example – The real world
During the passage of time before the expiry date of the options the market moves to $19.50 for futures and the delta value for the option premium increases to +0.60. The trader now requires 6 lots of futures contracts to maintain a neutral hedge position.

The trader now has to buy an additional futures contract at $19.50. The trader's position is now:

Transactions	Price,$	Delta position	
Sell 10 lots Call options	0.80	–10 x 0.6	= –6
Buy 5 lots futures	19.00	+5 x 1.0	= +5
Buy 1 lot futures	19.50	+1 x 1.0	= +1
		Net position	= 0

As the futures price has now risen, on expiry, the holder exercises the right to buy the underlying instrument.

The trader has to deliver 10 long futures positions at $19.00 and covers this by buying futures at $19.50.

Costs to trader	**$**
1. To deliver 10 lots of $19.00 futures and cover by buying 10 lots $19.50 futures: Loss = 10 x 0.50 x 1000	–5,000
2. To sell 5 lots of $19.00 futures To sell 1 lot of $19.50 futures Profit = 5 x 0.50 x 1000 1 x 0 x 1000	+2,500
3. Option premium received	+8,000
Net profit	**$5,500**

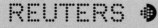

Example – Things get worse!

The futures position now soars to $22.00 and the delta moves to 0.9 – deep ITM. The trader now needs to buy 9 lots of futures to maintain a neutral hedge. In practice the trader would have been continually hedging his position as the market moved. At expiry the trader's position now looks like this:

Transactions	Price,$	Delta position	
Sell 10 lots Call options	0.80	–10 x 0.9	= –9
Buy 5 lots futures	19.00	+5 x 1.0	= +5
Buy 1 lot futures	19.50	+1 x 1.0	= +1
Buy 1 lot futures	20.00	+1 x 1.0	= +1
Buy 1 lot futures	20.50	+1 x 1.0	= +1
Buy 1 lot futures	21.50	+1 x 1.0	= +1
		Net position	= 0

The holder definitely exercises the right to buy the underlying instrument at expiry!

The trader has to deliver 10 long futures positions at $19.00 and covers this by buying futures at $22.00.

Costs to trader $
1. To deliver 10 lots of $19.00 futures and cover
    by buying 10 lots $22.00 futures:
    Loss = 10 x 3.00 x 1000   –30,000

2. To sell 5 lots of $19.00 futures
    To sell 1 lot of $19.50, $20.00, $20.50, $21.50 futures
    Profit = 5 x 3.00 x 1000   +15,000
    1 x 2.50 x 1000   +2,500
    1 x 2.00 x 1000   +2,000
    1 x 1.50 x 1000   +1,500
    1 x 0.50 x 1000   +500

3. Option premium received   +8,000

                                        Net loss   **$500**

By using a delta hedge the trader has turned a potential loss of $30,000 into a relatively minor one of $500.

This last example serves to illustrate how large amounts can be lost using options and the importance of having to constantly monitor and hedge option positions. In other words the example illustrates the importance of **risk management** when using options.

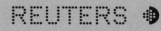

The Other Sensitivities

Although the delta and delta hedging are normally the most important considerations in assessing option positions, this is only the case when there are relatively **minor changes in the price of the underlying instrument**. The relationship between premium and changes in the underlying instrument price are not linear. This non-linearity in delta gives rise to the next of the greeks.

Gamma

This is the rate at which the delta value of an option increases or decreases as a result of a move in the price of the underlying instrument.

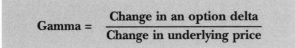

$$\text{Gamma} = \frac{\text{Change in an option delta}}{\text{Change in underlying price}}$$

For example, if a call option has a delta of 0.50 and a gamma of 0.05, then a rise of ±1 in the underlying means the delta will move to 0.55 for a price rise and 0.45 for a price fall. Gamma is rather like the rate of change in the speed of a car – its acceleration – in moving from a standstill, up to its cruising speed, and braking back to a standstill.

Gamma is greatest for an ATM option (cruising) and falls to zero as an option moves deeply ITM and OTM (standstill). The chart below illustrates the relationship between delta and gamma for a call option.

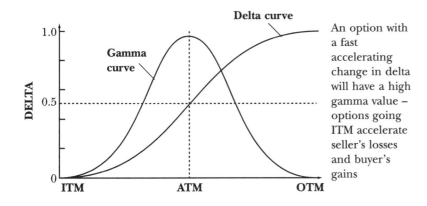

An option with a fast accelerating change in delta will have a high gamma value – options going ITM accelerate seller's losses and buyer's gains

Vega

This is a measure of the sensitivity of an option price to changes in market volatility. It is the change of an option premium for a given change – typically 1% – in the underlying volatility.

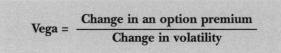

$$\text{Vega} = \frac{\text{Change in an option premium}}{\text{Change in volatility}}$$

If an option has a vega of 0.10 and the implied volatility is 12%, then a change in volatility to 13% means a premium change of 10 ticks. Vega has values between zero and infinity and falls over time – vega is high for ATM options with long expiry times. The higher the volatility in the underlying market, the greater the chance the option will be exercised at a profit and therefore the higher the price of the premium.

What practical use is the vega to a trader? If a trader maintains a delta neutral position, then it is possible to trade options purely in terms of volatility – the trader is not exposed to changes in underlying prices. The following chart shows how option curve prices are bands representing a 1% change in volatility. The longer an option has to expiry, the wider the band is and the further out it is placed from the expiry line. The following chart illustrates the situation for a call option.

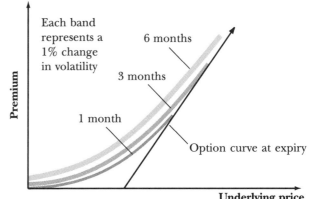

Theta

This variable measures the rate at which an option price curve shifts towards its expiry line.

$$\text{Theta} = \frac{\text{Change in an option premium}}{\text{Change in time to expiry}}$$

You have already seen that as the expiry date of an option approaches then its time value decays. At expiry the option has no time value, only intrinsic value. Theta is almost always a negative value. If an option has a theta value of –0.05, it will lose 5 ticks in price for every day lapsed. As an option approaches expiry, theta increases.

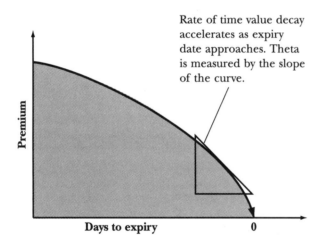

Rate of time value decay accelerates as expiry date approaches. Theta is measured by the slope of the curve.

Rho

The interest cost of funding a position in the underlying is part of the model for pricing options.

Rho measures the change in an option's price per unit increase – typically 1% – in the cost of funding the underlying.

$$\text{Rho} = \frac{\text{Change in an option premium}}{\text{Change in cost of funding underlying}}$$

In general rho tends to be small except for long-dated options.

You have already seen that as the cost of funding the underlying increases, call premiums rise and put premiums fall.

Writers of calls using delta hedging need to buy equivalent futures positions and therefore pass this cost on to the call buyers. Writers of puts need to sell equivalent futures positions to hedge and therefore adjust the premiums to take into account any increased interest benefits to put buyers.

The screen here is for call options on cash for Deutschemarks.

The screen here is for put options on Deutschemark futures.

PHO D MARK OPTIONS · FOA

Contract Definition

View by	○ RIC ● Name
Contract	PHO D MARK OPTIONS
Type	● Calls ○ Puts

Underlying Pricing Definition

Volatility	OTC Implied Bid
Underlying Price Field	Close
Underlying Price	0.5909

Option Display

CALLS	Volatility	Delta	Gamma	Vega	Theta	Rho
XDM Jun7 57.0 C	9.1563	0.9518	0.0431	0.0001	-0.0001	0.0003
XDZ Jun7 57.5 C	9.1563	0.9002	0.0768	0.0003	-0.0001	0.0003
XDM Jun7 58.0 C	9.1563	0.8163	0.1174	0.0004	-0.0001	0.0003
XDZ Jun7 58.5 C	9.1563	0.6991	0.1543	0.0005	-0.0001	0.0002
XDM Jun7 59.0 C	9.1563	0.5573	0.1752	0.0006	-0.0001	0.0002
XDZ Jun7 59.5 C	9.1563	0.4089	0.1726	0.0006	-0.0001	0.0001
XDM Jun7 60.0 C	9.1563	0.2735	0.1479	0.0005	-0.0001	0.0001
XDZ Jun7 60.5 C	9.1563	0.1657	0.1107	0.0004	-0.0001	0.0001
XDM Jun7 61.0 C	9.1563	0.0906	0.0726	0.0002	-0.0001	0.0000
XDZ Jun7 61.5 C	9.1563	0.0446	0.0418	0.0001	-0.0000	0.0000

IMM DEUTSCHE MARK · FFOA

Contract Definition

View by	○ RIC ● Name
Contract	IMM DEUTSCHE MARK
Expiry	DEUTSCHE MK Jun7
Type	○ Calls ● Puts

Underlying Pricing Definition

Volatility	OTC Implied Bid
Underlying Price Field	Last Trade
Underlying Price	0.5914

Option Display

PUTS	Volatility	Delta	Gamma	Vega	Theta	Rho
DM Jun7 57 P	9.2062	-0.0200	0.0269	0.0001	-0.0000	-0.0000
DM Jun7 57.5 P	9.2062	-0.0582	0.0646	0.0001	-0.0000	-0.0000
DM Jun7 58 P	9.2062	-0.1379	0.1223	0.0003	-0.0001	-0.0000
DM Jun7 58.5 P	9.2062	-0.2695	0.1834	0.0004	-0.0001	-0.0000
DM Jun7 59 P	9.2062	-0.4432	0.2191	0.0005	-0.0001	-0.0000
DM Jun7 59.5 P	9.2062	-0.6270	0.2097	0.0004	-0.0001	-0.0000
DM Jun7 60 P	9.2062	-0.7840	0.1617	0.0003	-0.0001	-0.0000
DM Jun7 60.5 P	9.2062	-0.8928	0.1011	0.0002	-0.0000	-0.0000
DM Jun7 61 P	9.2062	-0.9541	0.0514	0.0001	0.0000	-0.0000
DM Jun7 61.5 P	9.2062	-0.9825	0.0214	0.0000	0.0000	-0.0000

Notice the following:
1. The delta for the ATM strike of 59.0 is +0.5573
2. The ITM options have high delta values
   The OTM options have low delta values
3. The gamma is maximum for the ATM option and falls to zero for deep ITM and OTM options

Notice the following:
1. The delta for the ATM strike of 59.0 is –0.4432
2. The ITM options have high delta values
   The OTM options have low delta values
3. The gamma is maximum for the ATM option and falls to zero for deep ITM and OTM options

Exchange v OTC Traded Options

By now you should know that options can be exchange and OTC traded and you should know the basic differences between the two methods of trading. In some markets there is direct competition between exchange and OTC traded options. Although exchange based trading reduces or removes some of the risks involved in trading derivatives using a clearing house, the growth of OTC instruments has been dramatic in recent years.

Exchange Traded Options

The modern origins of exchange traded options started in 1973 when CBOE was established. Most exchanges now trade a wide variety of options which have futures as the underlying instrument in most cases. A few options are available for cash or physical delivery such as cash currency options on the Philadelphia Stock Exchange (PHLX).

Exchange traded options on futures trade in exactly the same manner as for futures trading. The key elements of exchange traded options are as follows:

- Trading takes place via open outcry in pits on the exchange floor
- The contracts are standardised and have exchange-set monthly or three monthly expiry dates to correspond with the expiry dates for the underlying futures contracts
- A clearing house takes opposite sides of all transactions thus guaranteeing the performance of all contracts

The following list includes some of the more common options on financial and commodity cash and futures contracts traded on exchanges worldwide:

- Interest rates
- Currencies
- Stock indices
- Individual equities
- Metals – base and precious
- Energy products
- Commodities – softs, grains, fibres and livestock

OTC Traded Options

Before CBOE was established most options were traded on an OTC basis, either over the telephone or via a broker. As OTC contracts are privately negotiated deals they can be very flexible which is very popular in volatile markets. One of the biggest disadvantages associated with OTC contracts is that of credit risk. The counterparties to every OTC trade have to satisfy themselves that the other side are able to honour their side of the deal.

In providing OTC options professional market-makers provide liquidity to the markets and include options for the following underlying instruments:

- US T-Bonds
- Interest rate products
- Currencies
- Stock indices
- Precious metals
- Energy products

Some of the more recent developments in the OTC options markets include the following:

- **Asian** or average price options

- **Spread options** – these are options on the price differentials between two related products such as crude oil/gasoline or T-Bonds/T-Notes

- **Long dated options** for up to 5 years

 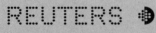

Trading Strategies for Options

There are many strategies available to market players trading options, some have exotic names and some are complex in operation. This section deals only with some of the simpler strategies used – if you can understand these then it may help if you need to consider the more complex trades.

One method of determining the strategy to be used is to consider the simple risk/reward basis of an option. If you consider this aspect alone there are four basic strategies available:

- Limited risk – Limited reward

- Unlimited risk – Limited reward

- Limited risk – Unlimited reward

- Unlimited risk – Unlimited reward

By selecting the risk/reward basis required a trader can determine the type of option to trade.

Another classification of option strategies depends on the market expectations of the underlying price movement.

Market expectations	Market expectations of underlying price	Typical options
Bullish	Increase	Long Call Short Put
Bearish	Decrease	Long Put Short Call
Neutral	No significant increase or decrease	Combination of Calls and Puts

It is also worth remembering that option strategies will differ depending on the market player. Hedgers buy and sell options to counteract the adverse affects of price movements whereas speculators use the instruments to profit from expected price behaviours.

You have already seen the use of profit/loss charts in relation to various options. These charts are very useful when considering the effects of using particular trading strategies. However, there are two further points to note when using these charts.

1. Break-even point. This is an important position on the chart as it indicates the point at which the potential to profit from the option begins.

Break-even point = Strike price ± premium

2. In the profit/loss charts used for the remainder of this section only the chart at expiry is used. This has been done for clarity. However, as you have seen already on other charts of premiums against the underlying price, option prices are actually curves which move toward the expiry line with time. The following charts illustrate these curves.

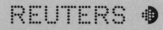

Long Call

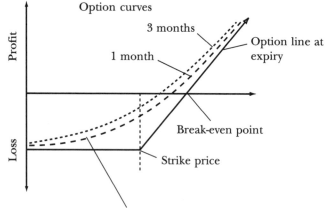

Option curves

3 months

1 month

Option line at expiry

Profit

Loss

Break-even point

Strike price

The position and shape of these curves vary depending on the time to expiry and volatility. The greater/less the time to expiry the further out/closer in the curve. The greater/less the volatility the further out/closer in and the wider/narrower the band.

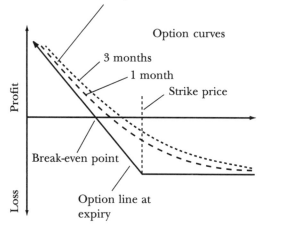

Option curves

3 months

1 month

Strike price

Profit

Loss

Break-even point

Option line at expiry

The four simplest option strategies which have been mentioned in this section are:

- Long call

- Short put

- Long put

- Short call

These strategies are now described in a little more detail to help your understanding of the conditions under which they are used, the risks and rewards involved and examples of the type of market player who might use the particular trading strategy.

Following these basic four strategies there are brief descriptions of some of the more sophisticated strategies which you may encounter. These are:

- Spreads

- Strangles

- Straddles

- Synthetic futures and options

There are many more sophisticated option trading strategies than are mentioned here. If you need to know more about these, refer to the Further Resources listing at the end of this section.

Long Call – Buy a Call	
Market view	Buyers seek to profit from, or protect against, price **rises** in the underlying. **Bullish** view of the market.
Volatility view	Expected to **increase**. **Bullish** view.
Risks	Limited to premium.
Rewards	Unlimited profit potential at expiry in a rising market.
Break-even point	Strike price + premium
Delta	Increases to +1 as underlying prices rise.
Users	The more bullish the market expectations, the deeper OTM the call should be bought. In other words the higher the strike price should be for the call buyer.
Example	An oil refiner is concerned that crude oil prices may rise but he does not want to lock in a firm price by purchasing a futures contract. The refiner therefore buys an IPE Brent Crude oil $16.00 call with a premium of $1.00 per barrel.

At expiry the profit/loss chart for the Long Call looks like this:

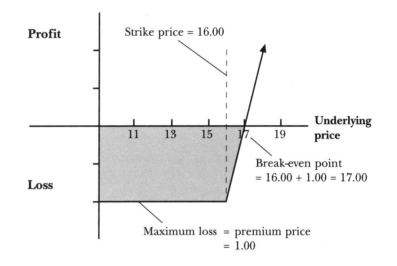

Market price	Outcome
> 17.00	Profit increases and is unlimited as market price rises
17.00	Break-even point
16.00 – 17.00	Loss which decreases as market price increases
< 16.00	Loss is limited to a maximum of the premium price

Short Put – Sell a Put	
Market view	Sellers seek to profit from, or protect against, price **rises** in the underlying. **Neutral/slightly bullish** view of the market.
Volatility view	Expected to **decrease**. **Bearish** view.
Risks	Unlimited loss potential at expiry in a falling market.
Rewards	Limited to premium.
Break-even point	Strike price – premium
Delta	Increases to +1 as underlying prices fall.
Users	The more bullish the market expectations, the deeper ITM the Put should be sold to maximise the premium earned. In other words the higher the strike price should be for the Put writer.
Example	A speculator has seen that the share prices of XYZ Corporation have fallen from 600p to 550p in a recent downturn. Although there is concern in the market, the speculator does not think the price will drop below 500p and will probably move up soon. To profit from this view the speculator sells a XYZ 500Put with a premium of 50p.

At expiry the profit/loss chart for the short put looks like this:

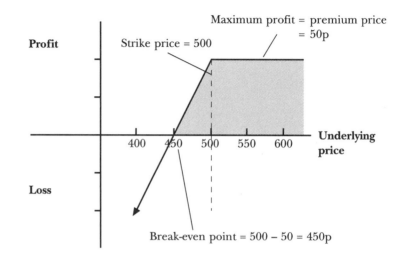

Market price	Outcome
> 500	Maximum profit is equal to the premium
450 – 500	Profit increases as market price increases
450	Break-even point
< 450	Loss increases as market price decreases and is unlimited

Short Call – Sell a Call	
Market view	Sellers seek to profit from, or protect against, price **falls** in the underlying. **Neutral/slightly bearish** view of the market.
Volatility view	Expected to **decrease**. **Bearish** view.
Risks	Unlimited loss potential at expiry in a rising market.
Rewards	Limited to premium.
Break-even point	Strike price ± premium
Delta	Increases to –1 as underlying prices rise.
Users	The more bearish the market expectations, the deeper ITM the Call should be sold. In other words the lower the strike price should be for the Call writer.
Example	A fund manager investing in T-Bonds wishes to enhance the yield on her portfolio. She has the view that market prices will remain stable or fall slightly over the next few months. The current T-Bond price is $100 and so the manager sells a 100Call option with a premium of $4. If the option is exercised the manager would deliver T-Bonds from her portfolio, otherwise the premium received enhances her profits.

At expiry the profit/loss chart for the short call looks like this:

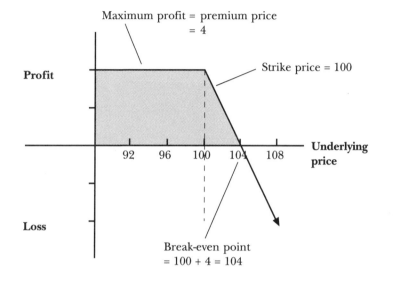

Market price	Outcome
> 104	Loss increases as market price increases and is unlimited
104	Break-even point
100 – 104	Profit increases as market price decreases
< 100	Maximum profit is equal to the premium

Options Contracts

Long Put – Buy a Put	
Market view	Buyers seek to profit from, or protect against, price **falls** in the underlying. **Bearish** view of the market.
Volatility view	Expected to **increase**. **Bullish** view.
Risks	Limited to premium.
Rewards	Unlimited profit potential at expiry in a falling market.
Break-even point	Strike price – premium
Delta	Increases to –1 as underlying prices fall.
Users	The more bearish the market expectations, the deeper OTM the put should be bought. In other words the lower the strike price should be for the put buyer.
Example	A US machinery company has concluded a deal to supply a UK company with machine parts but the payment for the parts will be made in GBP on delivery in 3 months. At the current exchange rate of 1.6000 the deal is profitable to the US company. However, the US company suspects that the exchange rate may fall in 3 month's time. The company therefore buys a 1.6000GBP put option with a premium of 2 cents per GBP.

At expiry the profit/loss chart for the long put looks like this:

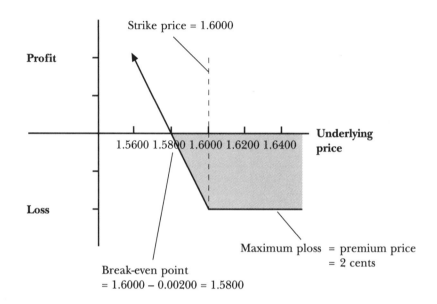

Market price	Outcome
> 1.6000	Maximum loss is equal to the premium
1.6000 – 1.5800	Loss decreases as spot decreases
1.5800	Break-even point
< 1.5800	Profit increases as spot decreases and is unlimited

Straddles

A straddle is the simultaneous buying or selling of options of **different** types with the **same** strike price.

Long straddle	
Simultaneously	**Buy** a **put** and **buy** a **call** with the **same strike** price.
Market view	Significant price changes, but unsure of direction.
Risks	Limited to total premium paid.
Rewards	If prices rise the call option can be exercised with unlimited profit potential. If prices fall the put option can be exercised with unlimited profit potential.
Example	Buy 1 March 5.00 Call .10 Buy 1 March 5.00 Put .10

Short straddle	
Simultaneously	**Sell** a **put** and **sell** a **call** with the **same strike** price.
Market view	Little or no movement in prices.
Risks	If prices rise the holder of the call has the right to exercise the option with the potential of unlimited loss for the writer. If prices fall the holder of the put has the right to exercise the option with the potential of unlimited loss for the writer.
Rewards	Limited to total premium received.
Example	Sell 1 March 5.00 Call .10 Sell 1 March 5.00 Put .10

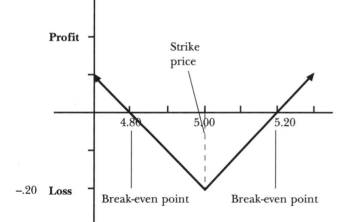

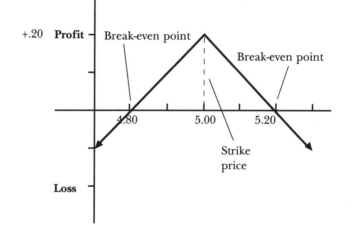

Options Contracts

Strangles

A strangle is the simultaneous buying or selling of options of **different** types with **different** strike prices.

Long strangle	
Simultaneously	**Buy** a **put** with a **low strike** price and **Buy** a **call** with a **high strike** price.
Market view	The expectations are that there will be a major movement in the market but its direction is not known. The cost of a strangle is cheaper than a straddle because the strikes are more OTM and therefore cost less.
Risks	Limited to net premium paid.
Rewards	Profit potential is unlimited if prices rise or fall although the movement in either direction must be substantial to profit.
Example	Buy 1 March 3.00 Put .05 Buy 1 Mrach 4.00 Call .10

Short strangle	
Simultaneously	**Sell** a **call** with a **high strike** price and **Sell** a **put** with a **low strike** price.
Market view	The expectations are that there will be a major movement in the market but its direction is not known. The cost of a strangle is cheaper than a straddle because the strikes are more OTM and therefore cost less.
Risks	Loss potential is unlimited if prices rise or fall although the movement in either direction must be substantial for losses to occur.
Rewards	Limited to net premium received.
Example	Sell 1 March 3.00 Put .05 Sell 1 March 4.00 Call .10

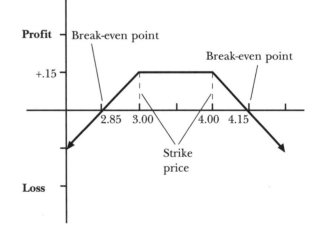

Spreads

A spread is the simultaneous buying and selling of options of the **same** type with **different** strike prices.

Bull Call spread – Long Call spread	
Simultaneously	**Buy** a **call** with a **low strike** price and **Sell** a **call** with a **high strike** price.
Market view	The expectations are that the market will rise to a certain level. The buyer of this Call spread wishes to take advantage of a bullish opinion but at the same time reducing the premium cost by selling a call which has the effect of limiting the potential profit if the underlying rises and limiting losses if it falls.
Risks	Limited to net premium paid.
Rewards	Limited to the difference between the two strike prices less net premium received.
Example	Buy 1 April 4.00 Call .50 Sell 1 April 4.50 Call .30

Bear Put spread – Long Put spread	
Simultaneously	**Buy** a **put** with a **high strike** price and **Sell** a **put** with a **low strike** price.
Market view	The expectations are that the market will fall to a certain level. The buyer of this Put spread wishes to take advantage of a bearish opinion but at the same time reducing the premium cost by selling a put which has the effect of limiting the loss exposure if the underlying rises and limiting profit if it falls.
Risks	Limited to the difference between the two strike prices less net premium received.
Rewards	Limited to net premium paid.
Example	Buy 1 June 5.50 Put .45 Sell 1 June 5.00 Put .18

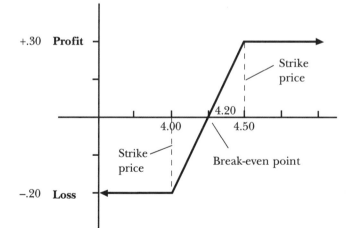

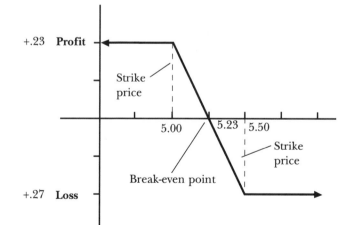

See if you can find out what Butterfly, Condor, Ratio spread and Ladder option strategies are and how they are used.

Your notes

Synthetic Futures and Options

If futures and options positions are considered in terms of going long/going short for the underlying instruments then it is possible to create 'synthetic' futures and options positions.

Example

If a long call is combined with a short put, both on underlying futures, what is the resulting position?

Option	This means	On exercise	Resulting futures position
Long Call	Buy a call	The buyer buys the underlying futures	**Go long**
Short Put	Sell a put	The seller sells the underlying futures	**Go short**

But what is a **long futures** contract?

On expiry	Resulting futures position
The buyer buys the futures contract	**Go long**
The seller sells the futures contract	**Go short**

If you compare the resulting buyer/seller positions you can see that synthetically:

Long Call + Short Put = Long futures

In a similar way you can deduce the following synthetic combinations shown in the chart here.

Long Call	+	Short Put	=	Long futures
Short Call	+	Long Put	=	Short futures
Long Put	+	Long futures	=	Long Call
Short Put	+	Short futures	=	Short Call
Long Call	+	Short futures	=	Long Put
Short Call	+	Long futures	=	Short Put

As an exercise in algebra this may be of interest but are synthetic positions of any use in the markets? The answer is yes, because synthetic option positions can provide more cost effective hedges than using a straightforward futures position as the following example illustrates.

Example

A cocoa consumer needs to hedge against anticipated future price increases. One way of hedging is to buy a futures contract which has unlimited profit potential if prices rise, but what if prices fall for any reason?

Using the chart above a combination of a long call and a short put options on futures is the equivalent of a long futures position. But is it more cost effective to use the synthetic position?

The consumer looks at the derivative prices and premiums.

> May Futures Cocoa is trading at $1300 per ton
> May 1300 call premium is $32 per ton to buy
> May 1300 put premium is $33 per ton to sell

If the consumer buys the call and sells the put the net premium income is 33 − 32 = $1. This income effectively lowers the cost of the long futures position to $1299 per ton – a small saving.

By using a combination of options and futures it is therefore possible to hedge any position required.

The Importance of Options

As with other derivative instruments a direct comparison of statistics for exchange traded and OTC options is not easy.

The data used for comparisons here has been drawn from the following organisations:

- Bank for International Settlements (BIS)

- Commodities Futures Trading Commission (CFTC)

- International Swaps and Derivatives Association (ISDA)

- The exchanges

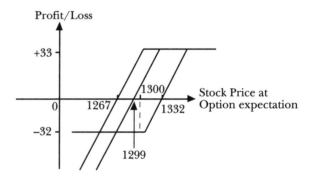

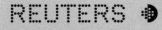

OTC v Exchange Traded Options

Although comparisons are difficult, the BIS has provided a number of reports from which the following statistics are drawn. The chart below summarises some of the data.

Options traded	Outstandings USD billion	Average daily turnover USD billion
OTC		
Currency	2,379	41
Interest Rate	3,548	21
Equity & Equity Index	527	–
Commodity	109	–
Exchange based		
Currency	80	2.6
Interest Rate	3,290	124
Equity & Equity Index	287	–
Commodity = Gold	50	–

BIS: Central Bank Survey of Foreign Exchange and Derivative Market Activity 1995

1. The most important OTC and exchange traded options, in terms of notional amounts outstanding, are interest rate options.

2. Although currency options are traded OTC and on exchanges, exchange trading is relatively minor compared with OTC trading both in terms of average daily turnover and notional amounts outstanding.

Exchange Traded Options

Comparison of the following charts of turnover for exchange traded futures and options shows that futures trading dominates the markets. The recent BIS report for financial derivatives also indicates that the best year, in terms of turnover, for trading financial derivatives was 1994. The report also indicates that trading interest rate derivatives dominates the markets.

Futures turnover – notional principal USD billions					
Instrument	1991	1992	1993	1994	1995
Interest rate	995.6	1409.7	1750.0	2732.7	2589.1
Currency	26.8	23.2	27.5	32.9	31.9
Equity Index	77.8	59.7	71.7	93.8	114.1
Total	**1100.2**	**1492.6**	**1849.2**	**2859.4**	**2735.1**

Options turnover – notional principal USD billions					
Instrument	1991	1992	1993	1994	1995
Interest rate	17.32	25.53	32.45	46.97	42.98
Currency	1.51	1.37	1.35	1.44	0.99
Equity Index	6.36	5.72	6.36	8.14	10.08
Total	**25.19**	**32.62**	**40.16**	**56.55**	**54.05**

BIS: International Banking and Financial Markets Developments 1997

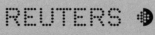

The market share of financial futures and options is shown in the charts below.

Market share of financial options in 1995:

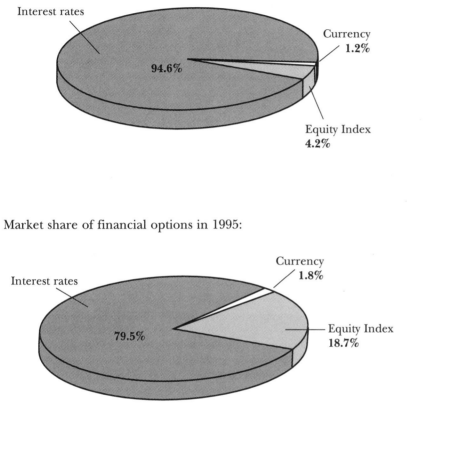

The following chart shows the volume of contracts traded on 22 worldwide exchanges. The smallest exchange was MACE with an options contract volume of 0.02 million, whereas the top exchange was CBOT trading 42.90 million option contracts. In terms of volumes of futures and options traded in 1995, CBOT was the largest exchange with a combined total of 209.42 million contracts.

Market share of financial options in 1995:

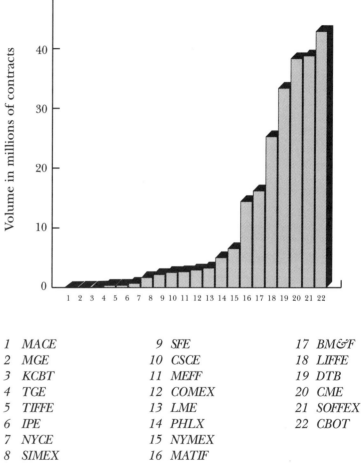

1	MACE	9	SFE	17	BM&F
2	MGE	10	CSCE	18	LIFFE
3	KCBT	11	MEFF	19	DTB
4	TGE	12	COMEX	20	CME
5	TIFFE	13	LME	21	SOFFEX
6	IPE	14	PHLX	22	CBOT
7	NYCE	15	NYMEX		
8	SIMEX	16	MATIF		

CFTC and Exchange data, 1995

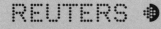

Options Contracts

It is clear from the statistics for exchanges that interest rate derivatives dominate the markets. The following chart of the top ten individual contracts, for the year to date April 1996, traded on worldwide exchanges shows that they were all financial derivatives contracts – two were for options.

Contract	Exchange	Volumes April 1995 - April 1996
3-Month Eurodollar	CME	33,151,598
Average Interest Rate Option	BBF	29,567,630
US T-Bonds	CBOT	29,519,887
S&P 100 Index Option	CBOE	21,419,286
Interest Rate	BM&F	18,537,128
US Dollar	BM&F	16,489,524
German Government Bund	LIFFE	14,969,359
Notional Bond	MATIF	13,042,395
3-Month Euromark	LIFFE	12,930,772
IBEX 35	MEFF	10,683,428

OTC Traded Options

The latest statistics available from ISDA indicate that in terms of notional amounts outstanding, Interest rate options – **Interest Rate Guarantees, IRGs**, and **Swaptions** are the second largest market.

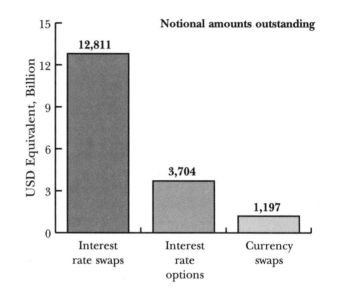

ISDA Summary of Market Survey Statistics: Year end 1995

For the interest rate options, contracts traded on the USD accounted for over half of the total in terms of notional amounts outstanding.

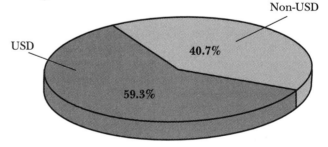

The following chart indicates the notional amounts outstanding for USD and non-USD for IRGs and Swaptions.

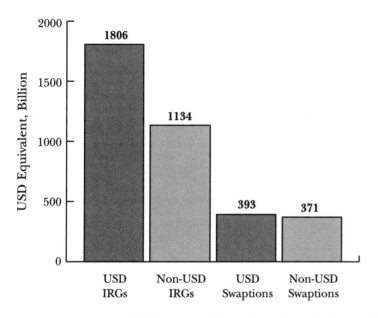

ISDA Summary of Market Survey Statistics: Year end 1995

Summary

You have now finished the third section of the book and you should have an understanding of the following:

- Options contracts – what they are and how they are traded

- The factors involved with pricing options, volatility and greeks

- Market players using options contracts – hedgers, speculators and arbitrageurs

- Some of the more basic trading strategies used by market players

- The importance of options trading

As a check on your understanding of this section, you should try the Quick Quiz Questions. You may also find the Overview Section to be a useful learning tool.

Quick Quiz Questions

1. Match the following statements concerning options on futures contracts:

   i) The right, but not obligation, to buy an underlying instrument in the future

   ii) The right, but not obligation, to sell an underlying instruments in the future

   iii) The right, but not obligation, to buy or sell an underlying instruments on or before a fixed date

   iv) The right, but not obligation, to buy or sell an underlying instruments which can only be exercised on a fixed date in the future

   a) A European option
   b) A Call option
   c) An American option
   d) A Put option

2. A Call option with a strike of $100 has a premium of $12 when the underlying share price is $110.

   i) What is the intrinsic value of the option?
   ii) What is the time value of the option?
   a) $0
   b) $2
   c) $10
   d) $12

   i ☐   ii ☐

3. Which one of the following statements describes the delta of an option?

   ☐ a) Change in option premium for a given change in period to expiry
   ☐ b) The change in the option premium for a given change in the underlying price
   ☐ c) The change in option premium for a given change in interest rate
   ☐ d) The change in option premium for a 1% change in the underlying volatility

4. The value of a call option falls with an increase in:

   ☐ a) Underlying price
   ☐ b) Strike price
   ☐ c) Volatility
   ☐ d) Time to expiry

5. Which one of the following factors has the greatest effect on the premium for an option?

   ☐ a) Volatility
   ☐ b) Interest rates
   ☐ c) Share prices
   ☐ d) Whether option is OTC or exchange traded

6. What type of option strategy does this profit/loss chart indicate?

   ☐ a) Long Call
   ☐ b) Short Call
   ☐ c) Short Put
   ☐ d) Long Put

   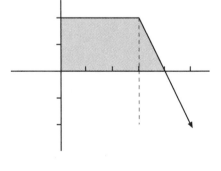

   You can check your answers on page 121.

Overview

Options Contracts

What Are Options?

- **Exchange Traded and OTC**

> An **option contract** confers the **right**, but not the obligation, to **buy (Call)** or **sell (Put)** a specific underlying instrument at a specific price – the **strike** or **exercise price** – up until or on a specific future date – the **expiry date**.

- **Calls/Puts – Buyers/Sellers – Holder/Writers**

```
                Options
                   |
        +----------+----------+
       Call                  Put
```

Buyer/holder Long Call	Seller/writer Short Call	Buyer/holder Long Put	Seller/writer Short Put
Right but not obligation to: • **Buy** underlying instrument • At the **strike price** • If the call is **exercised**	**Obligation** to: • **Sell** underlying instrument • At the **strike price** • If the holder decides to **buy**	**Right** but not obligation to: • **Sell** underlying instrument • At the **strike price** • If the put is **exercised**	**Obligation** to: • **Buy** underlying instrument • At the **strike price** • If the holder decides to **sell**

- **Options styles**
  - **American**
  - **European**
  - **Asian**

- **Options are characterised by:**
  - **The underlying instrument**
  - **A type – Call or Put**
  - **A style – American/European/Asian**
  - **A strike price**
  - **An expiry date**

Why Do Holders and Writers Use Options?

- **Hedgers**
  - **Market makers**
  - **Producers**
  - **Consumers**
  - **Speculators**
  - **Arbitrageurs**

How Options Work

- **Strike prices**
  - **At-The-Money (ATM)**
  - **In-The-Money (ITM)**
  - **Out-of-The-Money (OTM)**

	Call	Put
ITM	Underlying instrument price is **greater** than the strike price	Underlying instrument price is **less** than the strike price
ATM	Underlying instrument price is **equal to** or **near** the strike price	Underlying instrument price is **equal to** or **near** the strike price
OTM	Underlying instrument price is **less** than the strike price	Underlying instrument price is **greater** than the strike price

- **Premium, Intrinsic Value and Time Value**

> **Premium = Intrinsic Value + Time Value**

- **Call option**

> **Intrinsic Value = Underlying price – Strike price**

- **Put option**

> **Intrinsic Value = Strike price – Underlying price**

> **Time Value = Premium – Intrinsic Value**

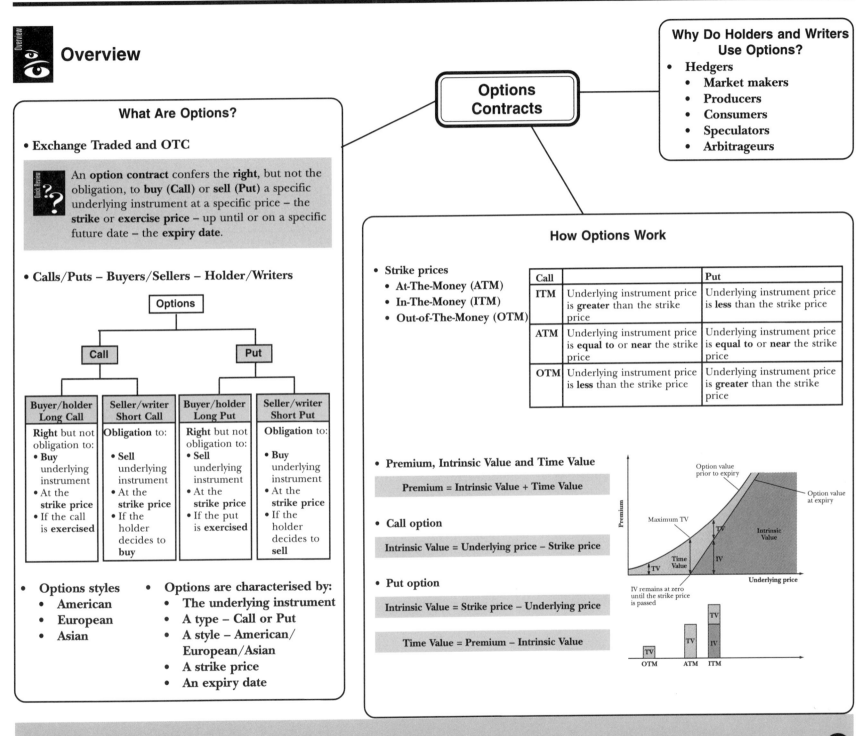

Overview

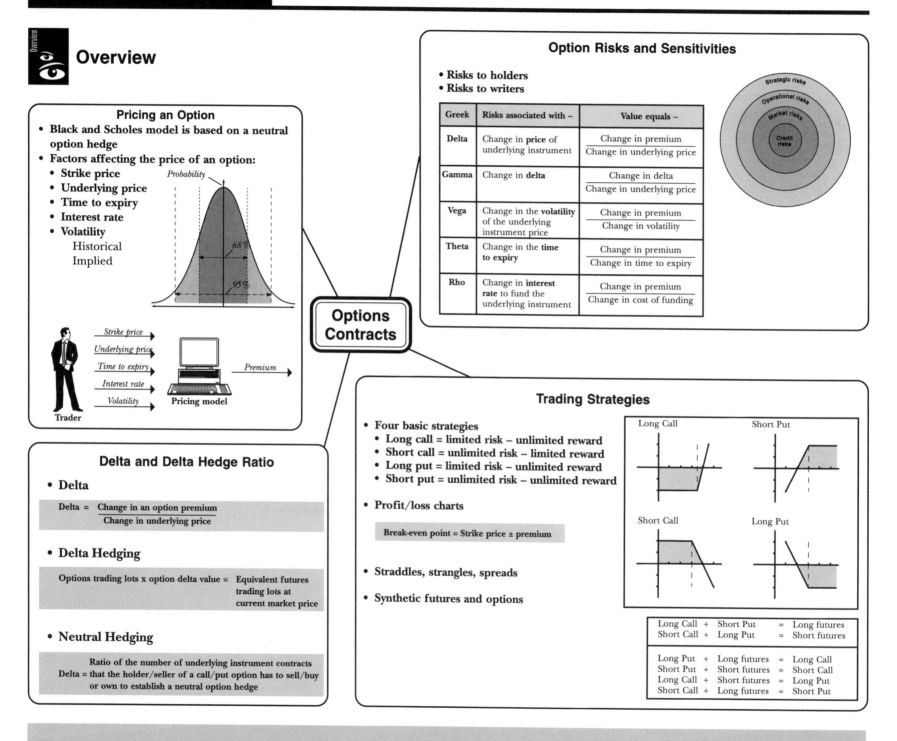

Pricing an Option

- Black and Scholes model is based on a neutral option hedge
- Factors affecting the price of an option:
  - **Strike price**
  - **Underlying price**
  - **Time to expiry**
  - **Interest rate**
  - **Volatility**
    - Historical
    - Implied

Probability

68%

95%

Strike price →
Underlying price →
Time to expiry →
Interest rate →
Volatility →

Pricing model → Premium →

Trader

Option Risks and Sensitivities

- **Risks to holders**
- **Risks to writers**

Greek	Risks associated with –	Value equals –
Delta	Change in **price** of underlying instrument	$\dfrac{\text{Change in premium}}{\text{Change in underlying price}}$
Gamma	Change in **delta**	$\dfrac{\text{Change in delta}}{\text{Change in underlying price}}$
Vega	Change in the **volatility** of the underlying instrument price	$\dfrac{\text{Change in premium}}{\text{Change in volatility}}$
Theta	Change in the **time to expiry**	$\dfrac{\text{Change in premium}}{\text{Change in time to expiry}}$
Rho	Change in **interest rate** to fund the underlying instrument	$\dfrac{\text{Change in premium}}{\text{Change in cost of funding}}$

Strategic risks
Operational risks
Market risks
Credit risks

Options Contracts

Delta and Delta Hedge Ratio

- **Delta**

  $$\text{Delta} = \frac{\text{Change in an option premium}}{\text{Change in underlying price}}$$

- **Delta Hedging**

  Options trading lots x option delta value = Equivalent futures trading lots at current market price

- **Neutral Hedging**

  Delta = Ratio of the number of underlying instrument contracts that the holder/seller of a call/put option has to sell/buy or own to establish a neutral option hedge

Trading Strategies

- **Four basic strategies**
  - **Long call = limited risk – unlimited reward**
  - **Short call = unlimited risk – limited reward**
  - **Long put = limited risk – unlimited reward**
  - **Short put = unlimited risk – unlimited reward**

- **Profit/loss charts**

  Break-even point = Strike price ± premium

- **Straddles, strangles, spreads**

- **Synthetic futures and options**

Long Call   Short Put

Short Call   Long Put

| Long Call | + | Short Put | = | Long futures |
| Short Call | + | Long Put | = | Short futures |

Long Put	+	Long futures	=	Long Call
Short Put	+	Short futures	=	Short Call
Long Call	+	Short futures	=	Long Put
Short Call	+	Long futures	=	Short Put

Quick Quiz Answers

		✓ or ✖
1.	i b ii d iii c iv a	❑
		❑
		❑
		❑
2.	i c i b	❑
		❑
3.	b	❑
4.	b	❑
5.	a	❑
6.	b	❑

How well did you score? You should have scored at least 8. If you didn't, you may need to study the materials again.

Further Resources

Books

Options, Futures and Exotic Derivatives
Eric Briys, John Wiley & Sons, Inc., 1998
ISBN   0 471 96909 5

The Conservative Investor's Guide to Trading Options
LeRoy Gross, John Wiley & Sons, Inc., projected pub date: Nov 1998
ISBN   0 471 31585 0

Getting Started in Options
Michael C. Thomsett, John Wiley & Sons, Inc., 3rd Edition 1997
ISBN   0 471 17758 X

McMillan on Options
Lawrence G. McMillan, John Wiley & Sons, Inc., 1996
ISBN   0 471 11960 1

The Options Course: High Profit & Low Stress Trading Methods
George A. Fontanills, John Wiley & Sons, Inc., 1998
ISBN   0 471 24950 5

Traded Options Simplified
Brian Millard, John Wiley & Sons, Inc., 4th Edition 1998
ISBN   0 471 96658 4

Understanding Options
Robert Kolb, John Wiley & Sons, Inc., 1995
ISBN   0 471 08554 5

Financial Derivatives: Hedging with Futures, Forwards, Options and Swaps
David Winstone, Chapman & Hall, 1995
ISBN   0 412 62770 1

Guide to Using the Financial Papers
Romesh Vaitiligam, FT/Pitman Publishing, 3rd Edition 1996
ISBN   0 273 62201 3

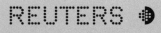

Further Resources (continued)

A – Z of International Finance
Stephen Mahoney, FT/Pitman Publishing, 1997
ISBN   0 273 62552 7

Options, Futures and Other Derivatives
John C. Hull, Prentice Hall International, 3rd Edition 1997
ISBN   0 13 264367 7

Publications

Chicago Mercantile Exchange
- A World Marketplace
- Options on Futures: An Introductory Guide
- Futures and Options Contract Highlights

Swiss Bank Corporation
- Financial Futures and Options
- Understanding Derivatives - Prospects Special Issue 1994
- Introduction to Foreign Exchange Options
- Options: The Fundamentals

Chicago Board of Trade
- Contract Specifications
- Financial Options Strategy Menu

London International Financial Futures and Options Exchange
- Summary of Futures and Options contracts
- LIFFE Options: A Guide to Trading Strategies
- An Introduction to Commodity Options

Credit Suisse
- A guide to foreign exchange and the money markets
  Credit Suisse Special Publications, Vol.80, 1992

Chicago Board Options Exchange
- Options Contract Specifications

New York Mercantile Exchange
- NYMEX Energy Options
- NYMEX Energy Options: Strategies at a Glance

New York Coffee Sugar & Cocoa Exchange
- Understanding Options on Futures

Options Clearing Corporation
- Characteristics and Risks of Standardised Options

Philadelphia Stock Exchange
- A User's Guide to Currency Options

Internet
RFT Web Site
- **http://www.wiley-rft.reuters.com**
This is the series' companion web site where additional quiz questions, updated screens and other information may be found.

Applied Derivatives Trading
- http://www.adtrading.com/
Have a look at the ADT Guide

Derivatives Research Unincorporated
- http://fbox.vt.edu:10021/business/finance/dmc/DRU/contents.html
A good collection of well explained articles

AIB: Derivatives in Plain English
- http://cgi-bin.iol.ie/aib/derivs-pe/

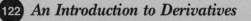

This section of the book should take about 75 minutes of study time. You may not take as long as this or you may take a little longer – remember your learning is individual to you.

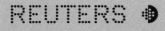

'A child of five would understand this. Send for a child of five.'

Groucho Marx (1895 – 1977)

 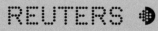

Introduction

In almost every financial market, market players are subject to price fluctuations in the underlying instruments or commodities which affect the derivatives they use. For example:

- Multinational corporations involved with major investment projects are affected by interest rates on their long term borrowing requirements

- Organisations involved with the import and export of goods and services are affected by fluctuating FX rates

- Airlines are subject to varying jet fuel prices

- Rises and falls in Stock Indices are very important to fund managers and institutional investors

Market players are constantly looking for ways to reduce the financial risks on their investments. They are looking to hedge against adverse price fluctuations and provide insurance for their transactions, particularly over a long period of time. Market players may also be willing to accept financial risks in order to profit from transactions.

There are a number of derivative contracts market players could use to provide the financial risk tools they require, for example, futures and options contracts. The main disadvantage associated with these instruments is that they are exchange traded and lack the kind of flexibility that many market players require.

A **swap** agreement or transaction is an OTC contract which meets the needs of many market players and is designed to exchange risks. But what is a swap?

 A **swap transaction** is the simultaneous buying and selling of a similar underlying asset or obligation of equivalent capital amount where the exchange of financial arrangements provides both parties to the transaction with more favourable conditions than they would otherwise expect.

 Before moving on, what features do you think market players require of OTC swaps which are not possible using exchange traded futures and options derivatives? Use the space here to jot down any thoughts you may have.

Swaps Transactions

This means that a swap is an OTC transaction between two parties in which the first party promises to make a payment to the second party. In turn the second party usually promises to make a simultaneous payment to the first party. The payments for both parties are calculated according to different formulas but paid according to an agreed set of future scheduled dates.

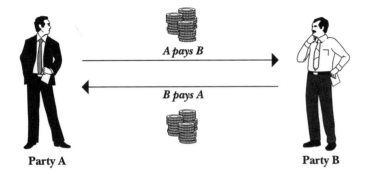

A pays B

B pays A

Party A   Party B

The type of swap described above is called a **plain vanilla** contract – it is without complications and straightforward both in principle and operation.

Swap agreements have been available for some time but the growth in use and importance of swaps really started in the early 1980s.

The beginning of the section described four different types of market player who are subject to financial risks. The varying needs of these market players give rise to the four main types of swap described in this section:

- Interest Rate Swaps (IRSs)

- Currency swaps – these are **not** the same as FX Swaps

- Commodity swaps

- Equity swaps

Payments in swaps can involve rates that are either **fixed** or **floating**. Fixed rates do not vary, for example, for bond coupons, whereas floating rates vary according to a reference index or rate, for example, LIBOR or for S&P 500 Index. The chart below summarises, in general terms, the payments made by both parties in each type of swap.

Swap	Party A payments based on:	Party B payments based on:
Interest rate	Fixed or floating interest rate	Fixed or floating interest rate
Currency	Interest on one currency	Interest on a different currency
Commodity	Price of a commodity index	Fixed rate or some other floating rate or price
Equity	Rate of return of a Stock Index	Fixed or floating rate or rate of return on another Stock Index

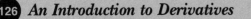

Swaps are privately negotiated OTC transactions which are the equivalent of a series of forward contracts each having the same price.

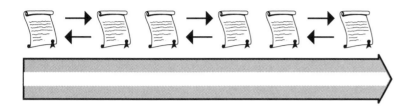

As the contracts are negotiated, the maturity period is agreed between both parties – swaps can have maturity periods for as long as is required but the most common cover periods up to 10 years. Long maturity periods are a distinct advantage over trading futures and options contracts which have relatively short term expiry dates. For example, an airline wishing to hedge jet oil prices over two years would have to trade a strip of at least 8 futures contracts to cover a single 2-year swap agreement. Using a swap agreement can be much more cost effective both in terms of fees and time.

Although swap agreement terms and conditions are privately negotiated there are two professional bodies who issue standard documentation relating to swaps. These are the:

- **British Bankers Association (BBA)**

- **International Swap and Derivatives Association (ISDA)**. ISDA was established in 1985 as a global trade association representing market players using OTC interest rate, currency, commodity and equity swaps, together with related products such as interest rate options and swaptions – options on swaps. Reuters is a member of ISDA.

Both organisations' documentation attempts to attach some form of standardisation to contract terms and conditions. ISDA also provides data and statistics on the swaps markets in general.

Swaps have always been important in the derivatives markets and are now used by a wide range of market players to:

- **Hedge** exposure on –
  - Interest rates
  - FX transactions
  - Commodity prices
  - Equity investments
  - Any other type of underlying instrument

- **Speculate** in buying or selling swap contracts with a view to making a profit

Some of the benefits to market players of using swaps are listed here:

- **Lowering of funding costs**. Swaps can/may provide access to markets which the market players may not normally have access to, for example, borrowing foreign currency at domestic rates.

- **Flexibility**. The OTC nature of swaps means that contracts have an almost limitless number of ways of being drawn up to suit both parties involved.

- **Single-transaction**. A single OTC swap agreement can cover payment periods over as long a maturity period as required – commonly up to 10 years. Using other short term derivatives to cover the required maturity period may involve a number of contracts incurring extra costs and organisation.

- **Insurance**. Swaps are used to exchange risk and are used as a form of insurance for market risk.

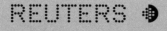

Swaps Transactions

The disadvantages of swaps are that the contracts are non-standardised and that they cannot be used for other financial purposes – they cannot be traded. There is also the issue of credit risk when transacting swaps. Whereas futures and options contracts involve a clearing house that guarantees the transactions, swaps involve counterparty risk. Will the parties to a contract both meet their scheduled payments? For example, if a counterparty defaults on an interest payment, then the market player concerned still has to pay the interest due on the underlying loan on which the swap is based. Just as for other derivatives, there are also market, legal and operational risks to take into account when transacting swaps.

The following chart compares the main differences between futures /options contracts with swaps.

Futures/options	Swaps
• Exchange traded	• Privately negotiated OTC
• Standardised contracts	• Customised agreements
• Available to private investors	• Only entered into by multinational corporations and banks
• Trading counterparties are anonymous	• Counterparties must be known to both sides
• Clearing house guarantees trade – no credit exposure	• Counterparty risks – credit exposure can be collateralised to minimise exposure

To summarise, the swap market is traditionally concerned with:

Swapping a financial advantage which one market player has in one market for an equivalent advantage to another market player in a different market.

The resulting exchange of payments associated with the swap benefits both sides of the swap.

But how are each of the different types of swap used in practice? Read on.

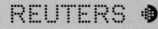

Interest Rate Swaps (IRSs)

Although the use of other types of swaps pre-dates Interest Rate Swaps by at least ten years, IRSs are now the most common and important swap transacted.

> An **Interest Rate Swap** is an agreement between counterparties in which each party agrees to make a series of payments to the other on agreed future dates until maturity of the agreement. Each party's interest payments are calculated using different formulas by applying the agreement terms to the **notional principal** amount of the swap.

With IRSs the notional principal **seldom** changes hands – it is only used as a reference point for calculating payments.

In effect this means that the interest rate basis for a debt or investment, for both parties, is changed **without** altering the underlying principal obligation – the loan or investment. It is also important to note that the interest rate payments are based on the **same currency**.

So how do IRSs work in practice? The following example describes the simplest type of IRS – the **plain vanilla** swap. In this case the swap involves **fixed-for-floating** interest payments.

Example – a plain vanilla IRS
Consider the following situation:

XYZ is a multinational corporation with a credit rating of BBB. XYZ needs to borrow $50 million for 5 years. The Treasury Department would prefer a **fixed rate** loan in order to predict future funding costs. In other words XYZ wants to hedge its interest rate exposure. Because of its credit rating, XYZ can only manage to raise a loan on a **floating rate** basis of LIBOR + 1%. An alternative strategy would be for XYZ to issue a debt instrument with a high coupon rate of 10%.

AYZ is an international bank with AAA credit rating who also need to raise $50 million for 5 years. The bank would prefer a loan on a **floating rate** basis in order to control its profit margins on any interest rate gap. In other words the bank too wants to hedge its interest rate exposure. Because of its credit rating, AYZ can borrow at a **fixed rate** of 8.25% or a floating rate of LIBOR.

Rates	XYZ can borrow	AYZ can borrow
Fixed @	10.00%	8.25%
Floating @	LIBOR + 1%	LIBOR
Required basis	**Fixed**	**Floating**

As you will see, a swap between XYZ and AYZ will reduce interest rate payments on both sides. The principal amounts on both sides are not swapped – the $50 million is the notional principal used to calculate interest rate payments.

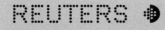

Both XYZ and AYZ obtain funds which are favourable to them and then swap the interest rate payments. So XYZ takes out their loan on a floating basis of LIBOR + 1%, whilst AYZ borrows at 8.25% on a fixed basis. The swap is therefore on a fixed-for-floating basis for a 5 year maturity period.

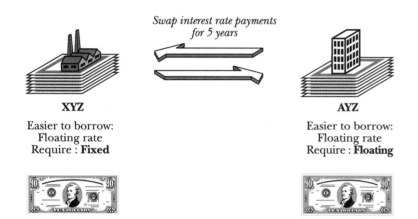

Swap interest rate payments for 5 years

XYZ

Easier to borrow:
Floating rate
Require : **Fixed**

AYZ

Easier to borrow:
Floating rate
Require : **Floating**

In practice, for each scheduled future payment date, only one payment is made. It is the **net difference** between payments in the same currency that is paid one way or the other. It is for this reason that IRSs are sometimes known as **contracts for difference**.

The result of swapping interest rate payments is that both parties should pay interest at net rates **lower** than otherwise available to them. This is how the IRS works...

a) XYZ borrows at a floating rate of LIBOR + 1%

b) AYZ borrows at a fixed rate of 8.25%

c) XYZ and AYZ enter into an IRS agreement for a notional principal amount of $50 millions for 5 years where:

- XYZ makes **fixed rate** payments of 9.75% to AYZ
- AYZ makes **floating rate** payments of LIBOR + 1% to XYZ
  XYZ pays this higher fixed rate to AYZ to compensate the bank for entering the swap.

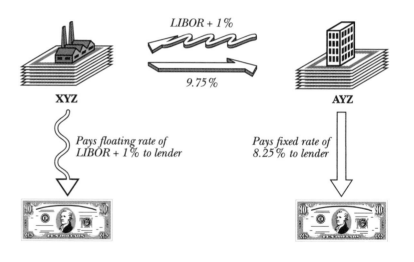

LIBOR + 1%

9.75%

XYZ

AYZ

Pays floating rate of LIBOR + 1% to lender

Pays fixed rate of 8.25% to lender

How do both sides benefit from the swap? Have a look at the chart below to see the savings both XYZ and AYZ make.

	XYZ	AYZ
Pays out	9.75% + LIBOR + 1%	8.25% + LIBOR + 1%
Receives in	LIBOR + 1%	9.75%
Payments =	9.75%	LIBOR ± 0.5%
Without swap costs	10.00%	LIBOR
Savings	**0.25%**	**0.50%**

Another way of considering the swap is as follows:

- Without the swap both XYZ and AYZ pay a total of 10.00% + LIBOR in interest rate charges

- With the swap both parties pay a total of 9.25% + LIBOR in charges

Thus, by using the swap, there is a net savings of 0.75% split 0.25%/0.50% in favour of the bank, which is the organisation with the better credit rating.

Summary of Interest Rate Swaps

- An IRS is an exchange or swap of interest rate payments calculated according to different formulas on the same notional principal amount.

- No exchange of principal occurs during the swap – no funds are lent or borrowed between the counterparties as part of the swap.

- Interest rate payments are usually netted and only the difference is paid to one party or the other.

- Any underlying loan or deposit is not affected by the swap. The swap is a separate transaction.

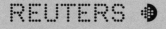

Currency Swaps

These derivatives are very similar, in principle, to IRSs and are often combined with them in use.

The two principle differences between Currency swaps and IRSs are the following:

- The interest payments are made in different currencies.

- There is an exchange of principal, usually at both the beginning and at maturity of the agreement. These exchanges are usually made at the original spot rate.

 A **Currency swap** is an agreement between counterparties in which one party makes payments in one currency and the other party makes payments in a different currency on agreed future dates until maturity of the agreement.

The periodic payments made by the counterparties may be based on either fixed or floating rates for both currencies.

The swap allows both parties to limit the effects of FX rates or lower financing costs in the required foreign currency. A currency swap is not the same transaction as an FX swap. FX swaps involve the simultaneous purchase and sale, or sale and purchase, of one currency against another for two value dates. Currency swaps can involve a schedule of payments over a long maturity period.

Currency swaps are OTC agreements that have been available since the 1970s but the first major long term currency swap took place in 1981 between the World Bank and IBM.

Before moving on try the activity opposite.

 From your current understanding of swaps what do you think happened in the currency swap between the World Bank and IBM? Jot down any general ideas you may have here.

IBM

World Bank

Example – a simple currency swap

Suppose the World Bank and IBM currency swap was happening now:

The World Bank needs to borrow Swiss francs (CHF) on a long term basis to fund various projects but in the current market is being quoted high interest rates. However the bank can borrow US dollars (USD), long term, at very favourable rates.

IBM, on the other hand, has a high standing in the Swiss markets and can borrow long term CHF at favourable rates but needs USD for several major projects.

The solution to both organisations' long term foreign currency funding needs is to enter into a currency swap. IBM borrows CHF and the World Bank borrows USD. The organisations then swap both the principal amounts and the interest payments. At maturity of the swap the principal amounts are re-exchanged.

The outcome is that IBM pays a lower rate 'borrowing' USD than it would have done in the FX markets, and the World Bank pays a lower rate on 'borrowing' CHF than it would have done. Both organisations benefit from their respective advantageous positions in different markets.

IBM and the World Bank could have issued fixed rate debt instruments and then converted the capital. Or, they could have issued Eurobonds. Why choose a currency swap?

In its simplest form a currency swap is in effect a spot transaction combined with a series of forward FX transactions.

This is how the currency swap works...

Exchange of principal amounts
At the start of the swap IBM and the World Bank both borrow equivalent amounts of currency and exchange these principal amounts of currency at an agreed exchange rate. The exchange rate is usually taken as spot. Another possibility is that notional amounts of foreign currency could have been exchanged where no actual delivery of currency takes place. This is the spot transaction stage of the currency swap:

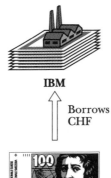
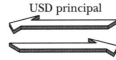

USD principal

CHF principal

IBM   **World Bank**

Borrows   **Spot transaction**   Borrows
CHF   USD

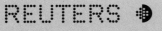

Counterparties exchange interest rate payments

During the period of the swap IBM and the World Bank exchange interest payments based on the principal amounts at the respective interest rates agreed at the start of the swap. These rates may be based on fixed or floating rates and the payment periods may be annual or semi-annual. The agreed payment periods are usually dependent on the interest payment periods of the underlying loans.

Re-exchange of principal amounts

On maturity of the swap IBM and the World Bank re-exchange the principal amounts at the original exchange rate.

The net effect of the currency swap is that IBM converts a CHF denominated loan into one for USD and the World Bank converts its USD loan into one for CHF.

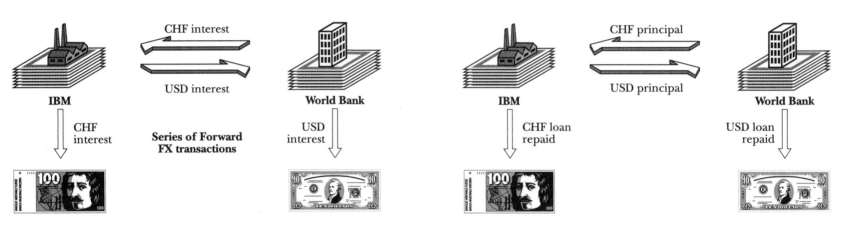

The receipt of CHF from the World Bank offsets IBM's payment of interest on its CHF loan and similarly the World Bank's receipt of USD offsets its USD interest payments.

In the example that has been used here for a swap between IBM and the World Bank, the interest rates used to determine the swap payments are fixed rates – this type of swap is also known as a **fixed-to-fixed** currency swap.

However, some currency swaps utilise floating rates for one or both of the currencies involved. Swaps of this type are called **cross-currency** swaps. For example, with a fixed-to-floating cross currency swap, fixed interest rate payments in one currency are swapped for floating rate interest rate payments in a different currency.

Summary of Currency Swaps

- A currency swap usually involves an exchange of currencies between counterparties at the outset of the agreement and at its maturity. If no exchange takes place at the outset, then there must be an exchange at maturity. Because exchange of principal takes place there is an additional credit risk attached to the transaction.

- Interest payments between the counterparties are usually paid in full.

- Interest payments on the two currencies can be calculated on a fixed or floating basis for both currencies, or payments for one currency can be on a fixed basis and floating for the other.

Commodity Swaps

The most common examples of commodity swaps involve plain vanilla OTC agreements for a fixed-for-floating exchange of risk. These are purely financial transactions in which **no delivery** of the physical commodity is involved.

> A **Commodity swap** is an agreement between counterparties in which at least one set of payments involved is set by the price of the commodity or by the price of a commodity index.

Commodity swaps are used by many consumers and producers of commodities to hedge price rises over a long term period. For example, bread and biscuit producers hedge grain prices, whilst airlines hedge jet fuel prices.

Since the Gulf War 1990 - 1991 fixed-for-floating **Energy swaps** for oil products have been increasingly more important in the derivatives markets.

Producers and consumers of commodities are often linked to long term contracts to buy or sell where the delivery price is determined by an index price. This means that the price at delivery is not known until a short time beforehand or until the actual delivery date. Under these conditions there is a considerable floating price risk.

The following example concerning an airline illustrates how a commodity swap – an energy swap in this case – works.

Example – a plain vanilla commodity swap

XYZ Airline needs to fix or set ticket prices for up to a year forward which are used to help predict its future revenue. Fuel prices represent approximately 35% of an airline's operating costs so any price fluctuations can seriously affect its profits if ticket prices are fixed. Also, airlines are committed usually to buy jet fuel on long term monthly delivery contracts. These contracts assure delivery but the delivery price is set based on an average monthly index price – typically Platts prices are used.

XYZ Airline has therefore a fixed revenue from ticket sales but operating costs which can fluctuate widely. How can the airline eliminate or reduce this floating price risk?

There are a number of derivatives XYZ could transact to hedge its risk, for example, futures and options. However, an energy swap is the most likely instrument as it provides a flexible, long term OTC contract.

Airlines often enter into swap contracts of two years maturity involving payment periods every 6 months where they either pay or receive a cash amount determined by the value of a specific Platts index oil price. The swap contract relates to a specific amount of oil which the airline is either contracted to take physical delivery of or is bought on the spot market.

By entering into an energy swap agreement the airline effectively locks in the price of its fuel for the two year period.

 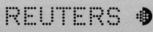

This is how the commodity swap works...

a) The airline enters into a swap with a bank

The airline, who has the floating price risk, buys an energy swap from the AYZ bank and agrees to pay a fixed price to the bank for a series of scheduled payments for the maturity period of the swap.

The seller of the swap, AYZ bank, agrees to pay the airline guaranteed payments based on a Platts oil price index for each scheduled period.

Platts oil index price

Fixed price

AYZ

XYZ

Buys oil at spot or contract price based on Platts

b) Counterparties exchange payments

The difference in payments is netted and a cash amount is paid either to the airline or to the bank.

If oil prices go down, then the airline benefits from lower spot or contract prices but they pay the difference between the fixed and floating prices to the bank.

If oil prices increase, then the airline pays more for the fuel but the bank pays the airline the difference between the fixed and floating prices. This receipt offsets the increased fuel costs.

The overall effect of the energy swap is that the airline has fixed its costs. The following chart illustrates the process.

 ← →

| Oil price falls to **$8** | XYZ pays AYZ a fixed price of **$10** | Oil price rises to **$11** |

XYZ pays AYZ $2 – the net difference between paying $10 and receiving $8.

XYZ pays $8 for oil.

Total cost for oil for XZY = $8 + $2
= $10

XYZ receives $1 from AYZ – the net difference between paying $10 and receiving $11.

XYZ pay $11 for oil.

Total cost for oil for XYZ = $11 – $1
= $10

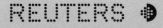

Swaps Transactions

There is an increasing use of swaps for base metals such as Copper, Aluminium and Nickel which involve an intermediary – a market-maker. This is in effect a **double swap** where the credit risk is taken on by the market maker rather than between the producer and consumer directly.

The screens below display a chain of last prices for **Brent Crude oil swaps**.

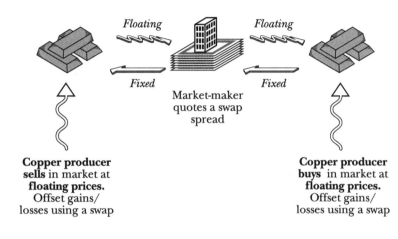

Floating   *Floating*

Fixed   *Fixed*

Market-maker quotes a swap spread

Copper producer sells in market at **floating prices.**
Offset gains/ losses using a swap

Copper producer buys in market at **floating prices.**
Offset gains/ losses using a swap

```
09:26 06NOV97          EUROPEAN NAPHTHA SWAPS      UK30507      EURO/SWAP/NAP

              Cargo swap    Crack spread

Nov-97         197.25          2.52
Dec-97         196.50          2.39
Jan-98         195.50          2.31
Feb-98         194.50          2.30

1Q98           195.36          2.40
2Q98           189.84          2.10

Notes:
Cargo CIF NWE swaps $ per tonne.
Crack spread versus IPE Brent $ per barrel.
Naphtha conversion 8.9 barrels = 1 tonne
Editorial contact: Keyvan Hedvat Tel: 171 542 8185
```

Summary of Commodity Swaps

- A commodity swap is usually a plain vanilla agreement which is purely financial involving **no delivery** of the physical commodity.

- Market players on the floating price side usually buy and sell under contract terms which are linked to a commodity index such as Platts for oil products. This means that the actual delivery price is not known until, at or near delivery.

- Market players on the fixed price side accept the high degree of risk involved in volatile commodity markets. They usually offset their risk by taking opposite positions in the forwards or futures markets.

O#BRT-SWAP	Brent Swaps								
Commodity	Del.Date	Last		Srce	Terms	Loc	Ccy	Units	Date
BRENT-SWAP-1M	Nov	↑ 19.66	+0.22		FOB S.VOE	EUR	USD	BBL	06NOV97
BRENT-SWAP-2M	Dec	↑ 19.69	+0.20		FOB S.VOE	EUR	USD	BBL	06NOV97
BRENT-SWAP-3M	Jan	↑ 19.66	+0.22		FOB S.VOE	EUR	USD	BBL	06NOV97
BRENT-SWAP-4M	Feb	↑ 19.55	+0.24		FOB S.VOE	SVoe	USD	BBL	06NOV97
BRENT-SWAP-5M	Mar	↑ 19.44	+0.15		FOB	EUR	USD	BBL	06NOV97
BRENT-SWAP-6M	Apr	↑ 19.33	+0.14		FOB	EUR	USD	BBL	06NOV97
BRENT-SWAP-1Q	1Q98	↑ 19.55	+0.21		FOB S.VOE	EUR	USD	BBL	06NOV97
BRENT-SWAP-2Q	2Q98	↑ 19.23	+0.15		FOB S.VOE	EUR	USD	BBL	06NOV97
BRENT-SWAP-3Q	3Q98	↑ 19.00	+0.15		FOB S.VOE	EUR	USD	BBL	06NOV97
BRENT-SWAP-4Q	4Q98	↑ 18.82	+0.17		FOB S.VOE	EUR	USD	BBL	06NOV97
BRENT-SWAP-5Q	1Q99	↑ 18.67	+0.17		FOB S.VOE	EUR	USD	BBL	06NOV97
BRENT-SWAP-6Q	2Q99	↑ 18.59	+0.17		FOB	EUR	USD	BBL	06NOV97
BRENT-SWAP-1Y	1998	↑ 19.16	+0.17		FOB S.VOE	EUR	USD	BBL	06NOV97
BRENT-SWAP-2Y	1999	↑ 18.61	+0.16		FOB S.VOE	EUR	USD	BBL	06NOV97
BRENT-SWAP-3Y	2000	↑ 18.59	+0.17		FOB S.VOE	EUR	USD	BBL	06NOV97
BRENT-SWAP-4Y	2001	↑ 18.60	+0.17		FOB S.VOE	EUR	USD	BBL	06NOV97
BRENT-SWAP-5Y	2002	↑ 18.62	+0.17		FOB S.VOE	EUR	USD	BBL	06NOV97

Equity Swaps

Equity swaps provide fund managers, portfolio managers and institutional investors with a method of transferring assets, particularly cross-country, without incurring the high fees involved in the buying and selling transactions. The swap also provides a means of avoiding the complexities of foreign regulations, taxes, dividend payments etc relating to overseas equity markets.

An **Equity swap** is an agreement between counterparties in which at least one party agrees to pay the other a rate of return based on a stock index, according to a schedule of future dates for the maturity period of the agreement. The other party makes payments based on a fixed or floating rate, or another stock index. The payments are based on an agreed percentage of an underlying notional principal amount.

The following example concerning a US portfolio manager illustrates how an equity swap works.

Example – a plain vanilla equity swap

A US portfolio manager at XYZ Inc has a fund which currently consists entirely of US stocks. The manager believes she should diversify into the German market and buy German blue-chip company stocks. She is prepared to allocate 15% of her portfolio to German stocks. What can she do?

She could sell 15% of her US stock holdings and use the funds to buy German stocks. However, this would incur high transaction costs in both buying and selling together with the added complications of holding foreign instruments.

The manager avoids both the high costs and foreign complications by entering into a plain vanilla Equity swap with a **swap bank**, AYZ. A swap bank is simply a commercial or investment bank who specialises in swap deals.

This is how the equity swap works...

a) The manager enters into a swap with a bank
The manager agrees the notional principal amount is equivalent to 15% of the market value of her portfolio market value and that payments will be made on a quarterly basis.

b) Counterparties exchange payments
The portfolio manager pays the S&P 500 Stock Index rate of return based on the notional principal to AYZ every quarter. In return AYZ pay the manager the DAX Stock Index rate of return for the same notional principal every quarter.

XYZ

DAX rate

S&P 500 rate

AYZ

National principal equivalents to 15% of portfolio

The overall result of the swap is that the portfolio manager has in effect sold US stock and bought German stock for a notional value of 15% of her portfolio.

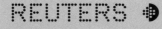

One difference between equity swaps and other types of swaps is that one party can be responsible for both payments. How can this be? In the example, suppose there is a simultaneous fall in the S&P 500 and a rise in the DAX. If the S&P 500 falls, then the portfolio has effectively been devalued, for example, to 14% of the notional principal. This means the portfolio manager will have to compensate AYZ for this loss. On the other side AYZ has to pay an amount on a revalued portfolio, for example, to 16% of the notional principal because the DAX has gone up. This means that AYZ is paying on a portfolio size which is greater than agreed. So the portfolio manager also has to compensate the bank for the difference in DAX payments.

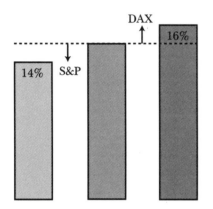

There are a number of ways equity swaps can be structured to cater to different needs.

- **Fixed and variable notional principal amounts**
  A fixed notional principal means that the portfolio is rebalanced periodically to maintain the same percentage allocation as agreed originally.

  A variable notional principal amount means that the portfolio is not rebalanced and grows or declines from the original according to the markets.

- **Currency risk**
  If a currency risk is unacceptable then the portfolio manager will require the payments be based on the DAX return applied to a USD notional principal.

  However, if a currency risk is acceptable then payments are based on a DEM notional principal. If the final payments are to be in USD, then the DEM would need to be exchanged in the spot FX market.

- **Specialised basis for payments**
  It is possible to structure an equity swap so that payments are made on specific stock market sectors or even on individual stocks, although the latter case is unusual.

Summary of Equity Swaps

- At least one payment is based on the rate of return of a Stock Index for an agreed percentage of a notional principal amount.

- Equity swaps in effect transfer assets without involving the physical buying and selling of equities or other financial instruments.

- Equity swaps provide an effective method of entering into overseas equity markets without the restraints and complications of actually trading abroad.

The Importance of Swaps

Swaps are agreements between two parties to exchange risks and as such they are now very important derivative risk management tools.

The latest statistics available from ISDA indicate that in terms of the notional principal outstanding, interest rate swaps are by far the most important type of swap transacted – almost $13,000 billion notional at the end of 1995. The chart below indicates the relative figures for interest rate swaps, currency swaps and interest rate options – these options include all types, for example, swaptions.

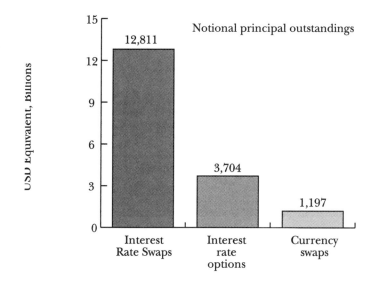

ISDA Summary of Market Survey Statistics: Year end 1995

Within the currency swaps the most important currency pairs involved in the transactions are shown in the data below.

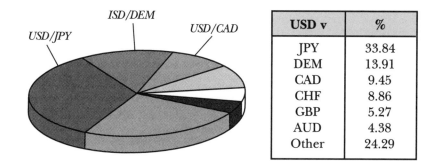

USD v	%
JPY	33.84
DEM	13.91
CAD	9.45
CHF	8.86
GBP	5.27
AUD	4.38
Other	24.29

The following table indicates the types of users responsible for the notional principal outstandings globally for both IRSs and currency swaps.

Business User Type	Interest Rate Swaps, % of market	Currency Swaps, % of market
Corporations	**24**	**32**
Banks	**53**	**37**
Investment institutions	7	6
Governments	9	21
Other	7	4
Total	100	100

Summary

You have now finished the fourth section of the book and you should have an understanding of the importance of swaps and in particular the principles underlying the following:

- Interest Rate Swaps (IRSs)

- Currency swaps

- Commodity swaps

- Equity swaps

As a check on your understanding of this section, you should try the Quick Quiz Questions. You may also find the Overview Section to be a useful learning tool.

Your notes

Quick Quiz Questions

Your notes

1. In an interest rate swap, principal amounts are usually:

   ❑ a) Exchanged at the end date
   ❑ b) Exchanged at the start date
   ❑ c) Not exchanged
   ❑ d) Exchanged at the end of the first swap period

2. A currency swap usually involves an exchange of currencies between counter parties at the start of the contract and at maturity. Is this statement true or false?

   ❑ a) True
   ❑ b) False

3. A commodity swap is usually a plain vanilla agreement which is purely financial involving **delivery** of the physical commodity. Is this statement true or false?

   ❑ a) True
   ❑ b) False

4. Which one of the following statements best describes a double swap?

   ❑ a) A swap where both counterparty payments are fixed
   ❑ b) A swap where both counterparty payments are floating
   ❑ c) A swap which involves a market-maker
   ❑ d) A swap which involves assets in two different markets

You can check your answers on page 145.

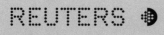

Swaps Transactions

Overview

Interest Rate Swaps (IRSs)

An **Interest Rate Swap** is an agreement between counterparties in which each party agrees to make a series of payments to the other on agreed future dates until maturity of the agreement. Each party's interest payments are calculated using different formulas by applying the agreement terms to the **notional principal** amount of the swap.

Summary of Interest Rate Swaps

- An IRS is an exchange or swap of interest rate payments calculated according to different formulas on the same notional principal amount.

- No exchange of principal occurs during the swap – no funds are lent or borrowed between the counterparties as part of the swap.

- Interest rate payments are usually netted and only the difference is paid to one party or the other.

- Any underlying loan or deposit is not affected by the swap. The swap is a separate transaction.

Currency Swaps

A **Currency swap** is an agreement between counterparties in which one party makes payments in one currency and the other party makes payments in a different currency on agreed future dates until maturity of the agreement.

Summary of Currency swaps

- A Currency swap usually involves an exchange of currencies between counterparties at the outset of the agreement and at its maturity. If no exchange takes place at the outset, then there must be an exchange at maturity. Because exchange of principal takes place there is an additional credit risk attached to the transaction.

- Interest payments between the counterparties are usually paid in full.

- Interest payments on the two currencies can be calculated on a fixed or floating basis for both currencies, or payments for one currency can be on a fixed basis and floating for the other.

Introduction

Definitions

A **swap transaction** is the simultaneous buying and selling of a similar underlying asset or obligation of equivalent capital amount where the exchange of financial arrangements provides both parties to the transaction with more favourable conditions than they would otherwise expect.

Types – fixed/floating

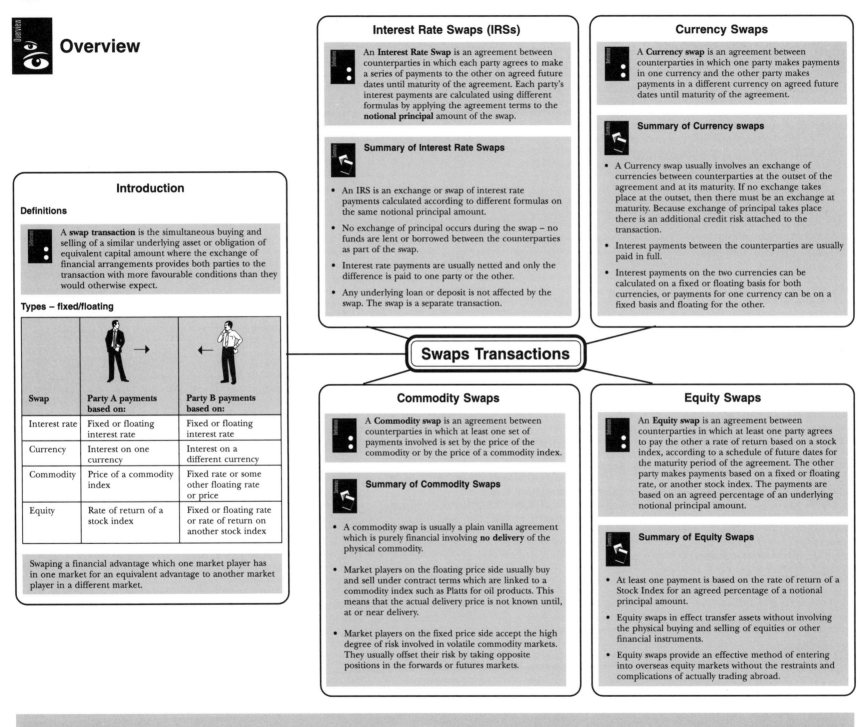

Swap	Party A payments based on:	Party B payments based on:
Interest rate	Fixed or floating interest rate	Fixed or floating interest rate
Currency	Interest on one currency	Interest on a different currency
Commodity	Price of a commodity index	Fixed rate or some other floating rate or price
Equity	Rate of return of a stock index	Fixed or floating rate or rate of return on another stock index

Swaping a financial advantage which one market player has in one market for an equivalent advantage to another market player in a different market.

Swaps Transactions

Commodity Swaps

A **Commodity swap** is an agreement between counterparties in which at least one set of payments involved is set by the price of the commodity or by the price of a commodity index.

Summary of Commodity Swaps

- A commodity swap is usually a plain vanilla agreement which is purely financial involving **no delivery** of the physical commodity.

- Market players on the floating price side usually buy and sell under contract terms which are linked to a commodity index such as Platts for oil products. This means that the actual delivery price is not known until, at or near delivery.

- Market players on the fixed price side accept the high degree of risk involved in volatile commodity markets. They usually offset their risk by taking opposite positions in the forwards or futures markets.

Equity Swaps

An **Equity swap** is an agreement between counterparties in which at least one party agrees to pay the other a rate of return based on a stock index, according to a schedule of future dates for the maturity period of the agreement. The other party makes payments based on a fixed or floating rate, or another stock index. The payments are based on an agreed percentage of an underlying notional principal amount.

Summary of Equity Swaps

- At least one payment is based on the rate of return of a Stock Index for an agreed percentage of a notional principal amount.

- Equity swaps in effect transfer assets without involving the physical buying and selling of equities or other financial instruments.

- Equity swaps provide an effective method of entering into overseas equity markets without the restraints and complications of actually trading abroad.

Quick Quiz Answers

		✓ or ✖
1.	c	❑
2.	a	❑
3.	b	❑
4.	c	❑

How well did you score? You should have scored at least 3. If you didn't, you may need to study the materials again.

Further Resources

Books
Understanding Swaps
John F. Marshall and Kenneth R. Kapner, John Wiley & Sons, Inc., 1993
ISBN 0 471 30827 7

Derivatives: The Theory and Practice of Financial Engineering
Paul Wilmott, John Wiley & Sons, Inc., 1998
ISBN 0 471 98389 6

Derivatives Handbook: Risk Management and Control
Edited by: Robert J. Schwartz and Clifford W. Smith, John Wiley & Sons, Inc., 1997
ISBN 0 471 15765 1

New Financial Instruments
Julian Walmsley, John Wiley & Sons, Inc., 2nd Edition 1998.
ISBN 0 471 12136 3

Financial Derivatives: Hedging with Futures, Forwards, Options and Swaps
David Winstone, Chapman & Hall, 1995
ISBN 0 412 62770 1

A – Z of International Finance
Stephen Mahoney, FT/Pitman Publishing, 1997
ISBN 0 273 62552 7

Options, Futures and Other Derivatives
John C. Hull, Prentice Hall International, 3rd Edition 1997
ISBN 0 13 264367 7

Publications
Credit Suisse
- A guide to foreign exchange and the money markets
  Credit Suisse Special Publications, Vol.80, 1992

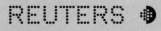

Further Resources (continued)

Your notes

Internet
RFT Web Site
- **http://www.wiley-rft.reuters.com**

This is the series' companion web site where additional quiz questions, updated screens and other information may be found.

Derivatives Research Unincorporated
- http://fbox.vt.edu:10021/business/finance/dmc/DRU/contents.html

A good collection of well explained articles

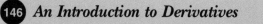
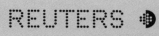

This section of the book should take about one hour of study time. You may not take as long as this or you may take a little longer – remember your learning is individual to you.

'Everyman is a maker of his fortune'

Sir Richard Steele (1672 – 1729)

 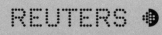

Introduction

Recent spectacular losses incurred by large multinational banks trading derivatives have arisen basically as a lack of financial control. These losses serve as reminders that trading derivatives is no different from other transactions in that there are always risks associated with the financial markets.

Derivatives are important financial instruments for risk management because they allow risks on an underlying asset to be separated and traded. Hedgers use derivatives as a form of insurance to manage their risks. Speculators, who provide liquidity to the markets, also need to manage their risks carefully.

Any institution involved with financial transactions needs an effective risk management process. The main considerations for such a process are:

- A comprehensive risk management approach

- Detailed guidelines governing risk taking and credit limits

- Efficient control, monitoring and reporting systems

As has been mentioned, the risks associated with trading derivatives are, in general, no different from trading other instruments. However, derivatives do have characteristics which require special methods to assess and control the risks involved.

But what are these risks associated with financial transactions in general? Before moving on use the space opposite to write down any risks you already know about – no answers are given because the text that follows covers everything.

 In general, what types of risk affect a financial transaction? Write down your answers here.

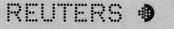

You may have mentioned a number of different types of risk. The following model encompasses four basic types of risk and places their level of importance as concentric rings with the most important at the centre.

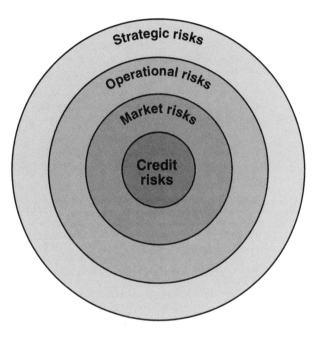

Each type of risk –
- **Credit**
- **Market**
- **Operational**
- **Strategic**

is now considered in more detail. If you mentioned another form of risk you may find it covered in the following text.

Credit Risk

Credit risk is the risk that a counterparty will fail to honour its agreed obligations.

In other words if the counterparty defaults, what would be the cost of **replacing** the transaction? For derivatives there are two replacement risks to be assessed.

- Current replacement cost of the transaction – **current exposure**

- Future replacement cost of the transaction – **potential exposure**

Financial institutions assess who they wish to trade with and how much they are willing to trade by establishing **credit limits** or **credit lines** for counterparties. These credit limits provide one way to manage this counterparty risk.

Credit risk is also dependent on the type of contract involved and the method of trading. For example, as you have already seen, credit risks for the holders and writers of options are different and credit risks for exchange traded derivatives are different from those traded OTC.

Exchange Traded Instruments
For these instruments credit risk is reduced to a minimum for the exchange members involved. This is because all matched trades on the exchange floor are cleared by a **clearing house**. The clearing house has a very high credit rating and operates a system of daily **margining** which settles any change in the value of an instrument on a daily basis. The whole process of exchange trading and the role of the clearing house is explained in more detail later.

Although credit risk for exchange members is virtually eliminated, any contract for the instrument between a client and the exchange member is still subject to credit risk.

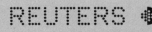

OTC Traded Instruments

In OTC markets the assessment of credit risk is very important and depends on the type of derivative involved.

If a bank sells an option for which the counterparty pays the premium in full at the start of the contract, then there is no counterparty credit risk.

If a bank buys a European style option, then there is a risk that the counterparty will not be able to pay if the option is exercised ITM at expiry. In addition, the bank does not know exactly what the value of the option will be if it is exercised ITM. In such cases the credit risk can only be calculated as a probability.

In OTC markets daily margin payments are not usually made. The credit risk associated with the derivative is therefore assessed as a gross replacement cost plus an estimate for any future changes in the contract value.

Market Risk

 Market risk results as a change in the value of a contract caused by any movements in the level or volatility of the market price of the underlying instrument.

Market risk is the reason **why** derivatives have gained so much importance as hedging and investment instruments. Derivatives are used expressly to cope with or take advantage of adverse price movements. However, derivatives are only affordable as a means of insurance because of the high degree of **leverage** involved. This means that losses as well as profits can be large but also that profits can become losses very quickly.

For these reasons derivatives market risks must be constantly managed using a **mark-to-market** process to evaluate open positions.

For exchange traded derivatives current market prices are available as a result of the way the exchange operates and disseminates information. However, OTC prices are not necessarily readily available owing to the very nature of the contracts. For OTC derivatives a pricing model such as Black and Scholes is used to calculate the current value of an instrument. But even this process carries a risk that incorrect parameters may be used in the model – a considerable difference in price can arise by using different volatilities.

Market risk is measured increasingly using a **Value-At-Risk, (VAR)** approach. This involves assessing the expected change in the value of a derivative resulting from a change of market movements with a pre-determined probability over a particular period of time. In the near future banks will be required both by the Bank for International Settlements (BIS) and their Central Bank to have an effective tool for measuring market risk. RiskMetrics, from J.P.Morgan, is such a tool. In collaboration with J.P.Morgan, Reuters can provide the software and documentation.

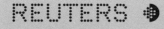

In addition to VAR assessments, many major institutions carry out simulations of extraordinary events such as a market crash to assess risk exposure – these are known as **stress tests**.

Finally within this area are **liquidity risks**. These are of two types:

- The risk that a financial institution cannot offset any position due to adverse market conditions or can offset the position at a price well outside the expected range.

- The risk that a financial institution cannot meet payment obligations on a settlement date or meet margin calls. This liquidity risk is particularly important when assessing the risk of American style options where exercise may take place before the due expiry date.

Operational Risk

This type of risk covers matters such as:

- **Settlement risk**

- **Legal risk**

- Deficiencies in information, monitoring and control systems which result in fraud, human error, system failures, management failures etc

Settlement Risk

Settlement risk arises as a result of the timing differences between when an institution either pays out funds or deliverable assets before receiving assets or payments from a counterparty.

Time differences between normal payment hours in different countries can create exposure gaps. This was demonstrated in 1974 when the closure of the private German Bank Herstatt took place in the afternoon, after payments of deutsche marks had been received by Herstatt, but before the corresponding US dollar payments in New York were due to be made. Settlement risk is often referred to as **Herstatt risk** for this reason.

It is important to note that compared with the FX markets, settlement risk for derivatives transactions is relatively small.

 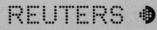

Legal Risk

> **Legal risk** arises when a contract is not legally enforceable.

There are a number of reasons which may result in this non-enforcement, including:

- Inadequate documentation

- The counterparty lacks the required authority to enter into the transaction

- The underlying transaction is not permissible

- Bankruptcy or insolvency of the counterparty changes the contract conditions

Strategic Risk

This arises from activities such as:

- Entrepreneurial behaviour of traders in financial institutions

- Misreading client requests

- Costs getting out of control

- Trading with inappropriate counterparties

As you can see, risk management is complex but if it is not carried our correctly then losses can be huge and lead to the downfall of even the most reputable of financial institutions.

Risk is inherent in trading derivatives but there are significant differences in trading OTC or on an exchange. Option risks have already been dealt with specifically in this book: *Section 4: Options – Option Risks and Sensitivities.*

As has already been mentioned, exchange trading virtually eliminates credit risk for exchange members which is often suggested as an advantage of exchange trading. The process of exchange trading, the role of the clearing house and margin are now described.

Exchange Trading

Whereas market players trading OTC derivatives range from small investors to traders for large financial institutions and can deal directly with each other, the individuals on the exchange floor are either members of the exchange or their representatives, or are exchange officials. On the exchange floor **only authorised traders** can execute a trade. This means that any market player wishing to buy or sell a derivative must trade via an exchange member which is a system which does not favour one market player over another. Different exchanges worldwide have different names for exchange members and their roles including commissioning broker, floor broker, pit broker, floor trader, pit trader, trader etc.

On many exchanges traders in a pit wear a distinctive red or coloured jacket which indicates the exchange member on whose behalf they trade. Traders also display badges indicating the type of contract they are allowed to trade and the exchange member they represent.

Traders on one of the CBOT floors

The process of trading a futures contract on LIFFE is now described – for other exchanges and other derivatives the process is much the same only differing slightly in detail.

Deciding to Trade

A market player decides he wants to buy a futures contract. The following sequence of events describes the decision to buy or not.

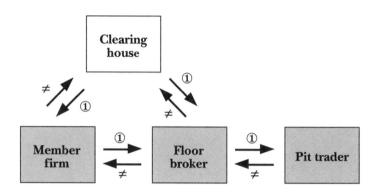

Step ①

The client telephones his request to a member firm – an executing broker – either directly to the exchange floor broker or to the broker's front office. The member firm must be a public order member – able to trade on behalf of the public. If the request is directly to the floor broker in a booth on the exchange floor, then the conversation is recorded by the exchange and can be used to resolve disputes. If the request is to the front office, then it is relayed to the firm's floor booth.

Step ②

The floor booth staff signal the client interest to the trader in the pit – at this stage it is not an order. The pit trader signals current prices back to the floor booth staff who in turn relay the information, directly or via the front office, back to the client. The client knows that the price is only firm for the time it is made – pit prices are constantly changing.

Making the Trade
The client decides to buy at the price relayed to him. This is what happens next:

Step ①
The details of the order, whether received directly or via the front office, are recorded in the floor booth on an **order slip** and **time stamped**. This is the first link in an audit trail and is important for monitoring purposes and resolving disputes.

Step ②
The floor broker instructs his pit trader of the order either by hand signals or by having the order slip taken to the trader by a booth clerk – a **yellow jacket**.

Step ③
Once the pit trader has received the order he must announce the bid or hit the offer in the pit by **open outcry**. Traders must physically be in the pit to trade and trading is carried out **fill or kill** – bids and offers must be filled immediately or they die. A combination of open outcry and hand signals are used to indicate a trader's intentions – hand signals are described later. Most exchanges now record trading activities both as sound and video.

Traders wishing to **buy/bid** shout orders as **price for lots**. For example, £4 for 15 means he is willing to buy 15 contracts @ £4 each.

Traders wishing to **sell/offer** shout orders as **lots for price**. For example, 15 for £4 means he is willing to sell 15 contracts @ £4 each.

In this case the bid is accepted and the order filled.

Step ④
Within the pit compliance with the exchange rules is ensured by the pit observers who wear **blue jackets**. If trading is carried out incorrectly, then the exchange officials can declare a trade void in the pit.

Step ⑤
Once the trade has been made an **exchange** or **floor contract** – a contract between the trader buying and the trader selling – is created immediately. Simultaneously a contract arises between the client and the member firm for the purchase of the futures contract in this case.

A pit observer reports the trade by microphone to the exchange staff. The bid/ask (offer) prices are displayed immediately on screens around the floor and disseminated to quote vendors such as Reuters or Telerate. This system ensures complete price transparency of the market.

What if a pit trader receives both buy and sell orders for the same contract from different clients? Most exchanges have rules governing such cross trades. In order to provide protection to clients and allow fair trading, exchange members are permitted to fill a proportion of cross trades but this has to be authorised by the exchange.

Traders on the floor of MONEP

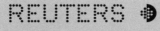

Completing the Order

Having completed the trade the following events take place:

Event ①

The trader completes a **trade card** which includes details such as price, contract month, counterparty, buy or sell etc. This card is taken to the floor booth and **time stamped**.

Event ②

The client is informed of the trade details by the member firm front office or floor booth staff. This action helps maintains the audit trail.

Event ③

Once the trade has been made floor staff of the member firm **match** the trade with the counterparty before the details are transferred to the **clearing house**.

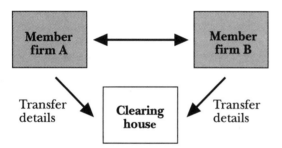

It should be noted that not all exchange members are members of the clearing house. Exchange members who are not members of the clearing house must get their trades cleared by a clearing member.

The diagrams following indicate the whole of the trading process and show a floor plan of one floor of CBOT which may help your understanding.

Your notes

The Trading Process

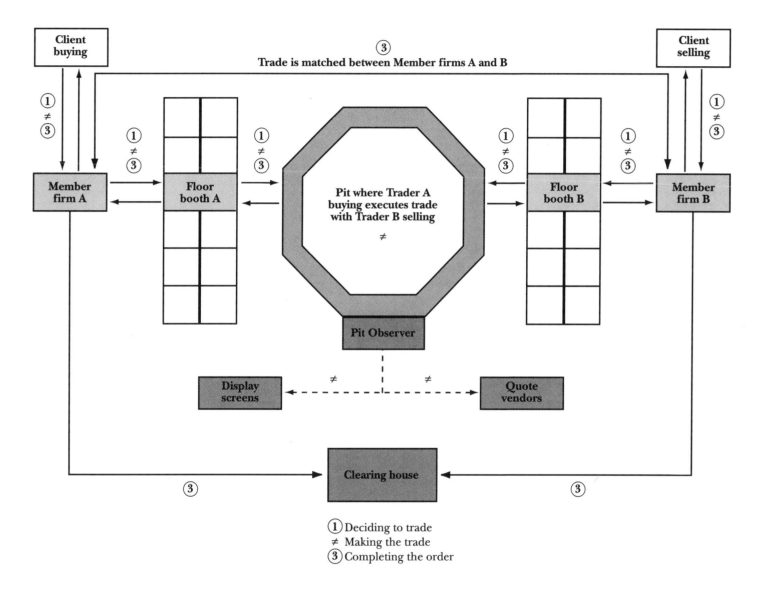

CBOT Floor Plan for Financial Derivatives

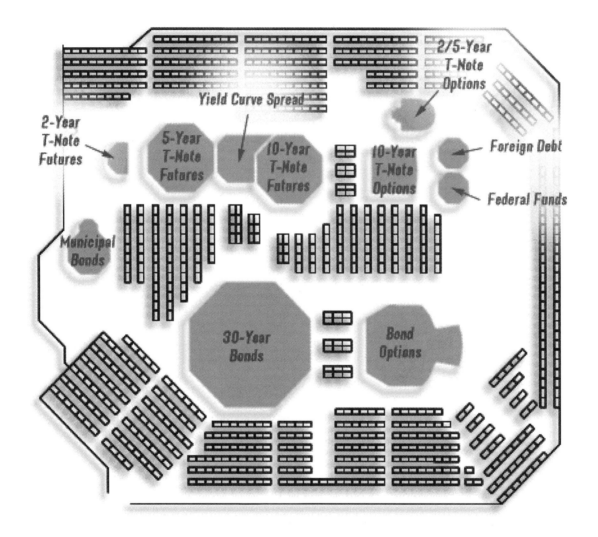

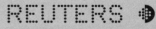

Hand Signals

On many of the exchange floors hand signals are used by traders as a means of complementing their communications and trading procedures. There are many different types of signals, some of which are specific to particular contracts. However, there are four basic types of information which hand signals are used to convey:

- **Buy or Sell**

      Buy – you see   **Sell** – you see
      the back of   the palm of
      the hand   the hand

- **Prices** – these are conveyed by signals **away** from the face

- **Quantity** – these use the same signals for prices but the hand is either on the **chin** or on the **forehead**

- **Month** – although traders usually trade for the 'front' month or the next month of the delivery cycle of a futures contract – **March, June, September** and **December** – each month does have its own signal

The delivery months are 3 months apart – if you are wondering why, have a look in *Section 2* of this workbook.

Prices

The price indicated by the trader is usually the last digit or digits as displayed on the electronic boards around the exchange floor.

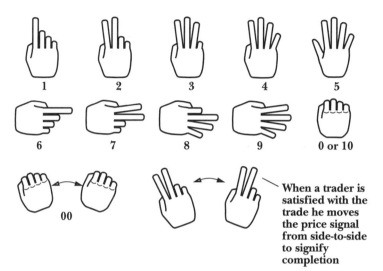

The price signals shown above are all for traders who are **buying** or in a **Bid** position – you see the back of their hand. For traders who are **selling** or in an **Offer (Ask)** position you would see the signs the other way round with the palm facing you.

      2   6

Quantity

Units are registered on the chin; tens on the forehead. Intermediate values are indicated using a combination of tens and units.

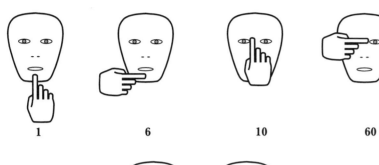

| 1 | 6 | 10 | 60 |

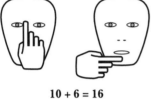

10 + 6 = 16

Months

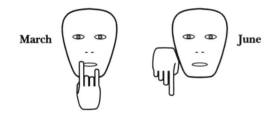

March   June

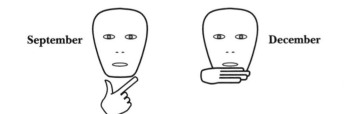

September   December

Your notes

Clearing Houses

Different exchanges worldwide use different clearing houses all of which perform similar functions. Clearing houses may be independent institutions such as the **London Clearing House (LCH)** in the UK, and the **Board of Trade Clearing Corporation (BOTCC)** in the US, which act for a number of exchanges or they may be part of a specific exchange such as for the CME.

The result of pit trading is an **exchange** or **floor contract** which is established between two traders. Simultaneously, if either trader is acting for a client, a separate **back-to-back** contract comes into effect between the executing member firm and the client. A back-to-back contract is **nothing** to do with the clearing house – the clearing house only clears contracts between clearing exchange members.

Once a trade has been matched it is registered with the Clearing house. The original exchange contract is now cancelled and replaced by **two** new **principal-to-principal** contracts:

- One contract is between the **clearing house** and the **buyer**

- The other contract is between the **clearing house** and the **seller**

In this way the clearing house acts as a **central counterparty** to both exchange members. In doing so, the clearing house guarantees the performance of all exchange contracts and thus virtually eliminates credit risk for exchange members. Obviously the clearing house takes on the credit risk but how does it manage this risk?

Clearing houses use a system of **margin** payments to ensure contract performance but before considering this have a look at the diagram opposite which illustrates the role of the clearing house.

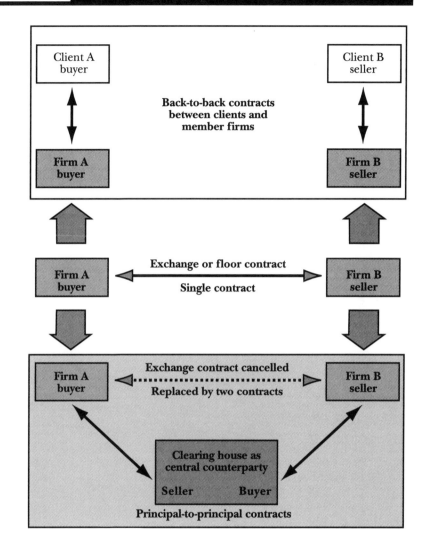

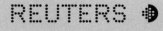

Margin Payments

Initial Margin

In general, a clearing house, in association with the exchange it acts for, set an initial margin level for contracts traded on the floor. Initial margins vary from exchange to exchange and from contract to contract, but typically they are 5 – 10% of the contract value.

The value of initial margin is calculated so that it should be sufficient to cover at least the maximum allowed price fluctuation per day which is set by the exchange and published. The initial margin can be deposited as funds for most major currencies or as financial instruments such as T-Bills and government bonds with an equivalent value.

Initial margin payments are quite small with respect to the value of the underlying contract. This means that highly **leveraged** positions can be established for a relatively small capital outlay.

Most futures contracts are closed out before expiry which means that once cleared, an equal and opposite position cancels the original contract with the clearing house. On closing out a position the clearing house returns the initial margin to the exchange member.

Variation Margin

Each day the futures contract is marked-to-market and its value calculated using the settlement price at the end of each trading day. This calculation may result in an increase or decrease in the contract value – in other words a profit or loss.

All profits and losses are credited to or debited from the counterparties' clearing house accounts daily. Any profits can be withdrawn. If a loss occurs, then extra margin called **variation margin** is paid to cover this loss. Payment of a variation margin ensures that the initial margin remains at a constant level. These payments are usually required in the same currency as that of the contract.

If a gain is made, then the member is allowed to withdraw the profits or keep then on deposit.

The clearing house carries out the collection/payment of all the calculated losses/profits daily.

For some contracts **maintenance margin** is set such that variation payments are only required when losses on a futures position fall below a specified level.

The system of margin payments described thus ensures that all parties including the clearing house acting as central counterparty can fulfil their contractual obligations.

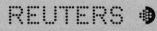

But how does variation margin work? Have a look at the following example.

Example

A broker buys one September LIFFE 3-month Short Sterling Interest Rate futures contract at 93.75 on 11th August. The contract is held for 5 days and closed out by selling one September contract for 94.98. The following chart indicates the amounts the broker's account is debited/credited on a daily basis. The total net variation margin for the contract is equal to the difference in the buy and sell prices – 123 ticks – but the profit of £1537.50 is not paid as a lump sum as you can see below.

Profits and losses are calculated using:

Profit/loss = No. of ticks x Tick value x No. of contracts
 = No. of ticks x £12.50 x 1

Date	Trade price	Net position	Closing poisition	Daily settlement	
				Credit,£	Debit,£
11.8	93.75	93.76	+0.01	12.50	
12.8		93.73	−0.03		37.50
13.8		94.02	0.29	362.50	
14.8		93.98	−0.04		50.00
15.8	94.98		1.00	1250.00	
				1625.00	87.50
Net gain of 123 ticks = profit of £1537.50					

It is important to note that clearing members have to margin their clients at levels no less than apply to their positions – in other words margin payments apply to the back-to-back contracts.

Margin Payments on Exchange Traded Options

On exchanges such as CBOT where the premium is paid in full when a position is opened, **no additional margin payments** are required for **buyers** or **holders** of options. The clearing house receives the premium once the buyer has paid it to the exchange member.

Writers of options, particularly uncovered options, have a potential unlimited loss risk. All exchanges operate some form of margin payment system for option sellers. As with futures the clearing house acts as the counterparty and guarantees the performance of the contract.

However some exchanges such as LIFFE trade options futures style. This means that both buyers and sellers pay margin. In this case the buyer does not pay a single premium payment at the outset of the contract but instead deposits initial margin.

Managing Risk and Trading

Summary

You have now finished the final section of the book and you should have an understanding of the following:

- What are derivatives?

- Why have derivatives at all?

- Who uses derivatives?

- How are derivatives traded and used?

In particular you should understand how you can answer these questions in relation to:

- Forward and futures contracts

- Options contracts

- Swaps transactions

- Managing risk and trading

As a check on your understanding of this section, you should try the Quick Quiz Questions. You may also find the Overview Section to be a useful learning tool.

Your notes

Quick Quiz Questions

1. When trading in futures contracts , the credit risk is always with:

   - ❑ a) The counterparty with whom your broker deals with in the pit
   - ❑ b) The broker you place your order with
   - ❑ c) The clearing house used by the exchange
   - ❑ d) None of the above

2. On exchange floors such as those operated by LIFFE and CME match the jacket colours worn by people according to their roles.

   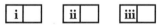

3. How is variation margin usually calculated on a futures contract?

   - ❑ a) By using a set % of the contract value
   - ❑ b) By using a calculation based on a worst case scenario
   - ❑ c) By using a set % of the initial value of the contract
   - ❑ d) By using a mark-to-market process at the end of each day

4. What is a cross trade?

   - ❑ a) When a trader consistently trades with the same trader across the pit
   - ❑ b) When the same trader has orders for both sides of the trade
   - ❑ c) When a trader trades the same contract for different months
   - ❑ d) When a trader trades in the same month for different contracts

5. Who are the risk takers in the futures markets?

You can check your answers on page 167.

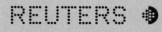

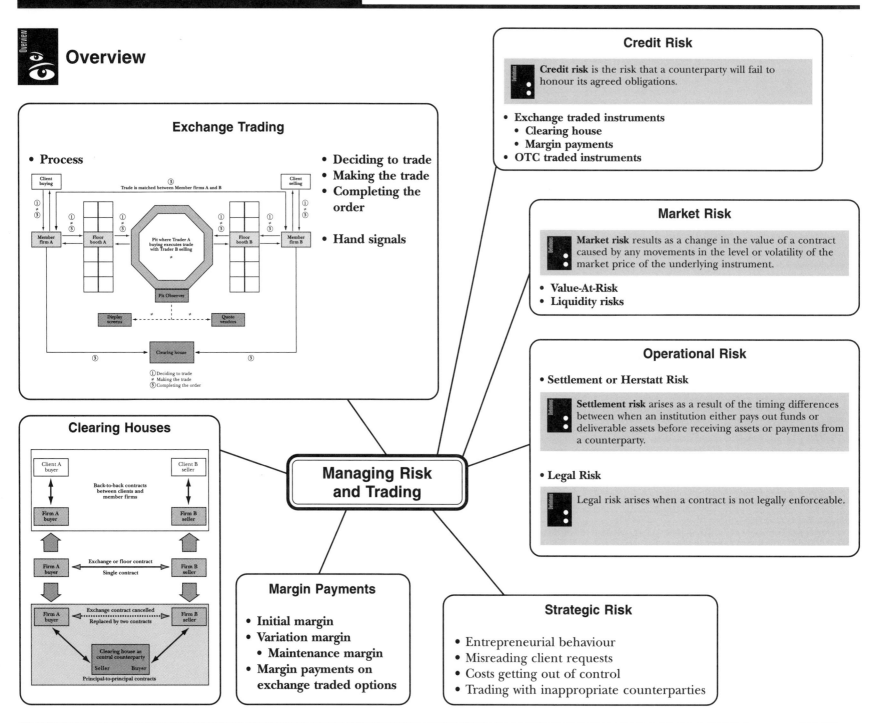

Overview

Exchange Trading

- Process

  - Deciding to trade
  - Making the trade
  - Completing the order

  - Hand signals

Client buying

Trade is matched between Member firms A and B

Client selling

Member firm A — Floor booth A — Pit where Trader A buying executes trade with Trader B selling — Floor booth B — Member firm B

Pit Observer

Display screens — Quote vendors

Clearing house

① Deciding to trade
≠ Making the trade
③ Completing the order

Clearing Houses

Client A buyer — Client B seller

Back-to-back contracts between clients and member firms

Firm A buyer — Firm B seller

Firm A buyer — Exchange or floor contract — Firm B seller
Single contract

Firm A buyer — Exchange contract cancelled / Replaced by two contracts — Firm B seller

Clearing house as central counterparty
Seller   Buyer

Principal-to-principal contracts

Managing Risk and Trading

Credit Risk

Credit risk is the risk that a counterparty will fail to honour its agreed obligations.

- Exchange traded instruments
  - Clearing house
  - Margin payments
- OTC traded instruments

Market Risk

Market risk results as a change in the value of a contract caused by any movements in the level or volatility of the market price of the underlying instrument.

- Value-At-Risk
- Liquidity risks

Operational Risk

- Settlement or Herstatt Risk

Settlement risk arises as a result of the timing differences between when an institution either pays out funds or deliverable assets before receiving assets or payments from a counterparty.

- Legal Risk

Legal risk arises when a contract is not legally enforceable.

Margin Payments

- Initial margin
- Variation margin
  - Maintenance margin
- Margin payments on exchange traded options

Strategic Risk

- Entrepreneurial behaviour
- Misreading client requests
- Costs getting out of control
- Trading with inappropriate counterparties

REUTERS

Quick Quiz Answers

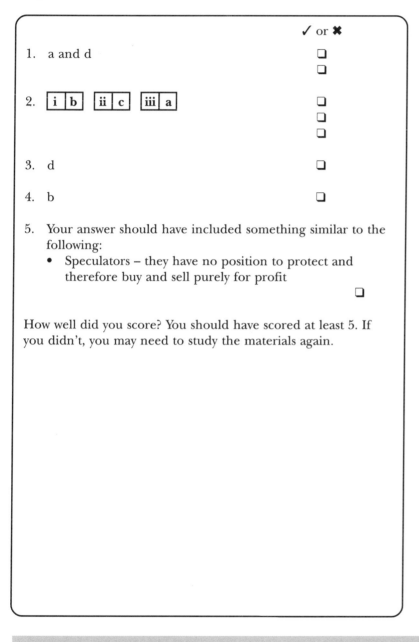

		✓ or ✗
1.	a and d	☐
		☐
2.	[i b] [ii c] [iii a]	☐
		☐
		☐
3.	d	☐
4.	b	☐

5. Your answer should have included something similar to the following:
   - Speculators – they have no position to protect and therefore buy and sell purely for profit

   ☐

How well did you score? You should have scored at least 5. If you didn't, you may need to study the materials again.

Further Resources

Books

Credit Derivatives: Trading & Management of Credit & Default Risk
Satyajit Das (ed.), John Wiley & Sons, Inc., 1998
ISBN   0 471 24856 8

Derivatives: The Wild Beast of Finance
Alfred Steinherr and Folkerts-Landau, John Wiley & Sons, Inc., 1998
ISBN   0 471 96544 8

Derivatives Handbook: Risk Management and Control
Edited by: Robert J. Schwartz and Clifford W. Smith, John Wiley & Sons, Inc., 1997
ISBN   0 471 15765 1

Merton Miller on Derivatives
Merton H. Miller, John Wiley & Sons, Inc., 1997
ISBN   0 471 18340 7

Risk Management
Emmett J. Vaughan, John Wiley & Sons, Inc., 1997
ISBN   0 471 10759 X

Risk Management and Analysis, Markets and Products
Carol Alexander, John Wiley & Sons, Inc., projected pub date Jan 1999
ISBN   0 471 97959 7

A Complete Guide to the Futures Markets: Fundamental Analysis, Technical Analysis, Trading, Spreads, and Options
Jack D. Schwager, John Wiley & Sons, Inc., 1984
ISBN   0 471 89376 5

Understanding Derivatives
Bob Reynolds, FT/Pitman Publishing, 1995
ISBN 0 273 61378 2

Publications
Options Clearing Corporation
- Characteristics and Risks of Standardised Options
- The Financial Guarantee

Further Resources (continued)

Chicago Mercantile Exchange
- A World Marketplace

Swiss Bank Corporation
- Understanding Derivatives - Prospects Special Issue 1994

Chicago Board of Trade
- Action in the Marketplace

London International Financial Futures and Options Exchange
- Managing Risk
- Hand signals

Internet
RFT Web Site
- **http://www.wiley-rft.reuters.com**

This is the series' companion web site where additional quiz questions, updated screens and other information may be found.

Your notes

Glossary of Options And Futures Related Terms

courtesy of Charles J. Kaplan, President of Equity Analytics, Ltd.

This is a slightly edited version of the Equity Analytics Glossary of Options And Futures Related Terms. The full version can be found on the internet at the URL address, *http://www.e-analytics.com/glossary/glossar9.htm.* The Publisher will not be responsible for any inaccuracies found in the glossary below. Queries should be addressed to Equity Analytics, Ltd. at *glossaries@equityanalytics.*com.

A

American-Style Option
An option contract that may be exercised at any time between the date of purchase and the expiration date. Most exchange-traded options in the United States are American-style.

Arbitrage
The simultaneous purchase and sale of identical or equivalent financial instruments or commodity futures in order to benefit from a discrepancy in their price relationship.

Assignment
The receipt of an exercise notice by an option writer (seller) that obligates him to sell (in the case of a call) or purchase (in the case of a put) the underlying security at the specified strike price.

At-The-Money
An option is at-the-money if the strike price of the option is equal to the market price of the underlying security.

B

Back Months
The futures or options on futures months being traded that are furthest from expiration.

Bear
One who believes prices will move lower.

Bear Market
A market in which prices are declining.

Bid
The price that the market participants are willing to pay.

Bull
One who expects prices to rise.

Bull Market
A market in which prices are rising.

Buy On Close
To buy at the end of a trading session at a price within the closing range.

Buy On Opening
To buy at the beginning of a trading session at a price within the opening range.

C

Call
An Option contract that gives the holder the right to buy the underlying security at a specified price for a certain, fixed period of time.

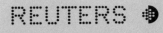

Capped-Style Option
A capped option is an option with an established profit cap. The cap price is equal to the option's strike price plus a cap interval for a call option or the strike price minus a cap interva for a put option. A capped option is automatically exercised when the underlying security closes at or above (for a call) or at or below (for a put) the Option's cap price.

Class Of Options
Option contracts of the same type (call or put) and Style (American, European or Capped) that cover the same underlying security.

Close, The
The period at the end of the trading session. Sometimes used to refer to the Closing Range (or Range). The high and low prices, or bids and offers, recorded during the period designated as the official close.

Closing Purchase
A transaction in which the purchaser's intention is to reduce or eliminate a short position in a given series of options.

Closing Sale
A transaction in which the seller's intention is to reduce or eliminate a long position in a given series of options.

Commission (or Round Turn)
The one-time fee charged by a broker to a customer when a futures or options on futures position is liquidated either by offset or delivery.

Contract
Unit of trading for a financial or commodity future. Also, actual bilateral agreement between the parties (buyer and seller) of a futures or options on futures transaction as defined by an exchange.

Contract Month
The month in which futures contracts may be satisfied by making or accepting delivery.

Covered Call Option Writing
A strategy in which one sells call options while simultaneously owning an equivalent position in the underlying security or strategy in which one sells put options and simultaneously is short an equivalent position in the underlying security.

D

Day Order
An order that is placed for execution during only one trading session. If the order cannot be executed that day, it is automatically cancelled.

Day Trading
Establishing and liquidating the same position or positions within one day's trading. The day is ended with no established position in the market.

Deferred
Another term for "back months."

Delivery
The tender and receipt of an actual commodity or financial instrument, or cash in settlement of a futures contract.

Derivative Security
A financial security whose value is determined in part from the value and characteristics of another security. The other security is referred to as the underlying security.

E

Equity Options
Options on shares of an individual common stock.

European-Style Options
An option contract that may be exercised only during a specified period of time just prior to its expiration.

Exercise
To implement the right under which the holder of an option is entitled to buy (in the case of a call) or sell (in the case of a put) the underlying security.

Exercise settlement amount
The difference between the exercise price of the option and the exercise settlement value of the index on the day an exercise notice is tendered, multiplied by the index multiplier.

Expiration Cycle
An expiration cycle relates to the dates on which options on a particular underlying security expire. A given option, will be assigned to one of three cycles, the January cycle, the February cycle or the March cycle. LEAPS are not included in this cycle.

Expiration Date
Date on which an option and the right to exercise it, cease to exist.

Expiration Time
The time of day by which all exercise notices must be received on the expiration date.

F

Floor Broker
An exchange member who is paid a fee for executing orders for Clearing Members or their customers. A Floor Broker executing orders must be licensed by the exchange he is working on.

Floor Trader
An exchange member who generally trades only for his/her own account or for an account controlled by him/her. Also referred to as a "local."

Futures
A term used to designate all contracts covering the purchase and sale of financial instruments or physical commodities for future delivery on a commodity futures exchange.

Futures Commission Merchant
A firm or person engaged in soliciting or accepting and handling orders for the purchase or sale of futures contracts, subject to the rules of a futures exchange and, who, in connection with solicitation or acceptance of orders, accepts any money or securities to margin any resulting trades or contracts. The FCM must be licensed by the CFTC.

G

H

Hedge
A conservative strategy used to limit investment loss by effecting a transaction which offsets an existing position.

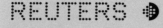

Holder
The party who purchased an option.

I

Initial Performance Bond
The funds required when a futures position (or a short options on futures position) is opened. Sometimes referred to as Initial Margin.

In-the-money
A call option is in-the-money if the strike price is less than the market price of the underlying security. A put option is in-the-money if the strike price is greater than the market price of the underlying security.

Intrinsic Value
The amount by which an option is in-the-money.

J, K

L

LEAPS
Long-Term Equity Anticipation Securities are long-term stock or index options. LEAPS are available in two types, calls and puts. They have expiration dates up to three years in the future.

Limit Order
An order given to a broker by a customer that specifies a price; the order can be executed only if the market reaches or betters that price.

Liquidation
Any transaction that offsets or closes out a long or short futures or options position.

Long Hedge (futures)
The purchase of a futures contract in anticipation of an actual purchase in the cash market. Used by processors or exporters as protection against and advance in the cash price

Long Position
An investors position where the number of contracts bought exceeds the number of contracts sold. He is a net holder.

M

Maintenance Performance Bond (Previously referred to a Maintenance Margin)
A sum, usually smaller than, but part of, the initial performance bond, which must be maintained on deposit in the customer's account at all times. If a customer's equity in any futures position drops to, or under, the maintenance performance bond level, a "performance bond call" is issued for the amount of money required to restore the customer's equity in the account to the initial margin level.

Margin Requirement For Options
The amount an uncovered (naked) option writer is required to deposit and maintain to cover a position. The margin requirement is calculated daily.

Mark-To-Market
The daily adjustment of margin accounts to reflect profits and losses.

Market Order
An order for immediate execution given to a broker to buy or sell at the best obtainable price.

Maximum Price Fluctuation (futures)
The maximum amount the contract price can change, up or down, during one trading session, as stipulated by Exchange rules.

Minimum Price Fluctuation
Smallest increment of price movement possible in trading a given contract, more commonly referred to as a "tick."

N

Nearby
The nearest active trading month of a futures or options on futures contract. It is also referred to as "lead month."

O

Offer
The price at which an investor is willing to sell a futures or options contract. Offset buying if one has sold, or selling if one has bought, a futures or options on futures contract.

Open Interest
Total number of futures or options on futures contracts that have not yet been offset or fulfilled by delivery. An indicator of the depth or liquidity of a market (the ability to buy or sell at or near a given price) and of the use of a market for risk- and/or asset-management.

Open Order
An order to a broker that is good until it is canceled or executed.

Opening Purchase
A transaction in which the purchaser's intention is to create or increase a long position in a given series of options.

Opening Sale
A transaction in which the seller's intention is to create or increase a short position in a given series of options.

Open interest
The number of outstanding option contracts in the exchange market or in a particular class or series.

Out-Of-The-Money
A call option is out-of-the-money if the strike price is greater than the market price of the underlying security. A put option is out-of-the-money if the strike price is less than the market price of the underlying security.

Out-Trades
A situation that results when there is some confusion or error on a trade. A difference in pricing, with both traders thinking they were buying, for example, is a reason why an out-trade may occur.

P

Performance Bond Call
Previously referred to as Margin Call. A demand for additional funds because of adverse price movement.

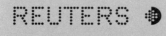

Glossary of Options And Futures Related Terms

Premium (options)
An options price has two components. They are the intrinsic value and time value. Premium is often referred to as time value. In the money call option - option strike 65. Underlying security is 67. Option price is 3. This is two points of intrinsic value and 1 point of premium. An out of the money call where the strike price is 65 and the underlying security is at 63 and the price of the option is 1½. The premium would be 1½, as there is no intrinsic value.

Premium (futures)
The excess of one futures contract price over that of another, or over the cash market price. Or, the amount agreed upon between the purchaser and seller for the purchase or sale of a futures option. Remember that purchasers pay the premium and sellers (writers) receive the premium.

Put
An option contract that gives the holder the right to sell the underlying security at a specified price for a fixed period of time.

R

Rally Reaction
A decline in prices following an advance. The opposite of rally. An upward movement of prices following a decline; the opposite of a reaction.

Registered Representative
A person employed by, and soliciting business for, a commission house or a broker dealer. Many times referred to as a broker.

Round-Turn (futures)
Procedure by which a long or short position is offset by an opposite transaction or by accepting or making delivery of the actual financial instrument or physical commodity.

S

Scalp
To trade for small gains. Scalping normally involves establishing and liquidating a position quickly, usually within the same day, hour or even just a few minutes.

Secondary Market
A market that provides for the purchase or sale of previously sold or bought options through closing transactions. Stock exchanges and the Over The Counter market are examples of the secondary market.

Series
All option contracts of the same class that also have the same unit of trade, expiration date and strike price.

Settlement Price (futures)
A figure determined by the closing range that is used to calculate gains and losses in futures market accounts. Settlement prices are used to determine gains, losses, margin calls, and invoice prices for deliveries.

Short Hedge
The sale of a futures contract in anticipation of a later cash market sale. Used to eliminate or lessen the possible decline in value of ownership of an approximately equal amount of the cash financial instrument or physical commodity.

Short Position
An investors position where the number of contracts sold exceeds the number of contracts bought. The person is a net seller.

Stop Order (Stop)
An order to buy or sell at the market when and if a specified price is reached.

REUTERS

Strike price
The stated price per share for which the underlying security may be purchased in the case of a call, or sold in the case of a put, by the option holder upon exercise of the option contract.

T

Time value
The portion of the option premium that is attributable to the amount of time remaining until the expiration of the option contract. Time value is whatever value the option has in addition to its intrinsic value. This is often referred to as premium.

Type
Describes either a put or call.

U

Uncovered call writing
A short call option position in which the writer does not own an equivalent position in the underlying security represented by his option contracts.

Uncovered put writing
A short put option position in which the writer does not have a corresponding short position in the underlying security or has not deposited, in a cash account, cash or cash equivalents equal to the exercise value of the put.

Underlying security
The security subject to being purchased or sold upon exercise of the option contract.

V

Volatility
A measure of the fluctuation in the market price of the underlying security. Mathematically, volatility is the annualized standard deviation of returns. See the sections in 'Options' which describes implied and historical volatility.

W

Writer
The seller of an option contract.

X, Y, Z

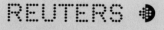

Glossary of Options And Futures Related Terms

Your notes

Directory of Futures & Options Exchanges

courtesy of Numa Financial Systems Ltd

The following directory is taken from the **Numa Directory of Futures & Options Exchanges** which can be found on the internet at the URL address, *http://www.numa.com/ref/exchange.htm.* The Publisher will not be responsible for any inaccuracies found in the listing below. Kindly address any queries to Numa Financial Systems Ltd via their home page at *http//www.numa.com.*

Argentina

Buenos Aires Stock Exchange
(Bolsa de Comercio de Buenos Aires)
Sarmiento 299, Buenos Aires
Tel: +54 1 313 3334
Fax: +54 1 312 9332
Email : cau@sba.com.ar
URL: http://www.merval.sba.com.ar

Merfox
(Mercados de Futuros y Opciones SA)
Samiento 299, 4/460, Buenos Aires
Tel: +54 1 313 4522
Fax: +54 1 313 4472

Buenos Aires Cereal Exchange
(Bolsa de Cereales de Buenos Aires)
Avenida Corrientes 127, Buenos Aires
Tel: +54 1 311 9540
Fax: +54 1 311 9540
Email : bolcerc@datamarkets.com.ar

Buenos Aires Futures Market
(Mercado a Termino de Buenos Aires SA)
Bouchard 454, 5to Piso, Buenos Aires
Tel: +54 1 311 47 16
Fax: +54 1 312 47 16

Rosario Futures Exchange
(Mercado a Termino de Rosario)
Cordoba 1402, Pcia Santa Fe, Rosario
Tel: +54 41 21 50 93
Fax: +54 41 21 50 97
Email : termino@bcr.com.ar

Rosario Stock Exchange
(Mercado de Valores de Rosario SA)
Cordoba Esquina Corrientes, Pcia Santa Fe, Rosario
Tel: +54 41 21 34 70
Fax: +54 41 24 10 19
Email : titulos@bcr.com.ar

Rosario Board of Trade
(Bolsa de Comercio de Rosario)
Cordoba 1402, Pcia Santa Fe, Rosario
Tel: +54 41 21 50 93
Fax: +54 41 21 50 97
Email : titulos@bcr.com.ar

La Plata Stock Exchange
(Bolsa de Comercio de La Plata)
Calle 48, No. 515, 1900 La Plata, Buenos Aires
Tel: +54 21 21 47 73
Fax: +54 21 25 50 33

Mendoza Stock Exchange
(Bolsa de Comercio de Mendoza)
Paseo Sarmiento 199, Mendoza
Tel: +54 61 20 23 59
Fax: +54 61 20 40 50

Cordoba Stock Exchange
(Bolsa de Comercio de Cordoba)
Rosario de Santa Fe 231, 1 Piso, Cordoba
Tel: +54 51 22 4230
Fax: +54 51 22 6550
Email : bolsacba@nt.com.ar

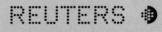

Mercado Abierto Electronico SA
(Mercado Abierto Electronico SA)
25 de Mayo 565, 4 Piso, Buenos Aires
Tel: +54 1 312 8060
Fax: +54 1 313 1445

Armenia

Yerevan Stock Exchange
22 Sarian Street, Yerevan Centre
Tel: +374 2 525 801
Fax: +374 2 151 548

Australia

Australian Stock Exchange
Exchange Centre, 20 Bond Street, Sydney
Tel: +61 29 227 0000
Fax: +61 29 235 0056
Email : info@asx.com.au
URL: http://www.asx.com.au

Sydney Futures Exchange
SFE
30-32 Grosvenor Street, Sydney
Tel: +61 29 256 0555
Fax: +61 29 256 0666
Email : sfe@hutch.com.au
URL: http://www.sfe.com.au

Austria

Austrian Futures & Options Exchange
(Osterreichische Termin Und Optionenborse)
OTOB
Strauchgasse 1-3, PO Box 192, Vienna
Tel: +43 1 531 65 0
Fax: +43 1 532 97 40
Email : contactperson@otob.ada.at
URL: http://www.wtab.at

Vienna Stock Exchange
(Wiener Borse)
Wipplingerstrasse 34, Vienna
Tel: +43 1 53 499
Fax: +43 1 535 68 57
Email : communications@vienna-stock-exchange.at
URL: http://www.wtab.at

Bahrain

Bahrain Stock Exchange
P.O. Box 3203, Manama
Tel: +973 261260
Fax: +973 256362
Email : bse@bahrainstock.com
URL: http://www.bahrainstock.com

Bangladesh

Dhaka Stock Exchange
Stock Exchange Building, 9E & 9F, Motijheel C/A, Dhaka
Tel: +880 2 956 4601
Fax: +880 2 956 4727
Email : info@dse.bdnet.net

Barbados

Securities Exchange of Barbados
5th Floor, Central Bank Building, Church Village, St Michael
Tel: +1809/1246 246 436 9871
Fax: +1809/1246 246 429 8942
Email : sebd@caribf.com

Belgium

Brussels Stock Exchange
(Societe de la Bourse de Valeurs Mobilieres de Bruxelles)
Palais de la Bourse, Brussels
Tel: +32 2 509 12 11
Fax: +32 2 509 12 12
Email : dan.maerten@pophost.eunet.be
URL: http://www.stockexchange.be

European Association of Securities Dealers Automated Quotation
EASDAQ
Rue des Colonies, 56 box 15, 1000 Brussels
Tel: +32 2 227 6520
Fax: +32 2 227 6567
Email : easdaq@tornado.be
URL: http://www.easdaq.be/

Belgian Futures & Options Exchange
BELFOX
Palais de la Bourse, Rue Henri Mausstraat, 2, Brussels
Tel: +32 2 512 80 40
Fax: +32 2 513 83 42
Email : marketing@belfox.be
URL: http://www.belfox.be

Antwerp Stock Exchange
(Effectenbeurs van Antwerpen)
Korte Klarenstraat 1, Antwerp
Tel: +32 3 233 80 16
Fax: +32 3 232 57 37

Bermuda

Bermuda Stock Exchange
BSE
Email : info@bse.com
URL: http://www.bsx.com

Bolivia

Bolivian Stock Exchange
(Bolsa Boliviana de Valores SA)
Av. 16 de Julio No 1525, Edif Mutual La Paz, 3er Piso, Casillia 12521, La Paz
Tel: +591 2 39 29 11
Fax: +591 2 35 23 08
Email : bbvsalp@wara.bolnet.bo
URL: http://bolsa-valores-bolivia.com

Botswana

Botswana Stock Exchange
5th Floor, Barclays House, Khama Crescent, Gaborone
Tel: +267 357900
Fax: +267 357901
Email : bse@info.bw

Brazil

Far-South Stock Exchange
(Bolsa de Valores do Extremo Sul)
Rua dos Andradas, 1234-8 Andar, Porte Alegre
Tel: +55 51 224 3600
Fax: +55 51 227 4359

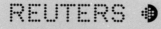

Santos Stock Exchange
(Bolsa de Valores de Santos)
Rua XV de Novembro, 111, Santos
Tel: +55 132 191 5119
Fax: +55 132 19 1800

Regional Stock Exchange
(Bolsa de Valores regional)
Avenida Dom Manuel, 1020, Fortaleza
Tel: +55 85 231 6466
Fax: +55 85 231 6888

Parana Stock Exchange
(Bolsa de Valores do Parana)
Rua Marechal Deodoro, 344-6 Andar, Curitiba
Tel: +55 41 222 5191
Fax: +55 41 223 6203

Minas, Espirito Santo, Brasilia Stock Exchange
(Blsa de Valores Minas, Espirito Santo, Brasilia)
Rua dos Carijos, 126-3 Andar, Belo Horizonte
Tel: +55 31 219 9000
Fax: +55 21 273 1202

Rio de Janeiro Stock Exchange
(Bolsa de Valores de Rio de Janeiro)
Praca XV de Novembro No 20, Rio de Janeiro
Tel: +55 21 271 1001
Fax: +55 21 221 2151
Email : info@bvrj.com.br
URL: http://www.bvrj.com.br

Sao Paolo Stock Exchange
(Bolsa de Valores de Sao Paolo)
Rua XV de Novembro 275, Sao Paolo
Tel: +55 11 233 2000
Fax: +55 11 233 2099
Email : bovespa@bovespa.com.br
URL: http://www.bovespa.com.br

Bahia, Sergipe, Alagoas Stock Exchange
(Bolsa de Valores Bahia, Sergipe, Alagoas)
Rua Conselheiro Dantas, 29-Comercio, Salvador
Tel: +55 71 242 3844
Fax: +55 71 242 5753

Brazilian Futures Exchange
(Bolsa Brasileira de Futuros)
Praca XV de Novembro, 20, 5th Floor, Rio de Janeiro
Tel: +55 21 271 1086
Fax: +55 21 224 5718
Email : bbf@bbf.com.br

The Commodities & Futures Exchange
(Bolsa de Mercadoris & Futuros)
BM&F
Praca Antonio Prado, 48, Sao Paulo
Tel: +55 11 232 5454
Fax: +55 11 239 3531
Email : webmaster@bmf.com.br
URL: http://www.bmf.com.br

Pernambuco and Paraiba Stock Exchange
(Bolsa de Valores de Pernambuco e Paraiba)
Avenida Alfredo Lisboa, 505, Recife
Tel: +55 81 224 8277
Fax: +55 81 224 8412

Bulgaria

Bulgarian Stock Exchange
1 Macedonia Square, Sofia
Tel: +359 2 81 57 11
Fax: +359 2 87 55 66
Email : bse@bg400.bg
URL: http://www.online.bg/bse

Canada

Montreal Exchange
(Bourse de Montreal)
ME
The Stock Exchange Tower, 800 Square Victoria, C.P. 61, Montreal
Tel: +1 514 871 2424
Fax: +1 514 871 3531
Email : info@me.org
URL: http://www.me.org

Vancouver Stock Exchange
VSE
Stock Exchange Tower, 609 Granville Street, Vancouver
Tel: +1 604 689 3334
Fax: +1 604 688 6051
Email : information@vse.ca
URL: http://www.vse.ca

Winnipeg Stock Exchange
620 - One Lombard Place, Winnipeg
Tel: +1 204 987 7070
Fax: +1 204 987 7079
Email : vcatalan@io.uwinnipef.ca

Alberta Stock Exchange
21st Floor, 300 Fifth Avenue SW, Calgary
Tel: +1 403 974 7400
Fax: +1 403 237 0450

Toronto Stock Exchange
TSE
The Exchange Tower, 2 First Canadian Place, Toronto
Tel: +1 416 947 4700
Fax: +1 416 947 4662
Email : skee@tse.com
URL: http://www.tse.com

Winnipeg Commodity Exchange
WCE
500 Commodity Exchange Tower, 360 Main St., Winnipeg
Tel: +1 204 925 5000
Fax: +1 204 943 5448
Email : wce@wce.mb.ca
URL: http://www.wce.mb.ca

Toronto Futures Exchange
TFE
The Exchange Tower, 2 First Canadian Place, Toronto
Tel: +1 416 947 4487
Fax: +1 416 947 4272

Cayman Islands

Cayman Islands Stock Exchange
CSX
4th Floor, Elizabethan Square, P.O Box 2408 G.T., Grand Cayman
Tel: +1345 945 6060
Fax: +1345 945 6061
Email : CSX@CSX.COM.KY
URL: http://www.csx.com.ky/

Chile

Santiago Stock Exchange
(Bolsa de Comercio de Santiago)
La Bolsa 64, Casilla 123-D, Santiago
Tel: +56 2 698 2001
Fax: +56 2 672 8046
Email : ahucke@comercio.bolsantiago.cl
URL: http://www.bolsantiago.cl

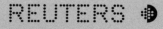

Bolsa Electronica de Chile
Huerfanos 770, Piso 14, Santiago
Tel: +56 2 639 4699
Fax: +56 2 639 9015
Email : info@bolchile.cl
URL: http://www.bolchile.cl

China

Wuhan Securities Exchange Centre
WSEC
2nd Floor, Jianghchen Hotel, Wuhan
Tel: +86 27 588 4115
Fax: +86 27 588 6038

China Zhengzhou Commodity Exchange
CZCE
20 Huanyuan Road, Zhengzhou
Tel: +86 371 594 44 54
Fax: +86 371 554 54 24

Shanghai Cereals and Oils Exchange
199 Shangcheng Road, Pudong New District, Shanghai
Tel: +86 21 5831 1111
Fax: +86 21 5831 9308
Email : liangzhu@public.sta.net.cn

China-Commodity Futures Exchange, Inc of Hainan
CCFE
Huaneng Building, 36 Datong Road, Haikou, Hainan Province
Tel: +86 898 670 01 07
Fax: +86 898 670 00 99
Email : ccfehn@public.hk.hq.cn

Guandong United Futures Exchange
JingXing Hotel, 91 LinHe West Road, Guangzhou
Tel: +86 20 8755 2109
Fax: +86 20 8755 1654

Shenzhen Mercantile Exchange
1/F Block B, Zhongjian Overseas Decoration , Hua Fu Road, Shenzhen
Tel: +86 755 3343 502
Fax: +86 755 3343 505

Shanghai Stock Exchange
15 Huang Pu Road, Shanghai
Tel: +86 216 306 8888
Fax: +86 216 306 3076

Beijing Commodity Exchange
BCE
311 Chenyun Building, No. 8 Beichen East Road, Chaoyang District, Beijing
Tel: +86 1 492 4956
Fax: +86 1 499 3365
Email : sunli@intra.cnfm.co.cn

Shenzhen Stock Exchange
203 Shangbu Industrial Area, Shenzhen
Tel: +86 755 320 3431
Fax: +86 755 320 3505

Colombia

Bogota Stock Exchange
BSE
Carrera 8, No. 13-82 Pisos 4-9, Apartado Aereo 3584, Santafe de Bogota
Tel: +57 243 6501
Fax: +57 281 3170
Email : bolbogot@bolsabogota.com.co
URL: http://www.bolsabogota.com.co

Medellin Stock Exchange
(Bolsa de Medellin SA)
Apartado Aereo 3535, Medellin
Tel: +57 4 260 3000
Fax: +57 4 251 1981
Email : 104551.1310@compuserve.com

Occidente Stock Exchange
(Bolsa de Occidente SA)
Calle 10, No. 4-40 Piso 13, Cali
Tel: +57 28 817 022
Fax: +57 28 816 720
Email : bolsaocc@cali.cetcol.net.co
URL: http://www.bolsadeoccidente.com.co

Costa Rica

National Stock Exchange
(Bolsa Nacional de Valores, SA)
BNV
Calle Central, Avenida 1, San Jose
Tel: +506 256 1180
Fax: +506 255 0131

Cote D'Ivoire (Ivory Coast)

Abidjan Stock Exchange
(Bourse des Valeurs d'Abidjan)
Avenue Marchand, BP 1878 01, Abidjan 01
Tel: +225 21 57 83
Fax: +225 22 16 57

Croatia (Hrvatska)

Zagreb Stock Exchange
(Zagrebacka Burza)
Ksaver 208, Zagreb
Tel: +385 1 428 455
Fax: +385 1 420 293
Email : zeljko.kardum@zse.hr
URL: http://www.zse.hr

Cyprus

Cyprus Stock Exchange
CSE
54 Griva Dhigeni Avenue, Silvex House, Nicosia
Tel: +357 2 368 782
Fax: +357 2 368 790
Email : cyse@zenon.logos.cy.net

Czech Republic

Prague Stock Exchange
PSE
Rybna 14, Prague 1
Tel: +42 2 2183 2116
Fax: +42 2 2183 3040
Email : marketing@pse.vol.cz
URL: http://www.pse.cz

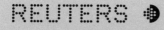

Denmark

Copenhagen Stock Exchange & FUTOP
(Kobenhavns Fondsbors)
Nikolaj Plads 6, PO Box 1040, Copenhagen K
Tel: +45 33 93 33 66
Fax: +45 33 12 86 13
Email : kfpost@xcse.dk
URL: http://www.xcse.dk

Ecuador

Quito Stock Exchange
(Bolsa de Valores de Quito CC)
Av Amazonas 540 y Carrion, 8vo Piso
Tel: +593 2 526 805
Fax: +593 2 500 942
Email : bovalqui@ecnet.ec
URL: http://www.ccbvq.com

Guayaquil Stock Exchange
(Bolsa de Valores de Guayaquil, CC)
Av. 9 de Octubre, 110 y Pinchina, Guayaquil
Tel: +593 4 561 519
Fax: +593 4 561 871
Email : bvg@bvg.fin.ec
URL: http://www.bvg.fin.ec

Egypt

Alexandria Stock Exchange
11 Talaat Harp Street, Alexandria
Tel: +20 3 483 7966
Fax: +20 3 482 3039

Cairo Stock Exchange
4(A) El Cherifeen Street, Cairo
Tel: +20 2 392 1402
Fax: +20 2 392 8526

El Salvador

El Salvador Stock Exchange
(Mercado de Valores de El Salvador, SA de CV)
6 Piso, Edificio La Centroamericana, Alameda Roosevelt No 3107,
San Salvador
Tel: +503 298 4244
Fax: +503 223 2898
Email : ggbolsa@gbm.net

Estonia

Tallinn Stock Exchange
Ravala 6, Tallinn
Tel: +372 64 08 840
Fax: +372 64 08 801
Email : tse@depo.ee
URL: http://www.tse.ee

Finland

Helsinki Stock Exchange
HSE
Fabianinkatu 14, Helsinki
Tel: +358 9 173 301
Fax: +358 9 173 30399
Email : mika.bjorklund@hex.fi
URL: http://www.hse.fi

 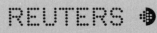

Finnish Options Exchange
(Suomen Optioporssi Oy)
FOEX
Erottajankatu 11, Helsinki
Tel: +358 9 680 3410
Fax: +358 9 604 442
Email : info@foex.fi
URL: http://www.foex.fi

Finnish Options Market
SOM
Keskuskatu 7, Helsinki
Tel: +358 9 13 1211
Fax: +358 9 13 121211
Email : webmaster@hex.fi
URL: http://www.som.fi

France

Paris Stock Exchange
(Bourse de Paris)
39 rue Cambon, Paris
Tel: +33 1 49 27 10 00
Fax: +33 1 49 27 13 71
Email : 100432.201@compuserve.com

MONEP
(Marche des Options Negociables de Paris)
MONEP
39, rue Cambon, Paris
Tel: +33 1 49 27 18 00
Fax: +33 1 9 27 18 23
URL: http://www.monep.fr

MATIF
(Marche a Terme International de France)
MATIF
176 rue Montmartre, Paris
Tel: +33 33 1 40 28 82 82
Fax: +33 33 1 40 28 80 01
Email : larrede@matif.fr
URL: http://www.matif.fr

Germany

Stuttgart Stock Exchange
(Baden-Wurttembergische Wertpapierborse zu Stuttgart)
Konigstrasse 28, Stuttgart
Tel: +49 7 11 29 01 83
Fax: +49 7 11 22 68 11 9

Hanover Stock Exchange
(Niedersachsische Borse zu Hanover)
Rathenaustrasse 2, Hanover
Tel: +49 5 11 32 76 61
Fax: +49 5 11 32 49 15

Dusseldorf Stock Exchange
(Rheinisch-Westfalische Borse zu Dusseldorf)
Ernst-Schneider-Platz 1, Dusseldorf
Tel: +49 2 11 13 89 0
Fax: +49 2 11 13 32 87

Berlin Stock Exchange
(Berliner Wertpapierborse)
Fasanenstrasse 85, Berlin
Tel: +49 30 31 10 91 0
Fax: +49 30 31 10 91 79

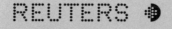

German Stock Exchange
(Deutsche Borse AG)
FWB
Borsenplatz 4, Frankfurt-am-Main
Tel: +49 69 21 01 0
Fax: +49 69 21 01 2005
URL: http://www.exchange.de

Hamburg Stock Exchange
(Hanseatische Wertpapierborse Hamburg)
Schauenburgerstrasse 49, Hamburg
Tel: +49 40 36 13 02 0
Fax: +49 40 36 13 02 23
Email : wertpapierboerse.hamburg@t-online.de

Deutsche Terminborse
DTB
Boersenplatz 4, Frankfurt-am-Main
Tel: +49 69 21 01 0
Fax: +49 69 21 01 2005
URL: http://www.exchange.de

Bavarian Stock Exchange
(Bayerische Borse)
Lenbachplatz 2(A), Munich
Tel: +49 89 54 90 45 0
Fax: +49 89 54 90 45 32
Email : bayboerse@t-online.de
URL: http://www.bayerischeboerse.de

Bremen Stock Exchange
(Bremer Wertpapierborse)
Obernstrasse 2-12, Bremen
Tel: +49 4 21 32 12 82
Fax: +49 4 21 32 31 23

Ghana

Ghana Stock Exchange
5th Floor, Cedi House, Liberia Road, PO Box 1849, Accra
Tel: +233 21 669 908
Fax: +233 21 669 913
Email : stockex@ncs.com.gh
URL: http://ourworld.compuserve.com/homepages/khaganu/
stockex.htm

Greece

Athens Stock Exchange
ASE
10 Sophocleous Street, Athens
Tel: +30 1 32 10 424
Fax: +30 1 32 13 938
Email : mailto:aik@hol.gr
URL: http://www.ase.gr

Honduras

Honduran Stock Exchange
(Bolsa Hondurena de Valores, SA)
1er Piso Edificio Martinez Val, 3a Ave 2a Calle SO, San Pedro Sula
Tel: +504 53 44 10
Fax: +504 53 44 80
Email : bhvsps@simon.intertel.hn

 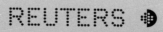

Hong Kong

Hong Kong Futures Exchange Ltd
HKFE
5/F, Asia Pacific Finance Tower, Citibank Plaza, 3 Garden Road
Tel: +852 2842 9333
Fax: +852 2810 5089
Email : prm@hfke.com
URL: http://www.hkfe.com

Hong Kong Stock Exchange
SEHK
1st Floor, One and Two Exchange Square, Central
Tel: +852 2522 1122
Fax: +852 2810 4475
Email : info@sehk.com.hk
URL: http://www.sehk.com.hk

Chinese Gold and Silver Exchange Society
Gold and Silver Commercial Bui, 12-18 Mercer Street
Tel: +852 544 1945
Fax: +852 854 0869

Hungary

Budapest Stock Exchange
Deak Ferenc utca 5, Budapest
Tel: +36 1 117 5226
Fax: +36 1 118 1737
URL: http://www.fornax.hu/fmon

Budapest Commodity Exchange
BCE
POB 495, Budapest
Tel: +36 1 269 8571
Fax: +36 1 269 8575
Email : bce@bce-bat.com
URL: http://www.bce-bat.com

Iceland

Iceland Stock Exchange
Kalkofnsvegur 1, Reykjavik
Tel: +354 569 9775
Fax: +354 569 9777
Email : gw@vi.is

India

Cochin Stock Exchange
38/1431 Kaloor Road Extension, PO Box 3529, Emakulam, Cochin
Tel: +91 484 369 020
Fax: +91 484 370 471

Bangalore Stock Exchange
Stock Exchange Towers, 51, 1st Cross, JC Road, Bangalore
Tel: +91 80 299 5234
Fax: +91 80 22 55 48

The OTC Exchange of India
OTCEI
92 Maker Towers F, Cuffe Parade, Bombay
Tel: +91 22 21 88 164
Fax: +91 22 21 88 012
Email : otc.otcindia@gems.vsnl.net.in

Jaipur Stock Exchange
Rajasthan Chamber Bhawan, MI Road, Jaipur
Tel: +91 141 56 49 62
Fax: +91 141 56 35 17

The Stock Exchange – Ahmedabad
Kamdhenu Complex, Ambawadi, Ahmedabad
Tel: +91 79 644 67 33
Fax: +91 79 21 40 117
Email : supvsr@08asxe

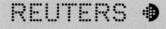

Delhi Stock Exchange
3&4/4B Asaf Ali Road, New Delhi
Tel: +91 11 327 90 00
Fax: +91 11 327 13 02

Madhya Pradesh Stock Exchange
3rd Floor, Rajani Bhawan, Opp High Court, MG Road, Indore
Tel: +91 731 432 841
Fax: +91 731 432 849

Magadh Stock Exchange
Industry House, Suinha Library Road,
Patna
Tel: +91 612 223 644

Pune Stock Exchange
Shivleela Chambers, 752 Sadashiv Peth, Kumethekar Road, Pune
Tel: +91 212 441 679

The Stock Exchange, Mumbai
Phiroze Jeejeebhoy Towers, Dalal Street, Bombay
Tel: +91 22 265 5860
Fax: +91 22 265 8121
URL: http://www.nseindia.com

Uttar Pradesh Stock Exchange
Padam Towers, 14/113 Civil Lines, Kanpur
Tel: +91 512 293 115
Fax: +91 512 293 175

Bhubaneswar Stock Exchange Association
A-22 Falcon House, Jharapara, Cuttack Road, Bhubaneswar
Tel: +91 674 482 340
Fax: +91 674 482 283

Calcutta Stock Exchange
7 Lyons Range, Calcutta
Tel: +91 33 209 366

Coimbatore Stock Exchange
Chamber Towers, 8/732 Avanashi Road, Coimbatore
Tel: +91 422 215 100
Fax: +91 422 213 947

Madras Stock Exchange
Exchange Building, PO Box 183, 11 Second Line Beach, Madras
Tel: +91 44 510 845
Fax: +91 44 524 4897

Ludhiana Stock Exchange
Lajpat Rai Market, Near Clock Tower, Ludhiana
Tel: +91 161 39318

Kanara Stock Exchange
4th Floor, Ranbhavan Complex, Koialbail, Mangalore
Tel: +91 824 32606

Hyderabad Stock Exchange
3-6-275 Himayatnagar, Hyderabad
Tel: +91 842 23 1985

Gauhati Stock Exchange
Saraf Building, Annex, AT Road, Gauhati
Tel: +91 361 336 67
Fax: +91 361 543 272

Indonesia

Jakarta Stock Exchange
(PT Bursa Efek Jakarta)
Jakarta Stock Exchange Building, 13th Floor, JI Jenderal Sudiman,
Kav 52-53, Jakarta
Tel: +62 21 515 0515
Fax: +62 21 515 0330
Email : webmaster@jsx.co.id
URL: http://www.jsx.co.id

 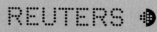

Surabaya Stock Exchange
(PT Bursa Efek Surabaya)
5th Floor, Gedung Madan Pemuda, 27-31 Jalan Pemuda, Surabaya
Tel: +62 21 526 6210
Fax: +62 21 526 6219
Email : heslpdesk@bes.co.id
URL: http://www.bes.co.id

Indonesian Commodity Exchange Board
(Badan Pelaksana Bursa Komoditi)
Gedung Bursa, Jalan Medan Merdeka Selatan 14, 4th Floor, Jakarta
Pusat
Tel: +62 21 344 1921
Fax: +62 21 3480 4426

Capital Market Supervisory Agency
(Baden Pelaksana Pasar Modal)
BAPEPAM
Jakarta Stock Exchange Building, 13th Floor, JI Jenderal Sudiman,
Kav 52-53, Jakarta
Tel: +62 21 515 1288
Fax: +62 21 515 1283
Email : bapepam@indoexchange.com
URL: http://www.indoexchange.com/bapepam

Iran

Tehran Stock Exchange
228 Hafez Avenue, Tehran
Tel: +98 21 670 309
Fax: +98 21 672 524
Email : stock@neda.net
URL: http://www.neda.net/tse

Ireland

Irish Stock Exchange
28 Anglesea Street, Dublin 2
Tel: +353 1 677 8808
Fax: +353 1 677 6045

Irish Futures & Options Exchange
IFOX
Segrave House, Earlsfort Terrace, Dublin 2
Tel: +353 1 676 7413
Fax: +353 1 661 4645

Israel

Tel Aviv Stock Exchange Ltd
TASE
54 Ahad Haam Street, Tel Aviv
Tel: +972 3 567 7411
Fax: +972 3 510 5379
Email : etti@tase.co.il
URL: http://www.tase.co.il

Italy

Italian Financial Futures Market
(Mercato Italiano Futures)
MIF
Piazza del Gesu' 49, Rome
Tel: +39 6 676 7514
Fax: +39 6 676 7250

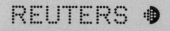

Italian Stock Exchange
(Consiglio de Borsa)
Piazza degli Affari, 6, Milan
Tel: +39 2 724 261
Fax: +39 2 864 64 323
Email : postoffice@borsaitalia.it
URL: http://www.borsaitalia.it

Italian Derivatives Market
IDEM
Piazza Affari 6, Milan
Tel: +39 2 72 42 61
Fax: +39 2 72 00 43 33
Email : postoffice@borsaitalia.it
URL: http://www.borsaitalia.it

Jamaica

Jamaica Stock Exchange
40 Harbour Street, PO Box 1084, Kingston
Tel: +1809 809 922 0806
Fax: +1809 809 922 6966
Email : jse@infochan.com
URL: http://www.jamstockex.com

Japan

Tokyo Commodity Exchange
(Tokyo Kogyoin Torihikijo)
TOCOM
10-8 Nihonbashi, Horidome-cho, Chuo-ku, 1-chome, Tokyo
Tel: +81 3 3661 9191
Fax: +81 3 3661 7568

Japan Securities Dealing Association
(Nihon Shokengyo Kyokai)
Tojyo Shoken Building, 5-8 Kayaba-cho, 1-chome, Nihonbashi, Tokyo
Tel: +81 3 3667 8451
Fax: +81 3 3666 8009

Osaka Textile Exchange
(Osaka Seni Torihikijo)
2-5-28 Kyutaro-machi, Chuo-ku, Osaka
Tel: +81 6 253 0031
Fax: +81 6 253 0034

Tokyo Stock Exchange
(Tokyo Shoken Torihikijo)
TSE
2-1 Nihombashi-Kabuto-Cho, Chuo-ku, Tokyo
Tel: +81 3 3666 0141
Fax: +81 3 3663 0625
URL: http://www.tse.or.jp

Kobe Raw Silk Exchange
(Kobe Kiito Torihiksho)
KSE
126 Higashimachi, Chuo-ku, Kobe
Tel: +81 78 331 7141
Fax: +81 78 331 7145

Kobe Rubber Exchange
(Kobe Gomu Torihiksho)
KRE
49 Harima-cho, Chuo-ku, Kobe
Tel: +81 78 331 4211
Fax: +81 78 332 1622

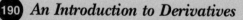

Nagoya Stock Exchange
(Nagoya Shoken Torihikijo)
NSE
3-17 Sakae, 3-chome, Naka-ku, Nagoya
Tel: +81 81 52 262 3172
Fax: +81 81 52 241 1527
Email : nse@po.iijnet.or.jp
URL: http://www.iijnet.or.jp/nse-jp/

Nagoya Textile Exchange
2-15 Nishiki 3 Chome, Naka-ku, Naka-ku, Nagoya
Tel: +81 52 951 2171
Fax: +81 52 961 6407

Osaka Securities Exchange
(Osaka Shoken Torihikijo)
OSE
8-l6, Kitahama, l-chome, Chuo-ku, Osaka
Tel: +81 6 229 8643
Fax: +81 6 231 2639
Email : osakaexc@po.iijnet.or.jp
URL: http://www.ose.or.jp

Tokyo Grain Exchange
(Tokyo Kokumotsu Shohin Torihikijo)
TGE
1-12-5 Nihonbashi, Kakigara-cho, l-Chome, Chuo-ku, Tokyo
Tel: +81 3 3668 9321
Fax: +81 3 3661 4564
Email : webmas@tge.or.jp
URL: http://www.tge.or.jp

Tokyo International Financial Futures Exchange
TIFFE
1-3-1 Marunouchi, Chiyoda-ku, Tokyo
Tel: +81 3 5223 2400
Fax: +81 3 5223 2450
URL: http://www.tiffe.or.jp

Hiroshima Stock Exchange
KANEX
14-18 Kanayama-cho, Naka-ku, Hiroshima
Tel: +81 82 541 1121
Fax: +81 82 541 1128

Fukuoka Stock Exchange
KANEX
2-14-2 Tenjin, Chuo-ku, Fukuoka
Tel: +81 92 741 8231
Fax: +81 92 713 1540

Niigata Securities Exchange
(Niigata Shoken Torihikijo)
1245 Hachiban-cho, Kamiokawame-don, Niigata
Tel: +81 25 222 4181
Fax: +81 25 222 4551

Sapporo Securities Exchange
(Sapporo Shoken Torihikijo)
5-14-1 Nishi-minami, I-jo, Chuo-ku, Sapporo
Tel: +81 11 241 6171
Fax: +81 11 251 0840

Kammon Commodity Exchange
(Kammon Shohin Torihikijo)
1-5 Nabe-cho, Shimonoseki
Tel: +81 832 31 1313
Fax: +81 832 23 1947

Kyoto Stock Exchange
KANEX
66 Tachiurinishi-machi, Higashinotoin-higashiiru, Shijo-dori,
Shimogyo-ku, Kyoto
Tel: +81 75 221 1171
Fax: +81 75 221 8356

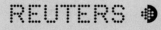

Maebashi Dried Cocoa Exchange
(Maebashi Kanken Torihikijo)
1-49-1 Furuichi-machi, Maebashi
Tel: +81 272 52 1401
Fax: +81 272 51 8270

Cubu Commodity Exchange
3-2-15 Nishiki, Naka-ku, Nagoya
Tel: +81 52 951 2170
Fax: +81 52 961 1044

Yokohama Raw Silk Exchange
(Yokohama Kiito Torihikijo)
Silk Centre, 1 Yamashita-cho, Naka-ku, Yokohama
Tel: +81 45 641 1341
Fax: +81 45 641 1346

Kansai Agricultural Commodities Exchange
KANEX
1-10-14 Awaza, Nishi-ku, Osaka
Tel: +81 6 531 7931
Fax: +81 6 541 9343
Email : kex-1@kanex.or.jp
URL: http://www.kanex.or.jp

Jordan

Amman Financial Market
PO Box 8802, Ammam
Tel: +962 6 607171
Fax: +962 6 686830
Email : afm@go.com.jo
URL: http://accessme.com/AFM/

Kenya

Nairobi Stock Exchange
PO Box 43633, Nairobi
Tel: +254 2 230692
Fax: +254 2 224200
Email : nse@acc.or.ke

Korea (South)

Korea Stock Exchange
KSE
33 Yoido-dong, Youngdeungpo-gu, Seoul
Tel: +82 2 3774 9000
Fax: +82 2 786 0263
Email : world@www.kse.or.kr
URL: http://www.kse.or.kr

Kuwait

Kuwait Stock Exchange
PO Box 22235, Safat, Kuwait
Tel: +965 242 3130
Fax: +965 242 0779

Latvia

Riga Stock Exchange
Doma Laukums 6, Riga
Tel: + 7 212 431
Fax: + 7 229 411
Email : rfb@mail.bkc.lv
URL: http://www.rfb.lv

Lithuania

National Stock Exchange of Lithuania
Ukmerges St 41, Vilnius
Tel: +370 2 72 14 07
Fax: +370 2 742 894
Email : office@nse.lt
URL: http://www.nse.lt

Luxembourg

Luxembourg Stock Exchange
(Societe Anonyme de la Bourse de Luxembourg)
11 Avenue de la Porte-Neuve
Tel: +352 47 79 36-1
Fax: +352 47 32 98
Email : info@bourse.lu
URL: http://www.bourse.lu

Macedonia

Macedonia Stock Exchange
MSE
Tel: +389 91 122 055
Fax: +389 91 122 069
Email : mse@unet.com.mk
URL: http://www.mse.org.mk

Malaysia

Kuala Lumpur Commodity Exchange
KLCE
4th Floor, Citypoint, Komplex Dayabumi, Jalan Sulta Hishamuddin,
Kuala Lumpur
Tel: +60 3 293 6822
Fax: +60 3 274 2215
Email : klce@po.jaring.my
URL: http://www.klce.com.my

Kuala Lumpur Stock Exchange
KLSE
4th Floor, Exchange Square, Off Jalan Semantan, Damansara
Heights, Kuala Lumpur
Tel: +60 3 254 64 33
Fax: +60 3 255 74 63
Email : webmaster@klse.com.my
URL: http://www.klse.com.my

The Kuala Lumpur Options & Financial Futures Exchange
KLOFFE
10th Floor, Wisma Chase Perdana, Damansara Heights, Jalan
Semantan, Kuala Lumpur
Tel: +60 3 253 8199
Fax: +60 3 255 3207
Email : kloffe@kloffe.com.my
URL: http://www.kloffe.com.my

Malaysia Monetary Exchange BHD
4th Floor, City Point, PO Box 11260, Dayabumi Complex, Jalan
Sultan Hishmuddin, Kuala Lumpur
Email : mme@po.jaring.my
URL: http://www.jaring.my/mme

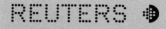

Malta

Malta Stock Exchange
27 Pietro Floriani Street, Floriana, Valletta 14
Tel: +356 244 0515
Fax: +356 244 071
Email : borza@maltanet.omnes.net

Mauritius

Mauritius Stock Exchange
Stock Exchange Commission, 9th Floor, SICOM Building, Sir
Celicourt Anselme Street, Port Louis
Tel: +230 208 8735
Fax: +230 208 8676
Email : svtradha@intnet.mu
URL: http://lynx.intnet.mu/sem/

Mexico

Mexican Stock Exchange
(Bolsa Mexicana de Valores, SA de CV)
Paseo de la Reforma 255, Colonia Cuauhtemoc, Mexico DF
Tel: +52 5 726 66 00
Fax: +52 5 705 47 98
Email : cinform@bmv.com.mx
URL: http://www.bmv.com.mx

Morocco

Casablanca Stock Exchange
(Societe de la Bourse des Valeurs de Casablanca)
98 Boulevard Mohammed V, Casablanca
Tel: +212 2 27 93 54
Fax: +212 2 20 03 65

Namibia

Namibian Stock Exchange
Kaiserkrone Centre 11, O Box 2401, Windhoek
Tel: +264 61 227 647
Fax: +264 61 248 531
Email : tminney@nse.com.na
URL: http://www.nse.com.na

Netherlands

Financiele Termijnmarkt Amsterdam NV
FTA
Nes 49, Amsterdam
Tel: +31 20 550 4555
Fax: +31 20 624 5416

AEX-Stock Exchange
AEX
Beursplein 5, PO Box 19163, Amsterdam
Tel: +31 20 550 4444
Fax: +31 20 550 4950
URL: http://www.aex.nl/

AEX-Agricultural Futures Exchange
Beursplein 5, PO Box 19163, Amsterdam
Tel: +31 20 550 4444
Fax: +31 20 623 9949

AEX-Options Exchange
AEX
Beursplein 5, PO Box 19163, Amsterdam
Tel: +31 20 550 4444
Fax: +31 20 550 4950
URL: http://www.aex-optiebeurs.ase.nl

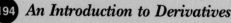

New Zealand

New Zealand Futures & Options Exchange Ltd
NZFOE
10th Level, Stock Exchange Cen, 191 Queen Street, Auckland 1
Tel: +64 9 309 8308
Fax: +64 9 309 8817
Email : info@nzfoe.co.nz
URL: http://www.nzfoe.co.nz

New Zealand Stock Exchange
NZSE
8th Floor Caltex Tower, 286-292 Lambton Quay, Wellington
Tel: +64 4 4727 599
Fax: +64 4 4731 470
Email : info@nzse.org.nz
URL: http://www.nzse.co.nz

Nicaragua

Nicaraguan Stock Exchange
(Bolsa de Valores de Nicaragua, SA)
Centro Financiero Banic, 1er Piso, Km. 5 1/2 Carretera Masaya
Email : info@bolsanic.com
URL: http://bolsanic.com/

Nigeria

Nigerian Stock Exchange
Stock Exchange House, 8th & 9th Floors, 2/4 Customs Street, Lagos
Tel: +234 1 266 0287
Fax: +234 1 266 8724
Email : alile@nse.ngra.com

Norway

Oslo Stock Exchange
(Oslo Bors)
OSLO
P.O. Box 460, Sentrum, Oslo
Tel: +47 22 34 17 00
Fax: +47 22 41 65 90
Email : informasjonsavdelingen@ose.telemax.no
URL: http://www.ose.no

Oman

Muscat Securities Market
Po Box 3265, Ruwi
Tel: +968 702 665
Fax: +968 702 691

Pakistan

Islamabad Stock Exchange
Stock Exchange Building, 101-E Fazal-ul-Haq Road, Blue Area, Islamabad
Tel: +92 51 27 50 45
Fax: +92 51 27 50 44
Email : ise@paknet1.ptc.pk

Karachi Stock Exchange
Stock Exchange Building, Stock Exchange Road, Karachi
Tel: +92 21 2425502
Fax: +92 21 241 0825
URL: http://www.kse.org

Lahore Stock Exchange Po Box 1315, 19 Khayaban e Aiwan e Iqbal, Lahore
Tel: +92 42 636 8000
Fax: +92 42 636 8484

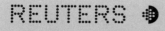

Panama

Panama Stock Exchange
(Bolsa de Valores de Panama, SA)
Calle Elvira Mendex y Calle 52, Edif Valarino, Planta Baja
Tel: +507 2 69 1966
Fax: +507 2 69 2457
URL: http://www.urraca.com/bvp/

Paraguay

Ascuncon Stock Exchange
(Bolsa de Valores y Productos de Ascuncion)
Estrella 540, Ascuncion
Tel: +595 21 442 445
Fax: +595 21 442 446
Email : bolsapya@pla.net.py
URL: http://www.pla.net.py/bvpasa

Peru

Lima Stock Exchange
(La Bolsa de Valores de Lima)
Pasaje Acuna 191, Lima
Tel: +51 1 426 79 39
Fax: +51 1 426 76 50
Email : web_team@bvl.com.pe
URL: http://www.bvl.com.pe

Philippines

Philippine Stock Exchange
Philippine Stock Exchange Cent, Tektite Road, Ortigas Centre, Pasig
Tel: +63 2 636 01 22
Fax: +63 2 634 51 13
Email : pse@mnl.sequel.net
URL: http://www.pse.com.ph

Manila International Futures Exchange
MIFE
7/F Producer's Bank Centre, Paseo de Roxas, Makati
Tel: +63 2 818 5496
Fax: +63 2 818 5529

Poland

Warsaw Stock Exchange
Gielda papierow, Wartosciowych w Warszawie SA, Ul Nowy Swiat 6/
12, Warsaw
Tel: +48 22 628 32 32
Fax: +48 22 628 17 54
Email : gielda@kp.atm.com.pl

Portugal

Oporto Derivatives Exchange
(Bolsa de Derivados do Oporto)
BDP
Av. da Boavista 3433, Oporto
Tel: +351 2 618 58 58
Fax: +351 2 618 56 66

Lisbon Stock Exchange
(Bolsa de Valores de Lisboa)
BVL
Edificio da Bolsa, Rua Soeiro Pereira Gomes, Lisbon
Tel: +351 1 790 99 04
Fax: +351 1 795 20 21
Email : webmaster@bvl.pt
URL: http://www.bvl.pt

Romania

Bucharest Stock Exchange
BSE
Doamnei no. 8, Bucharest
Email : bse@delos.ro
URL: http://www.delos.ro/bse/

Romanian Commodities Exchange
(Bursa Romana de Marfuri SA)
Piata Presei nr 1, Sector 1, Bucharest
Tel: +40 223 21 69
Fax: +40 223 21 67

Russian Federation

Moscow Interbank Currency Exchange
MICEX
21/1, Sadovaya-Spasskay, Moscow
Tel: +7 095 705 9627
Fax: +7 095 705 9622
Email : inmicex@micex.com
URL: http://www.micex.com/

Russian Exchange
RCRME
Myasnitskaya ul 26, Moscow
Tel: +7 095 262 06 53
Fax: +7 095 262 57 57
Email : assa@vc-rtsb.msk.ru
URL: http://www.re.ru

Moscow Commodity Exchange
Pavilion No. 4, Russian Exhibition Centre, Moscow
Tel: +7 095 187 83 07
Fax: +7 095 187 9982

St Petersburg Futures Exchange
SPBFE
274 Ligovski av., St Petersburg
Tel: +7 812 294 15 12
Fax: +7 812 327 93 88
Email : seva@spbfe.futures.ru

Siberian Stock Exchange
PO box 233, Frunze St 5, Novosibirsk
Tel: +7 38 32 21 06 90
Fax: +7 38 32 21 06 90
Email : sibex@sse.nsk.su

Moscow Central Stock Exchange
9(B) Bolshaya Maryinskaya Stre, Moscow
Tel: +7 095 229 88 82
Fax: +7 0995 202 06 67

Moscow International Stock Exchange
MISE
Slavyanskaya Pl 4, Bld 2, Moscow
Tel: +7 095 923 33 39
Fax: +7 095 923 33 39

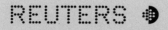

National Association of Securities Market Participants
(NAUF)
Floor 2, Building 5, Chayanova Street 15, Moscow
Tel: +7 095 705 90
Fax: +7 095 976 42 36
Email : naufor@rtsnet.ru
URL: http://www.rtsnet.ru

Vladivostock Stock Exchange
VSE
21 Zhertv Revolyutsii Str, Vladivostock
Tel: +7 4232 22 78 87
Fax: +7 4232 22 80 09

St Petersburg Stock Exchange
SPSE
274 Ligovsky pr, St Petersburg
Tel: +7 812 296 10 80
Fax: +7 812 296 10 80
Email : root@lse.spb.su

Saudi Arabia

Saudi Arabian Monetary Authority
SAMA
PO Box 2992, Riyadh
Tel: +966 1 466 2300
Fax: +966 1 466 3223

Singapore

Singapore Commodity Exchange Ltd
SICOM
111 North Bridge Road, #23-04/, Peninsula Plaza
Tel: +65 338 5600
Fax: +65 338 9116
Email : sicom@pacific.net.sg

Stock Exchange of Singapore
No. 26-01/08, 20 Cecil Street, The Exchange
Tel: +65 535 3788
Fax: +65 535 6994
Email : webmaster@ses.com.sg
URL: http://www.ses.com.sg

Singapore International Monetary Exchange Ltd
SIMEX
1 Raffles Place, No. 07-00, OUB Centre
Tel: +65 535 7382
Fax: +65 535 7282
Email : simex@pacific.net.sg
URL: http://www.simex.com.sg

Slovak Republic

Bratislava Stock Exchange
(Burza cenny ch papierov v Bratislave)
BSSE
Vysoka 17, Bratislava
Tel: +42 7 5036 102
Fax: +42 7 5036 103
Email : kunikova@bsse.sk
URL: http://www.bsse.sk

Slovenia

Commodity Exchange of Ljubljana
Smartinskal 52, PO Box 85, Ljubljana
Tel: +386 61 18 55 100
Fax: +386 61 18 55 101
Email : infos@bb-lj.si
URL: http://www.eunet.si/commercial/bbl/bbl-ein.html

Ljubljana Stock Exchange, Inc
LJSE
Sovenska cesta 56, Lbujljana
Tel: +386 61 171 02 11
Fax: +386 61 171 02 13
Email : info@jse.si
URL: http://www.ljse.si

South Africa

Johannesburg Stock Exchange
JSE
17 Diagonal Street, Johannesburg
Tel: +27 11 377 2200
Fax: +27 11 834 3937
Email : r&d@jse.co.za
URL: http://www.jse.co.za

South African Futures Exchange
SAFEX
105 Central Street, Houghton Estate 2198, Johannesburg
Tel: +27 11 728 5960
Fax: +27 11 728 5970
Email : jani@icon.co.za
URL: http://www.safex.co.za

Spain

Citrus Fruit and Commodity Market of Valencia
(Futuros de Citricos y Mercaderias de Valencia)
2, 4 Libreros, Valencia
Tel: +34 6 387 01 88
Fax: +34 6 394 36 30
Email : futuros@super.medusa.es

Spanish Options Exchange
(MEFF Renta Variable)
MEFF RV
Torre Picasso, Planta 26, Madrid
Tel: +34 1 585 0800
Fax: +34 1 571 9542
Email : mefrv@meffrv.es
URL: http://www.meffrv.es

Spanish Financial Futures Market
(MEFF Renta Fija)
MEFF RF
Via Laietana, 58, Barcelona
Tel: +34 3 412 1128
Fax: +34 3 268 4769
Email : marketing@meff.es
URL: http://www.meff.es

Madrid Stock Exchange
(Bolsa de Madrid)
Plaza de la Lealtad 1, Madrid
Tel: +34 1 589 26 00
Fax: +34 1 531 22 90
Email : internacional@bolsamadrid.es
URL: http://www.bolsamadrid.es

Barcelona Stock Exchange
Paseo Isabel II No 1, Barcelona
Tel: +34 3 401 35 55
Fax: +34 3 401 38 59
Email : agiralt@borsabcn.es
URL: http://www.borsabcn.es

Bilbao Stock Exchange
(Sociedad Rectora de la Bolsa de Valoes de Bilbao)
Jose Maria Olabarri 1, Bilbao
Tel: +34 4 423 74 00
Fax: +34 4 424 46 20
Email : bolsabilbao@sarenet.es
URL: http://www.bolsabilbao.es

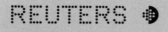

Valencia Stock Exchange
(Sociedad Rectora de la Bolsa de Valoes de Valencia)
Libreros 2 y 4, Valencia
Tel: +34 6 387 01 00
Fax: +34 6 387 01 14

Sri Lanka

Colombo Stock Exchange
CSE
04-01 West Bloc, World Trade Centre, Echelon Square, Colombo 1
Tel: +94 1 44 65 81
Fax: +94 1 44 52 79
Email : cse@sri.lanka.net
URL: http://www.lanka.net/cse/

Swaziland

Swaziland Stock Market
Swaziland Stockbrokers Ltd, 2nd Floor Dlan'ubeka House, Walker
St, Mbabane
Tel: +268 46163
Fax: +268 44132
URL: http://mbendi.co.za/exsw.htm

Sweden

The Swedish Futures and Options Market
(OM Stockholm AB)
OMS
Box 16305, Brunkebergstorg 2, Stockholm
Tel: +46 8 700 0600
Fax: +46 8 723 1092
URL: http://www.omgroup.com

Stockholm Stock Exchange Ltd
(Stockholm Fondbors AB)
Kallargrand 2, Stockholm
Tel: +46 8 613 88 00
Fax: +46 8 10 81 10
Email : info@xsse.se
URL: http://www.xsse.se

Switzerland

Swiss Options & Financial Futures Exchange AG
SOFFEX
Selnaustrasse 32, Zurich
Tel: +41 1 229 2111
Fax: +41 1 229 2233
Email : webmaster@swx.ch
URL: http://www.bourse.ch

Swiss Exchange
SWX
Selnaustrasse 32, Zurich
Tel: +41 1 229 21 11
Fax: +41 1 229 22 33
URL: http://www.bourse.ch

Taiwan

Taiwan Stock Exchange
Floors 2-10, City Building, 85 Yen Ping Road South, Taipei
Tel: +886 2 311 4020
Fax: +886 2 375 3669
Email : intl-aff@tse.com.tw
URL: http://www.tse.com.tw

 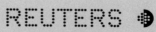

Thailand

The Stock Exchange of Thailand
SET
2nd Floor, Tower 1, 132 Sindhorn Building, Wireless Road, Bangkok
Tel: +66 2 254 0960
Fax: +66 2 263 2746
Email : webmaster@set.or.th
URL: http://www.set.or.th

Trinidad and Tobago

Trinidad and Tobago Stock Exchange
65 Independence Street, Port of Spain
Tel: +1809 809 625 5108
Fax: +1809 809 623 0089

Tunisia

Tunis Stock Exchange
(Bourse des Valeurs Mobilieres de Tunis)
Centre Babel - Bloc E, Rue Jean-Jacques Rousseau, Montplaisir,
Tunis
Tel: +216 1 780 288
Fax: +216 1 789 189

Turkey

Istanbul Stock Exchange
(Istanbul Menkul Kiymetler Borasi)
ISE
Istinye, Istanbul
Tel: +90 212 298 21 00
Fax: +90 212 298 25 00
Email : info@ise.org
URL: http://www.ise.org

United Kingdom

The London Securities and Derivatives Exchange
OMLX
107 Cannon Street, London
Tel: +44 171 283 0678
Fax: +44 171 815 8508
Email : petter.made@omgroup.com
URL: http://www.omgroup.com/

International Petroleum Exchange of London Ltd
IPE
International House, 1 St. Katharine's Way, London
Tel: +44 171 481 0643
Fax: +44 171 481 8485
Email : busdev@ipe.uk.com
URL: http://www.ipe.uk.com

London International Futures & Options Exchange
LIFFE
Cannon Bridge, London
Tel: +44 171 623 0444
Fax: +44 171 588 3624
Email : exchange@liffe.com
URL: http://www.liffe.com

London Metal Exchange
LME
56 Leadenhall Street, London
Tel: +44 171 264 5555
Fax: +44 171 680 0505
Email : lsnow@lmetal.netkonect.co.uk
URL: http://www.lme.co.uk

The Baltic Exchange
Tel: +44 171 623 5501
Fax: +44 171 369 1622
Email : enquiries@balticexchange.co.uk
URL: http://www.balticexchange.co.uk

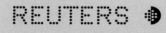

Directory of Futures & Options Exchanges

London Stock Exchange
LSE
Old Broad Street, London
Tel: +44 171 797 1000
Fax: +44 171 374 0504

Tradepoint Investment Exchange
35 King Street, London
Tel: +44 171 240 8000
Fax: +44 171 240 1900
Email : g171@dial.pipex.com
URL: http://www.tradepoint.co.uk

London Commodity Exchange
LCE
1 Commodity Quay, St. Katharine Docks, London
Tel: +44 171 481 2080
Fax: +44 171 702 9923
URL: http://www.liffe.com

United States

New York Stock Exchange
NYSE
11 Wall Street, New York
Tel: +1 212 656 3000
Fax: +1 212 656 5557
URL: http://www.nyse.com

Minneapolis Grain Exchange
MGE
400 S. Fourth St., Minneapolis
Tel: +1 612 338 6216
Fax: +1 612 339 1155
Email : mgex@ix.netcom.com
URL: http://www.mgex.com

Philadelphia Stock Exchange
PHLX
1900 Market Street, Philadelphia
Tel: +1 215 496 5000
Fax: +1 215 496 5653
URL: http://www.phlx.com

Kansas City Board of Trade
KCBT
4800 Main St., Suite 303, Kansas City
Tel: +1 816 753 7500
Fax: +1 816 753 3944
Email : kcbt@kcbt.com
URL: http://www.kcbt.com

Chicago Board Options Exchange
CBOE
400 S. LaSalle Street, Chicago
Tel: +1 312 786 5600
Fax: +1 312 786 7409
Email : investor_services@cboe.com
URL: http://www.cboe.com

Chicago Board of Trade
CBOT
141 West Jackson Boulevard, Chicago
Tel: +1 312 435 3500
Fax: +1 312 341 3306
Email : comments@cbot.com
URL: http://www.cbt.com

New York Mercantile Exchange
NYMEX
4 World Trade Center, New York
Tel: +1 212 938 222
Fax: +1 212 938 2985
Email : marketing@nymex.com
URL: http://www.nymex.com

REUTERS

Chicago Stock Exchange
CHX
One Financial Place, 440 S. LaSalle St, Chicago
Tel: +1 312 663 222
Fax: +1 312 773 2396
Email : marketing@chiacgostockex.com
URL: http://www.chicagostockex.com

MidAmerica Commodity Exchange
MIDAM
141 W. Jackson Boulevard, Chicago
Tel: +1 313 341 3000
Fax: +1 312 341 3027
Email : comments@cbot.com
URL: http://www.midam.com

Philadelphia Board of Trade
1900 Market Street, Philadelphia
Tel: +1 215 496 5357
Fax: +1 215 496 5653

The Cincinnati Stock Exchange
400 South LaSalle Street, Chicago
Tel: +1 312 786 8803
Fax: +1 312 939 7239

Boston Stock Exchange, Inc
BSE
38th Floor, One Boston Place, Boston
Tel: +1 617 723 9500
Fax: +1 617 523 6603
URL: http://www.bostonstock.com

Nasdaq Stock Market
1735 K Street NW, Washington DC
Tel: +1 202 728 8000
Fax: +1 202 293 6260
Email : fedback@nasdaq.com
URL: http://www.nasdaq.com

American Stock Exchange
AMEX
86 Trinity Place, New York
Tel: +1 212 306 1000
Fax: +1 212 306 1802
Email : jstephan@amex.com
URL: http://www.amex.com

New York Cotton Exchange
NYCE
4 World Trade Center, New York
Tel: +1 212 938 2702
Fax: +1 212 488 8135
URL: http://www.nyce.com

Pacific Stock Exchange, Inc
PSE
301 Pine Street, San Francisco
Tel: +1 415 393 4000
Fax: +1 415 393 4202
URL: http://www.pacificex.com

Chicago Mercantile Exchange
CME
30 S. Wacker Drive, Chicago
Tel: +1 312 930 1000
Fax: +1 312 930 3439
Email : info@cme.com
URL: http://www.cme.com

Coffee, Sugar & Cocoa Exchange Inc.
CSCE
4 World Trade Center, New York
Tel: +1 212 938 2800
Fax: +1 212 524 9863
Email : csce@ix.netcom.com
URL: http://www.csce.com

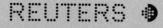

Venezuela

Maracaibo Stock Exchange
(Bolsa de Valores de Maracaibo)
Calle 96, Esq Con Avda 5, Edificio
Banco Central de Vene, Piso 9, Maracaibo
Tel: +58 61 225 482
Fax: +58 61 227 663

Venezuela Electronic Stock Exchange
(de Venezuela)
C·mara de Comercio de Valencia, Edif. C·mara de Comercio, Av.
Bolìvar, Valencia, Edo. Carabobo, Apartado 151
Tel: +58 57.5109
Fax: +58 57.5147
Email : set@venezuelastock.com
URL: http://www.venezuelastock.com

Caracas Stock Exchange
(Bolsa de Valores de Caracas)
Edificio Atrium, Piso 1 Calle Sorocaima, Urbanizacion, El Rosal,
Caracas
Tel: +58 2 905 5511
Fax: +58 2 905 5814
Email : anafin@true.net
URL: http://www.caracasstock.com

Yugoslavia

Belgrade Stock Exchange
(Beogradska Berza)
Omladinskih 1, 3rd Floor, PO Box 214, Belgrade
Tel: +381 11 19 84 77
Fax: +381 11 13 82 42
Email : beyu@eunet.yu

Zimbabwe

Zimbabwe Stock Exchange
5th Floor, Southampton House, Union Avenue, Harare
Tel: +263 4 736 861
Fax: +263 4 791 045

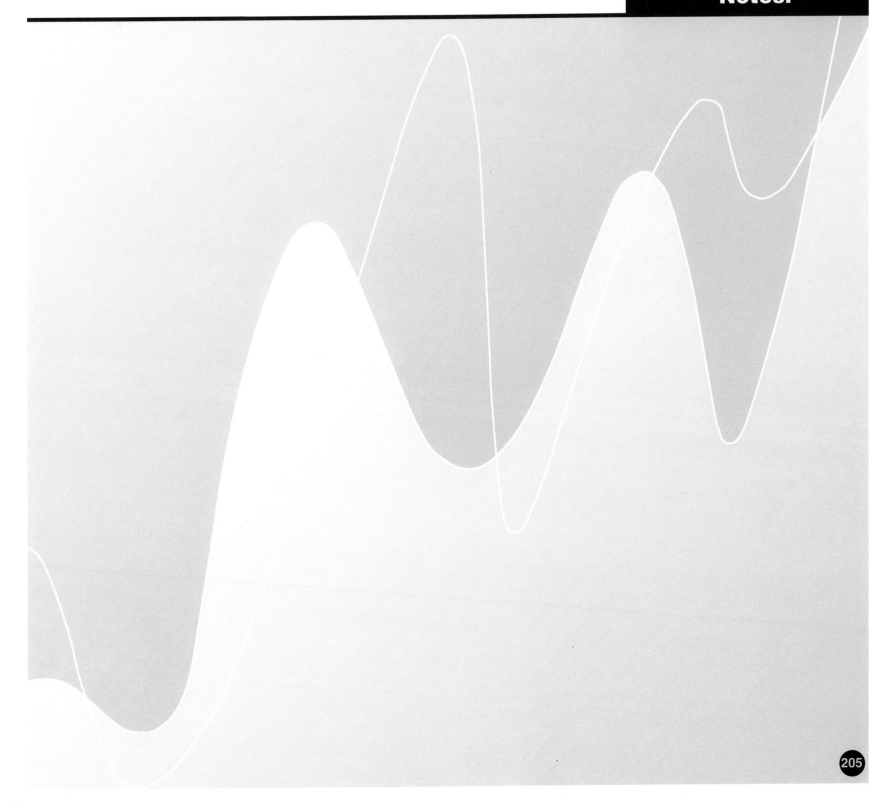

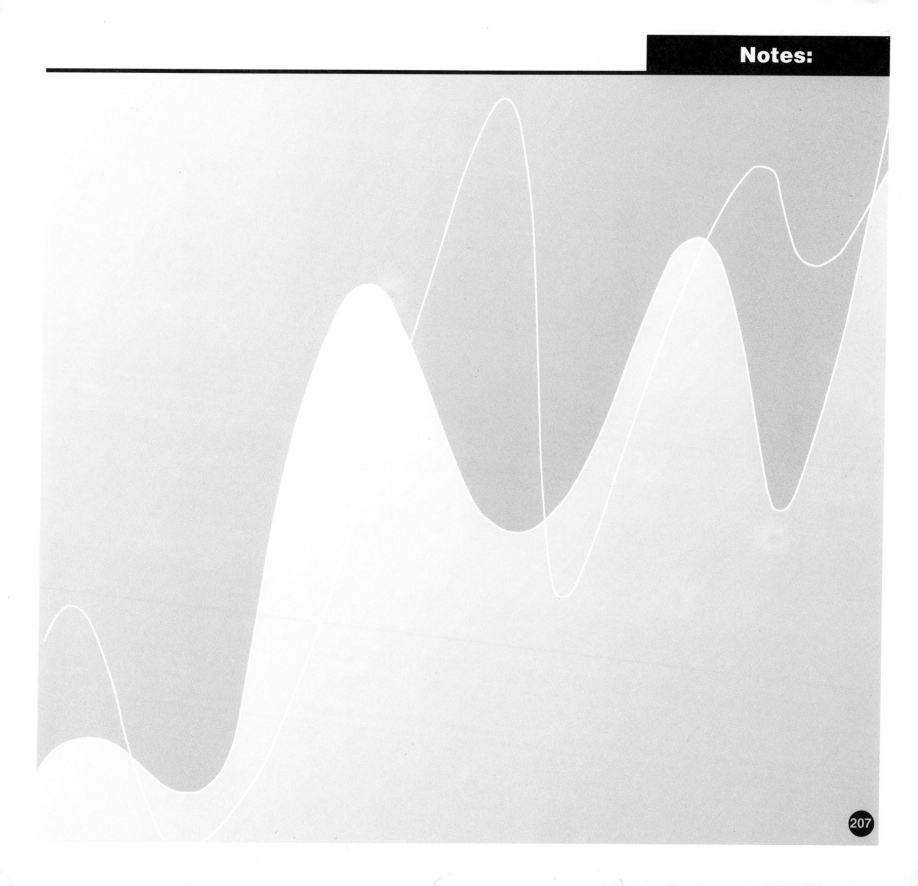

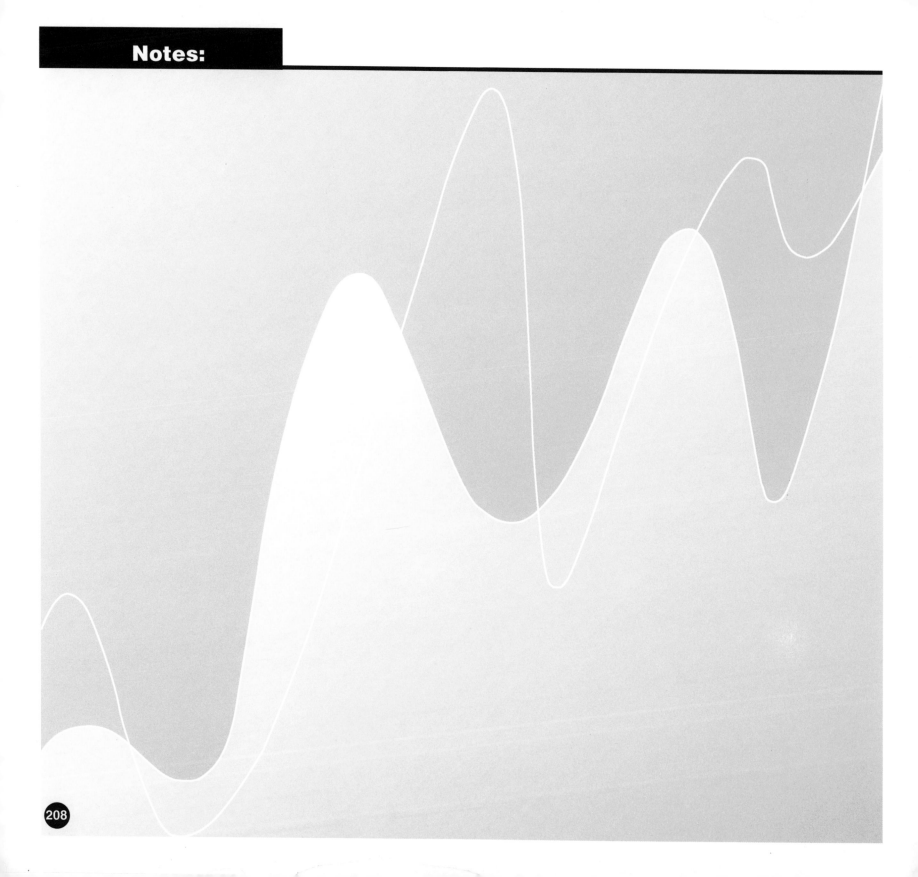

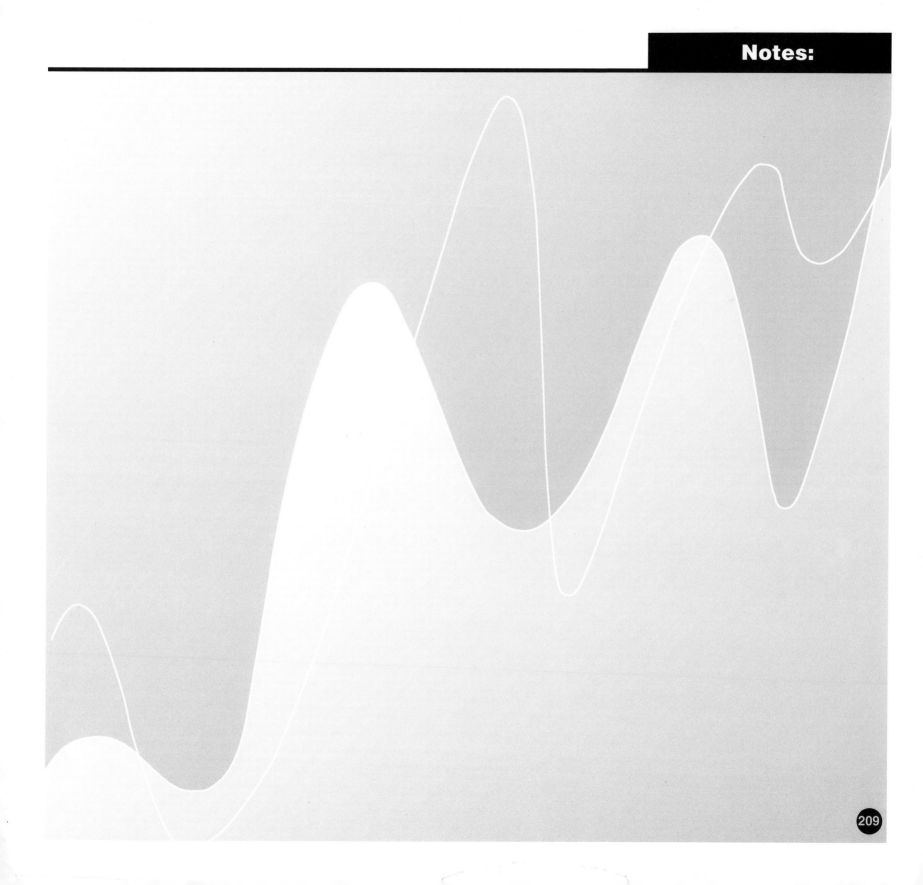

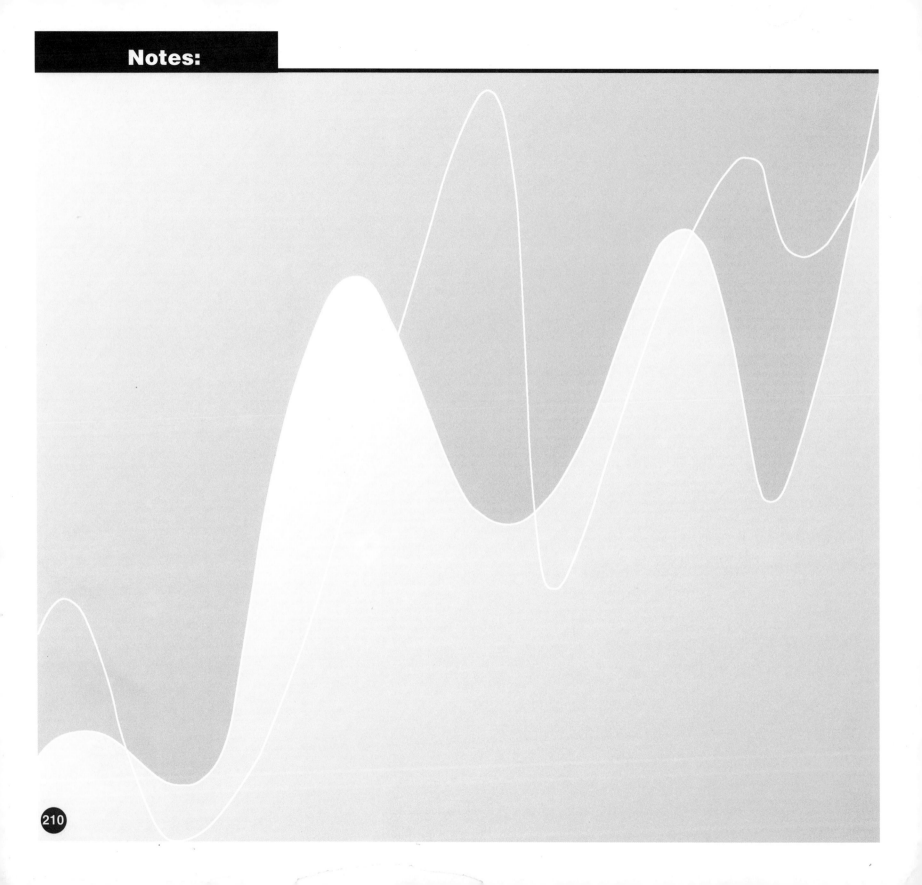

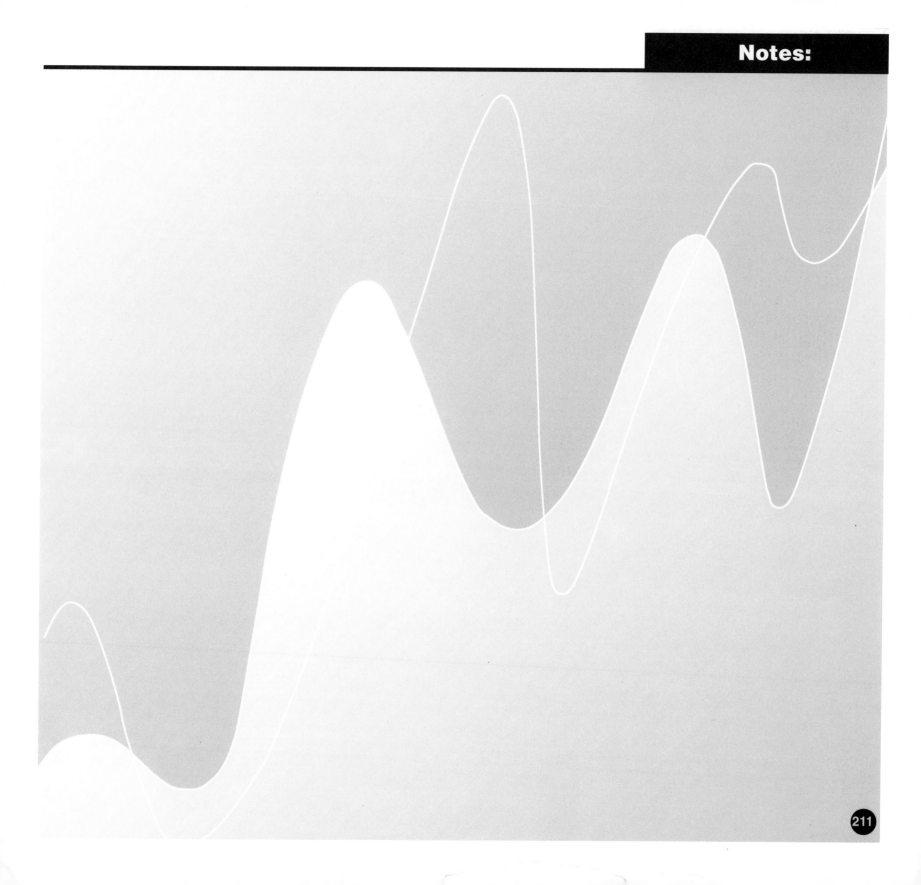

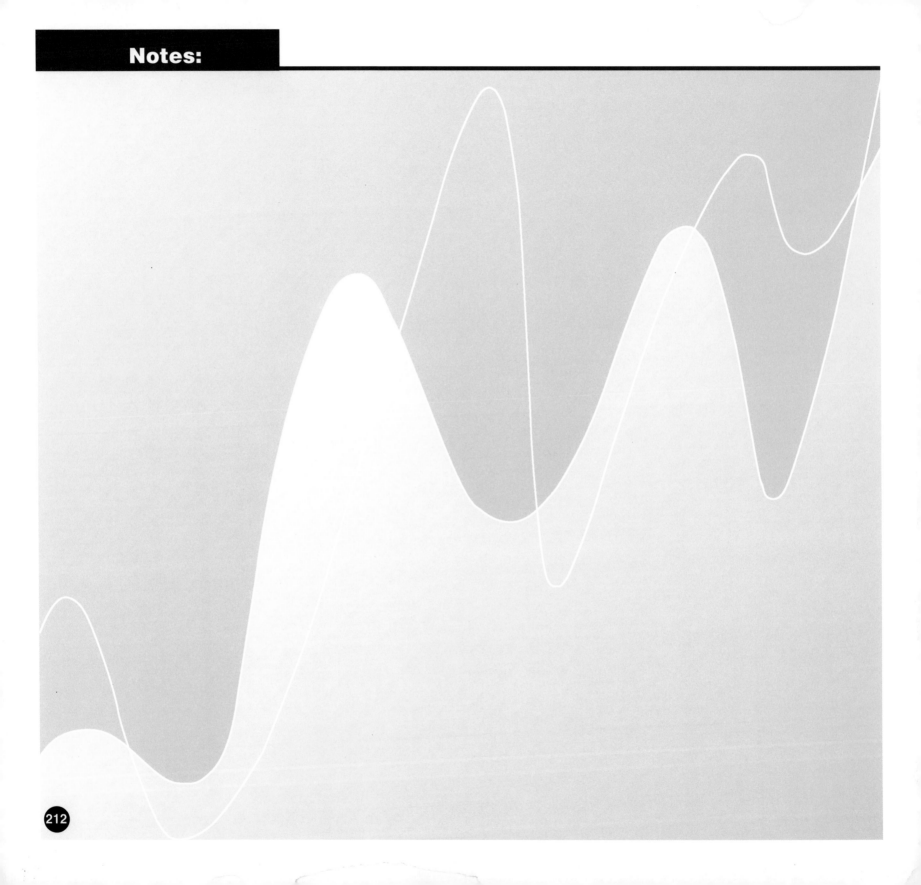